A NEW VISION FOR ISRAEL

Studying the Historical Jesus

It was once fashionable to claim that Jesus could not be known as a figure of history and that even if he could be known in that way the result would not be of interest for faith. Both contentions have been laid to rest over the past twenty years.

Scholarship has seen archaeological discoveries, advances in the study of Jewish and Hellenistic literature, a renewed interest in the social milieu of Judaism and Christianity, and critical investigation of the systematic relationship between those two religions (and others in the ancient world). In the midst of these discussions — and many others — Jesus has appeared again and again as a person who can be understood historically and who must be assessed before we can give any complete explanation of the history of the period in which he lived. As he and his movement are better understood, the nature of the faith that they pioneered has been more clearly defined.

Of course, the Jesus who is under investigation cannot simply be equated with whatever the Gospels say of him. The Gospels, composed in Greek a generation after Jesus' death, reflect the faith of early Christians who came to believe in him. Their belief included reference to historical data, but also included the interpretation of Jesus as it had developed after his time.

The critical tasks of coming to grips with the development of the New Testament, the nature of primitive Christian faith, and the historical profile of Jesus are all interrelated. The purpose of this series is to explore key questions concerning Jesus in recent discussion. Each author has already made an important contribution to the study of Jesus and writes for the series on the basis of expertise in the area addressed by his or her particular volume.

Of the many studies of Jesus that are available today, some are suspect in their treatment of primary sources and some do not engage the secondary literature appropriately. **Studying the Historical Jesus** is a series of contributions that are no less sound for being creative. Jesus is a figure of history as well as the focus of Christian theology: discussion of him should be accessible, rigorous, and interesting.

BRUCE CHILTON
Bard College

CRAIG A. EVANS
Trinity Western University

A New Vision for Israel

*The Teachings of Jesus in
National Context*

Scot McKnight

WILLIAM B. EERDMANS PUBLISHING COMPANY
GRAND RAPIDS, MICHIGAN / CAMBRIDGE, U.K.

© 1999 Wm. B. Eerdmans Publishing Co.

255 Jefferson Ave. S.E., Grand Rapids, Michigan 49503 /

P.O. Box 163, Cambridge CB3 9PU U.K.

Printed in the United States of America

04 03 02 01 00 99   7 6 5 4 3 2 1

Library of Congress Cataloging-in-Publication Data

McKnight, Scot.

A new vision for Israel: the teachings of Jesus in national context /

Scot McKnight.

p.   cm.

Includes bibliographical references and index.

ISBN 0-8028-4212-7 (paper)

1. Jesus Christ — Views on Judaism.

2. Judaism (Christian theology)

I. Title.

BT590.J8M34   1999

232.9′54 — dc21   98-43795

CIP

Unless otherwise noted, the Scripture quotations in this publication are from the
New Revised Standard Version of the Bible, copyright © 1989 by the Division of
Christian Education of the National Council of Churches of Christ in the U.S.A.,
and used by permission.

For Jim Panther

Contents

Preface

The most important development in recent studies of the historical Jesus has been the recognition that Jesus had a mission to the nation of Israel. In this sense, Jesus' mission was political to the core. By "political" I do not mean that Jesus was thinking in terms of political parties or of a revolt against either Rome or the reigning powers in Jerusalem. Scholarship today tends to see Jesus calling the nation to repent in light of a coming act of judgment by God, and in this respect Jesus' politics were national: he was concerned with Israel as a nation. His view of God, kingdom, and ethics was derived from this "national" or "political" mission. Ultimately, of course, he was concerned with Israel's salvation or judgment. This perception of Jesus and his context of mission has displaced older views of Jesus: that he was a Protestant liberal, a social revolutionary, a religious genius, or a misguided enthusiast. The implications of this development are enormous and give shape to this book.

In particular, I attempt in this study to present how the teachings of Jesus are to be understood in light of his mission to Israel. For those who are looking for a book simply on the teachings of Jesus, especially on how those teachings might relate to Christian faith today, this book might disappoint. It does, however, build upon the recent developments in historical Jesus studies that focus upon Jesus' aims and purposes. Most of these studies are concerned primarily with the *actions* of Jesus (his actions in the temple courts, his choosing of the Twelve, his miraculous cures, his exorcisms, etc.), though the implications of these actions for christology are not yet completely worked out (at least not here). This book will build upon this discussion of Jesus' intentions in light of his actions but will press the agenda one step farther by asking, In light of what we know about Jesus through his actions as they relate to Israel, how are we now to understand his teachings? When the national mission of Jesus becomes the orientation for his teachings, those teachings are suddenly brought into a bold new shape. Our study, then, is an exploration of how the teachings of Jesus are to be configured in light of his mission to the nation.

A word ought to be said here about my discussion partners. Since this book represents an initial foray into the teachings of Jesus as seen from the angle of his politics, it will restrict footnotes to only a few major schools of thought: the consistent eschatological orientation of Johannes Weiß and Albert Schweitzer; the Protestant liberalism of Adolf von Harnack and his successors; and German existentialist interpreters of Jesus, especially Rudolf Bultmann, Günther Bornkamm, and Hans Conzelmann. These three schools of thought have now been brought under serious criticism by the more national and political approaches of G. B. Caird, Marcus Borg, and N. T. Wright. In interacting with the major books about Jesus, I have mostly eschewed the more technical discussions found in journals and *Festschriften*.

In light of this purpose, the reader will not confront extensive exegetical analyses of only a few texts with their history of discussion but, rather, a broader canvassing of a larger sampling of the evidence. Debates about authenticity dominate Jesus studies today to the point where one's view of Jesus is ultimately decided by what evidence is counted as reliable. I have attempted here only a few discussions of this sort and have simply tried to show where such discussions might lead. I apologize for the scholarly compulsion to defend everything. Thus, I spare the reader a presentation that focusses on questions of reliability. Each logion of Jesus, of course, can be analyzed at length when matters of authenticity are raised. I have used data that I think are reliable or at least that cohere with what is considered reliable. More extensive analyses of fewer logia can be found elsewhere.

Though I find myself constantly discussing the contemporary significance of Jesus' teachings, the practical implications of what I present here have been largely omitted from the purview of this study. At times I have indicated the direction I might take, but bringing the issue of hermeneutics into this book would lengthen it beyond measure and would also divert the focus from understanding Jesus' teachings in their original political context.

When I was a doctoral student, my supervisor, Professor James D. G. Dunn, suggested that I read a little book by G. B. Caird entitled *Jesus and the Jewish Nation.* I did so, and the book jolted my perception of Jesus, though my work on Matthew kept me from pursuing the lines set out by Caird. While teaching the Synoptic Gospels to seminarians, my interests shifted away from the redactional and the literary and toward the historical; finally, I gave in, dropped my concerns with Matthew, and joined the legions who are now studying Jesus in historical context. Historical Jesus study today is actually the place many of us who were once Gospels students belong, since we were more often than not concerned with history than with the literary and narrative shapes. Three students of Caird — Marcus Borg, N. T. Wright, and Lincoln D. Hurst — have filled in many of the lines marked down by Caird, and I can but hope that this study continues their noble efforts by sketching how the teachings of Jesus fit into this orientation.

A recent move to an undergraduate setting at North Park University has stimulated my life in many ways, among them the sheer fun of teaching young minds about Jesus. Many of my students have expressed a sincere interest in this book and have asked to read portions. Their questions have forced me to look both at presentation and substance. I asked them to write down any questions they had when reading various sections of the book, and those questions have at times found their way into the book. I express my thanks especially to Scott Nelson, Anne Gustafson, Liz Smith, Dan Boehlje, and Leslie Gilbert. Karen Wenell not only read the manuscript but also graciously put together the bibliography during her own busy schedule. David Nystrom, my colleague and friend, looks over my shoulder with courteously critical eyes and has helped me in numerous ways, not the least of which was expressing confidence that I could teach undergraduates. Our librarians and staff have patiently and efficiently acquired sources for me, and they deserve my admiration, especially Sonia Bodi, Ann Briody, and Doug Pierce. I am grateful to Bruce Chilton and Craig Evans, not only for their important research in matters pertaining to Jesus, but especially for inviting me to contribute to this series. I wish here to record my sincere appreciation to my editor at Eerdmans, Dan Harlow, for his painstaking care in working with me on this manuscript. In addition, I extend my gratitude to Reinder Van Til for his enthusiasm for this study, even if it was a mutual enthusiasm for baseball books that initially drew us together.

I dedicate this book to my good friend, Jim Panther. Every summer, for two short weeks, Jim and I teach kids how to play baseball; he has guided the development of my son's baseball abilities, and he brings to my life a measure of realism and sanity. When his team won a thriller to take the IHSBCA summer state championship (July 1997), he brought to fruition the dreams of twenty young men and their parents. I speak on behalf of all the parents and kids: Thanks, Jim.

The burden of my writing is carried by my family. Evenings spent at the computer, all too frequent allusions to my research, discussions with one another in the living room when I mysteriously drift off, and conversations in the same room with so many others are endured lovingly and (usually) forgivingly by my dear wife Kris and our children, Laura and Lukas. In another preface I mentioned Lukas's Little League baseball team, and my academic friends have frequently asked about him. This time I honor his opportunity to catch for the University of Kansas and wish him the joy of the game.

It is my sincere prayer that this book will encourage more and more students to direct their studies toward Jesus as they confess with so many, *Ecce homo!*

Abbreviations

AB	Anchor Bible
ABD	*Anchor Bible Dictionary,* ed. D. N. Freedman
ABRL	Anchor Bible Reference Library
AGJU	Arbeiten zur Geschichte des antiken Judentums und des Urchristentums
AnBib	Analecta Biblica
ANRW	*Aufstieg und Niedergang der römischen Welt*
ASNU	*Acta seminarii neotestamentici upsaliensis*
BAGD	W. Bauer, W. F. Arndt, F. W. Gingrich, F. W. Danker, *Greek-English Lexicon of the New Testament*
BETL	Bibliotheca ephemeridum theologicarum lovaniensium
BGBE	Beiträge zur Geschichte der biblischen Exegese
Bib	*Biblica*
CBNT	Coniectanea Biblica, New Testament
CBQ	*Catholic Biblical Quarterly*
CRINT	Compendia rerum iudaicarum ad novum testamentum
DB	*Dictionary of the Bible,* ed. J. Hastings
DBW	Dietrich Bonhoeffer Werke
DJG	*Dictionary of Jesus and the Gospels,* ed. J. B. Green, S. McKnight, I. H. Marshall
ExpTim	*Expository Times*
FBBS	Facet Books, Biblical Series
GNS	Good News Studies

GP	Gospel Perspectives
HO	Handbuch der Orientalistik
HTKNT	Herder's Theologischer Kommentar zum Neuen Testament
HTKNTS	Herder's Theologischer Kommentar zum Neuen Testament, Supplementband
HTR	*Harvard Theological Review*
IDB	*Interpreter's Dictionary of the Bible,* ed. G. A. Buttrick
IRT	Issues in Religion and Theology
JBL	*Journal of Biblical Literature*
JSNT	*Journal for the Study of the New Testament*
JSNTSup	Journal for the Study of the New Testament — Supplement Series
JTS	*Journal of Theological Studies*
LCC	Library of Christian Classics
LD	Lectio divina
MNTS	McMaster New Testament Studies
NICNT	New International Commentary on the New Testament
NIDNTT	*New International Dictionary of New Testament Theology,* ed. C. Brown
NovT	*Novum Testamentum*
NovTSup	Novum Testamentum, Supplements
NTS	*New Testament Studies*
NTTS	New Testament Tools and Studies
OBO	Orbus biblicus et orientalis
OBT	Overtures to Biblical Theology
PEQ	*Palestine Exploration Quarterly*
PSJCO	Princeton Studies in Judaism and Christian Origins
RES	Religious Experience Series
RGG[3]	*Religion in Geschichte und Gegenwart*
SAC	Studies in Antiquity and Christianity
SBEC	Studies in the Bible and Early Christianity
SBFLA	*Studii biblici franciscani liber annuus*
SBLASP	*SBL Abstracts and Seminar Papers*
SBLEJL	SBL Early Judaism and Its Literature
SBS	Stuttgarter Bibelstudien
SBT	Studies in Biblical Theology
SCJ	Studies in Christianity and Judaism

SJT	*Scottish Journal of Theology*
SNTSMS	Society for New Testament Studies Monograph Series
SNTSU	Studien zum Neuen Testament und seiner Umwelt
SNTW	Studies of the New Testament and Its World
SOTBT	Studies in Old Testament Biblical Theology
Str-B	H. Strack, P. Billerbeck, *Kommentar zum Neuen Testament*
TDNT	*Theological Dictionary of the New Testament*, ed. G. Kittel and G. Friedrich
TDOT	*Theological Dictionary of the Old Testament*, ed. G. J. Botterweck, H. Ringgren, and H.-J. Fabry
THAT	*Theologisches Handwörterbuch zum Alten Testament*, ed. E. Jenni and C. Westermann
TLNT	*Theological Lexicon of the New Testament*
TNTC	Tyndale New Testament Commentary
TWNT	*Theologisches Wörterbuch zum Neuen Testament*, ed. G. Kittel and G. Friedrich
TynBul	*Tyndale Bulletin*
VTSup	Vetus Testamentum, Supplements
WBC	Word Biblical Commentary
WPC	Westminster Pelican Commentary
WUNT	Wissenschaftliche Untersuchungen zum Neuen Testament
ZNW	*Zeitschrift für die neutestamentliche Wissenschaft*

CHAPTER 1

The Vision of Jesus:
A Preliminary Sketch[1]

Prologue

Sometime between 7 and 4 B.C., Miriam, wife of Joseph, gave birth to her firstborn, a son, and he was given the name Jesus (Hebrew *Yeshua*). According to the Gospel records, the small family resided permanently in Nazareth of Lower Galilee (Luke 2:39-40) or, after a brief sojourn in Egypt (Matt. 2:13-15), relocated to Nazareth (Matt. 2:19-23). Growing up in Lower Galilee during the time of Herod Antipas had its own impact on Jesus,[2] as did the evident piety of his mother and father. The pi-

---

1. For the discussions, both about evidence and the secondary literature, see now J. P. Meier, *A Marginal Jew: Rethinking the Historical Jesus* (ABRL; 3 vols.; New York: Doubleday, 1991-). The six scholarly works on Jesus that have shaped my thinking, or that I think we must engage in order for the discussion to move forward are: J. Jeremias, *New Testament Theology: The Proclamation of Jesus* (trans. J. Bowden; New York: Charles Scribner's Sons, 1971); B. F. Meyer, *The Aims of Jesus* (London: SCM, 1979); E. P. Sanders, *Jesus and Judaism* (Philadelphia: Fortress, 1985); J. P. Meier, *A Marginal Jew*; N. T. Wright, *Jesus and the Victory of God* (Christian Origins and the Question of God, vol. 2; Minneapolis: Fortress, 1996); J. Becker, *Jesus von Nazaret* (New York: Walter de Gruyter, 1996). Another important study, though not as helpful since he places Jesus in a Cynic cast, is that of J. D. Crossan, *The Historical Jesus: The Life of a Mediterranean Jewish Peasant* (San Francisco: HarperSanFrancisco, 1991).

2. See esp. R. A. Horsley, *Galilee: History, Politics, People* (Valley Forge, Penn.: Trinity Press International, 1995); see also the older study of S. Freyne, *Galilee from Alexander the Great to Hadrian: A Study of Second Temple Judaism* (Wilmington, Del.: Glazier, 1980); idem, "Galilean Questions to Crossan's Mediterranean Jesus," in W. E. Arnal and M. Desjardins, eds., *Whose Historical Jesus?* (SCJ 7; Waterloo, Ont.: Wilfrid

ety of his parents would have included a disposition of covenantal fidelity and national support, not to mention hope for a restored Israel.[3] Jesus' occupation was apparently that of an artisan, either as a "stone mason," or "carpenter," or "woodworker" (Mark 6:3), but the Greek term behind these translations *(tekton)* does not necessarily indicate poverty. Within this world Jesus did not apparently strike his neighbors as anyone of special significance (cf. Mark 6:1-6a), though these hometown perceptions proved to be superficial.

Several features combined to make Jesus a noteworthy historical figure: his profound religious experience and wisdom, his commitment to celibacy (cf. Matt. 19:12; Mark 3:31-35),[4] his claim that the kingdom of God was now at work through himself and among his followers, his ability to capture audiences using parabolic stories, his breathtaking powers to heal and exorcise, his constant repudiation of sacred tradition symbolized in his practice of table fellowship, his last act in the temple courts, his decision to appoint twelve special leaders for his new community, and his ability both to command allegiance and to astound crowds with his teachings (even to the point of being called "rabbi").[5] The combination of these features eventually forced a decisive break with his hometown's religious ideals and those of the religious establishment. It was this break that inevitably led to his ignominious death on a cross. The penalty was crucifixion on the charge of sedition.

Jesus' life and mission took shape in interaction with a diverse Judaism. Options were many and orthodoxies were few, as can be seen in the manifold ways in which Judaism expressed itself. Thus, Jesus needs to be understood in the context of diverse apocalyptic movements and teachings: the sectarian Essenism of the Dead Sea Scrolls, the evolving

---

Laurier University Press, 1997) 63-91; idem, *Galilee, Jesus, and the Gospels: Literary Approaches and Historical Investigations* (Philadelphia: Fortress, 1988).

3. That Joseph and Mary named their sons after patriarchs expresses not only their fidelity to the covenant and Israel's heritage but also, perhaps, their hope for a future fullness to that covenant (cf. Mark 6:3). "James" is "Jacob" in Greek; "Joses" translates "Joseph"; "Judas" no doubt corresponds to "Judah," and "Simon" translates "Simeon." Jesus' hope for a restored Israel may indeed have been inherited from his parents.

4. That Jesus was celibate may reveal a pre-baptism consciousness of a special mission from God. See H. Schürmann, *Gottes Reich — Jesu Geschick: Jesu ureigener Tod im Licht seiner Basileia-Verkündigung* (Freiburg: Herder, 1983) 28-29. See also Meier, *A Marginal Jew*, 1.332-45.

5. See B. D. Chilton, *Pure Kingdom: Jesus' Vision of God* (Grand Rapids: Eerdmans, 1996) 103-7.

movement of Pharisaism that eventually took shape in a different but somewhat continuous form in rabbinic Judaism, and the social resistance and militaristic violence so characteristic of Galilee, that rabid nationalism which shows, at times, alarming connections with Jesus but which, no matter how the evidence be construed, can no longer be shown to be the formative influence on Jesus or his followers. Jesus did not have to choose one of these options to grow and flourish. Like so many Jews, he learned from the varieties of Judaism and developed in interaction with them.

A neglected feature in Jesus' development, which lies at the very heart of his mission, is the piety that was shaped through public readings and teachings from the Hebrew Bible, as well as its targumic rendering, about which scholarship is now so much more aware.[6] These scriptures and their various renderings mediated to Jesus, and his world, a plurality of Judaisms and approaches to the traditions of Israel.

Alongside Jesus there was John the Baptist. No significant prophet-like figure in Jewish history has been more neglected than John, even though he was a rival of Jesus for the nation's attention. In the beginning, Jesus was probably a disciple of John, though we may debate the nature of his discipleship. Jesus began his own work within the circle of John's prophetic and restorationist movement, a movement anchored in the vision of renewing Israel.[7] Whatever be said about John, his "crisis was one which would determine who among the

---

6. See B. D. Chilton, *A Galilean Rabbi and His Bible* (GNS 8; Wilmington, Del.: Glazier, 1984). Recent study argues that these readings probably did not take place in a building referred to as a "synagogue." Rather, "synagogue" probably refers to the public assembly of the Jewish community and it is in this context that targumic renderings would have had an influence on Jesus. For a recent survey of the issue of "synagogue," see Horsley, *Galilee*, 222-37.

7. On Jesus and John, see Meier, *A Marginal Jew*, 2.19-233; see also J. Weiß, *Die Predigt Jesu vom Reiche Gottes* (3d ed.; ed. F. Hahn; intro. R. Bultmann; Göttingen: Vandenhoeck & Ruprecht, 1964) 65-69. An English edition of Weiß's study is available as *Jesus' Proclamation of the Kingdom of God* (trans. and ed. R. H. Hiers and D. L. Holland; Chico, Calif.: Scholars Press, 1985); Meyer, *Aims of Jesus*, 111-28; Becker, *Jesus von Nazaret*, 37-99; R. L. Webb, *John the Baptizer and Prophet: A Socio-Historical Study* (JSNTSup 62; Sheffield: JSOT Press, 1991); idem, "John the Baptist and His Relationship to Jesus," in B. D. Chilton and C. A. Evans, eds., *Studying the Historical Jesus: Evaluations of the State of Current Research* (NTTS 19; Leiden: Brill, 1994) 179-229; J. E. Taylor, *The Immerser: John the Baptist within Second Temple Judaism* (Grand Rapids: Eerdmans, 1997) 261-316.

Jews belonged to the true Israel."[8] The early traditions about John witness to his call to the nation to repent before the coming judgment and to change the course of national life to reflect the kind of social justice envisioned by both Moses and the prophets:

> John said to the crowds that came out to be baptized by him, "You brood of vipers! Who warned you to flee from the wrath to come? Bear fruits worthy of repentance. Do not begin to say to yourselves, 'We have Abraham as our ancestor'; for I tell you, God is able from these stones to raise up children to Abraham. Even now the ax is lying at the root of the trees; every tree therefore that does not bear good fruit is cut down and thrown into the fire." And the crowds asked him, "What then should we do?" In reply he said to them, "Whoever has two coats must share with anyone who has none; and whoever has food must do likewise." Even tax collectors came to be baptized, and they asked him, "Teacher, what should we do?" He said to them, "Collect no more than the amount prescribed for you." Soldiers also asked him, "And we, what should we do?" He said to them, "Do not extort money from anyone by threats or false accusation, and be satisfied with your wages." (Luke 3:7-14)

To have watched, heard, and participated in John's prophetic movement would have awakened the hopes of the nation for the end of its exile and the dawn of its restoration. John surely stirred the eschatological fires of the expectant among Israel.

Jesus eventually separated himself from John, but Jesus cannot be understood until his relationship with John is clarified. Jesus' vision, message, and tactics were shaped by John. In particular, John's vision of an imminent judgment and the need to prepare Israel in light of that judgment fundamentally impacted Jesus and his teachings. It is this context of the historic prophets of Israel, John included, that gave

8. G. B. Caird, *Jesus and the Jewish Nation* (London: Athlone, 1965) 7. This study contributed significantly to developments in recent studies of the historical Jesus. Two of the major figures in contemporary Jesus research are both former students of Caird: N. T. Wright and M. Borg. Not to be neglected is the major role played by another Caird student: L. D. Hurst, who has made Caird's views more widely known by taking on the Herculean task of editing and completing, with meticuous care, Caird's NT theology; see G. B. Caird, *New Testament Theology* (completed and edited by L. D. Hurst; Oxford: Clarendon, 1994). This book finds its climax in a final section entitled "The Theology of Jesus," where Hurst's skillful hands were especially needed.

shape to the whole mission of Jesus: he saw himself as standing on their shoulders in a renewed prophetic call to the nation.

Alongside this context of the variety of Judaism and his relationship to John, we must also remember that Jesus was, after all, a human being. Orthodox confessions within Christianity, especially among the more conservative, have understandably focused on the extraordinary nature of Jesus' person and ministry. However theologically astute such a confession may be, the impact of this focus has been of a decidedly docetic nature when it comes to approaching Jesus as a historical figure. Christians may worship Jesus as God and they may attribute to him divine status, but in so doing they should not deny his fundamental humanity. Two recent scholars who rightly emphasize this point are G. B. Caird and Gerald F. Hawthorne.[9] Emphasizing Jesus' divinity at the expense of his humanity risks abstracting him from his Jewish context.[10] We cannot understand Jesus until we have put this human figure into his Jewish context, especially as it relates to John the Baptist.

A Political Vision

That both John and Jesus had a vision for the nation of Israel needs to be emphasized: neither John nor Jesus was thinking down the road thousands of years, to our own time, when Christianity would have gone through a multitude of mutations and denominations and when the Church would be interacting with cultures and ideologies so remote from that encountered in the land of Israel at the time of Herod Antipas. Both John and Jesus had a single vision: the restoration of Is-

9. I am thinking especially of G. B. Caird's posthumous *New Testament Theology* and G. F. Hawthorne's *The Power and the Presence: The Significance of the Holy Spirit in the Life and Ministry of Jesus* (Dallas: Word, 1991).

10. Further studies on the humanity of Jesus can be found in J. D. G. Dunn, *Jesus and the Spirit: A Study of the Religious and Charismatic Experience of Jesus and the First Christians as Reflected in the New Testament* (Philadelphia: Westminster, 1975; reprint, Grand Rapids: Eerdmans, 1997) 41-67; C. F. D. Moule, "The Manhood of Jesus in the New Testament," in S. W. Sykes and J. P. Clayton, eds., *Christ, Faith and History: Cambridge Studies in Christology* (Cambridge: Cambridge University Press, 1972) 95-110; reprint in W. R. Farmer, ed., *Crisis in Christology: Essays in Quest of Resolution* (Livonia, Mich.: Dove, 1995) 47-62.

rael. That is, they had one vision for their contemporary Israel, and that was for Israel to become what God had called it to be.

In this sense, a faithful portrait of Jesus must be in line with his vision for Israel and with the role he saw himself playing within that vision. Scholars have utilized many categories for assessing Jesus: God, Lord, messiah, king, teacher, social revolutionary, Cynic-like sage, and religious genius.[11] This study will proceed on the basis that Jesus thought of himself as in some sense king, messiah, and prophet. Each of these categories requires careful definition and elaboration, but the reader will have to go elsewhere for that.[12] The recent attempt by John P. Meier to put it all into one (rather lengthy) sentence speaks for many: Jesus is

a 1st-century Jewish eschatological prophet who proclaims an immi-nent-future coming of God's kingdom, practices baptism as a ritual of preparation for that kingdom, teaches his disciples to pray to God as 'abbā' for the kingdom's arrival, prophesies the regathering of all Israel (symbolized by the inner circle of his twelve disciples) and the inclusion of the Gentiles when the kingdom comes — but who at the same time makes the kingdom already present for at least some Isra-elites by his exorcisms and miracles of healing.[13]

Contemporary scholarship is nearly united in the view that Jesus' vision concerned Israel as a nation and not a new religion.[14] He wanted to consummate God's promises to Israel, and he saw this taking place in the land of Israel.

11. For my assessment of a few recent studies, see "Who Is Jesus?" in M. J. Wilkins and J. P. Moreland, eds., *Jesus under Fire: Crucial Questions about Jesus* (Grand Rapids: Zondervan, 1995) 51-72; the most thorough, up-to-date study is Wright, *Jesus and the Victory of God*, 3-124; see also Arnal and Desjardins, eds., *Whose Historical Jesus?*

12. On Jesus as king, see Sanders, *Jesus and Judaism;* on messiah, see J. D. G. Dunn, "Messianic Ideas and Their Influence on the Jesus of History," in J. H. Charlesworth, ed., *The Messiah: Developments in Earliest Christianity* (PSJCO; Minne-apolis: Fortress, 1992) 365-81; on prophet, see Wright, *Jesus and the Victory of God.* See further B. Witherington, *The Christology of Jesus* (Minneapolis: Fortress, 1990); Meyer, *Aims of Jesus,* 174-202.

13. Meier, *A Marginal Jew,* 2.454.

14. A good example of this is another student of G. B. Caird: M. Borg, *Conflict, Holiness and Politics in the Teachings of Jesus* (SBEC 5; New York: Edwin Mellen, 1984).

A Vision unto Death

Jesus did things that got him into trouble and caused controversy. His choice to participate in table fellowship with the unlikely,[15] his choice to do things on the Sabbath that were considered by others to be sacrilegious, and especially his act of turning tables upside down in the temple courts during a holy festival — each, in its own way, provoked heated controversy, accusations, and exchange, not to mention questionings, plots, and machinations on the part of the establishment.[16] Alongside these acts we should note his choice of the Twelve, surely a symbol for the restoration of the twelve tribes of Israel and the end-time reconstitution of Israel.[17] These deeds are to be understood in the category of "prophetic symbolic acts"[18] and not simply "acts of compassion" performed by one who, in needing and wanting to reach out to people in mercy, could not comprehend what all the fuss was about. In each of these acts, Jesus knew what he was doing and what others would say — and he did them because of what others *would* do and say! These acts reveal Jesus, at least in his mission and his self-understanding of his relation to God, as one who had a mission to Israel. His mission was not well received, and to this lack of reception Jesus responded with a warning about judgment prior to his death.[19]

The establishment, for whatever reasons (and the evidence is notoriously complex), brought Jesus down for blasphemy[20] and sedition, and had him crucified. Scholars have long debated how Jesus saw his

15. I use the term "unlikely" for those who followed Jesus but who would have been seen in Jesus' world as the most unlikely to have done so. Instead of the pure, holy, and respectful, the most unlikely figures responded to Jesus: tax collectors, Galilean peasants and fishermen, prostitutes, and the otherwise sinful.

16. See the suggestive study of G. N. Stanton, "Jesus of Nazareth: A Magician and a False Prophet Who Deceived God's People? " in J. B. Green and M. Turner, eds., *Jesus of Nazareth: Lord and Christ: Essays on the Historical Jesus and New Testament Christology* (Grand Rapids: Eerdmans, 1994) 164-80.

17. Meyer, *Aims of Jesus*, 153-54; Sanders, *Jesus and Judaism*, 95-106.

18. See M. D. Hooker, *The Signs of a Prophet: The Prophetic Actions of Jesus* (Harrisburg, Penn.: Trinity Press International, 1997).

19. A thorough analysis of the theme of judgment has recently been offered by M. Reiser, *Jesus and Judgment: The Eschatological Proclamation in Its Jewish Context* (trans. L. M. Maloney; Minneapolis: Fortress, 1997).

20. See D. L. Bock, "The Son of Man Seated at God's Right Hand and the Debate over Jesus' Blasphemy," in Green and Turner, eds., *Jesus of Nazareth*, 181-91.

own death. A sure aspect of Jesus' vision for the nation included an ordeal of tribulation through which the nation would have to pass before God's judgment and kingdom would materialize. It seems clear that Jesus saw his own death as part of that ordeal. We can be confident that the opponents of Jesus saw in his death a fitting end to his "failed national experiment" to call the nation to its knees in its final hour. Both sides of the story, then, fit the paradigm of a national mission: the opponents had him put to death because he was disturbing the nation's peace, and Jesus himself saw his mission in terms of calling that nation to repent so that it might avert its own doom. His occupation of the temple in the last week of his life shows how central the nation was to his mission. As Bruce D. Chilton, who has given significant attention to Jesus' temple incident, has stated: "However memorable Jesus' teaching may have been on its own merits, it was his crucifixion as a result of his occupation of the temple that became the centerpiece of the Gospels and of the movement that came to be called 'Christian.'"[21]

Not to be disconnected from the temple incident is the last meal Jesus had with his chosen few; what Jesus had protested in the temple incident (corrupt leadership; the need for a restored nation, a restored worship, and a restored covenant; a restoration on Mount Zion for the king) he actualized in a renewal of the covenant in the meal. When his followers took of the bread and the cup, they did so as new participants in the restored Israel (Mark 14:12-26 and parallels). This original context has unfortunately been long forgotten in most Christian celebrations of the Lord's Supper.

Before Jesus' teachings can be understood, then, the historian must make sense of Jesus' death. *That* Jesus was crucified will inevitably help us to situate his teachings in their proper place.[22] Unless Jesus was crucified for reasons totally unrelated to the course of his teachings and the patterns of his life prior to, and including, his final entry into Jeru-

---

21. Chilton, *Pure Kingdom*, 107. See also Chilton, *The Temple of Jesus: His Sacrificial Program within a Cultural History of Sacrifice* (University Park, Penn.: Pennsylvania State University Press, 1992). The incident in the temple has come under intensive scrutiny of late, beginning with Sanders, *Jesus and Judaism*, 61-67. The debate includes C. A. Evans, "Jesus' Action in the Temple: Cleansing or Portent of Destruction?" *CBQ* 51 (1989) 237-70; and Wright, *Jesus and the Victory of God*, 405-28.

22. The most enduring insight of Sanders' book *Jesus and Judaism* is his trenchant emphasis on the need to explain Jesus' life in light of its end: a crucifixion. His teachings need the same kind of attention.

salem, which seems ludicrous, those teachings deserve to be related to his death. And if Jesus' crucifixion stemmed from a desire on the part of the Jerusalem establishment to put away a threat to Jewish piety and the Jewish nation, then it follows that his teachings are anchored in politics and nationalism. No survey of Jesus' teachings is credible unless those teachings are related to his death. The Jesus constructed by historians must be a Jesus who is crucifiable.

The same must be said for the belief in his resurrection: Jesus' anticipation of his own death (Mark 8:31) was also an anticipation of his own vindication. Jesus believed that the true Israel, embodied in himself as the Son of Man, would not only be rejected but also vindicated before God in the face of all opposition. The teachings of Jesus carry this paradoxical theme: rejection at the hands of God's people will result in vindication by God before this same people. Jesus saw this rejection and vindication in the categories of his own death and resurrection, and in the destruction of Jerusalem, an event which simultaneously judged and delivered. Accordingly, Jesus not only saw his death as the inevitable result of his mission to Israel, he chose to die and gave himself for his nation in that last week as part of his plea that the nation repent. In so offering himself, Jesus must have believed that God would vindicate his work. His death, then, was a national sacrifice, offered to God on Israel's behalf, the death of one "for the many" (Mark 10:45).

The National Context of Jesus' Vision

One-sided political approaches to Jesus, whether of the pacifist sort[23] or the zealot type (e.g., that of S. G. F. Brandon or George W. Buchanan),[24] must be corrected with an approach to Jesus that anchors

---

23. At times J. H. Yoder strolls away from Jesus' nationalistic orientation toward too pietistic an outlook; see his *The Politics of Jesus* (2d ed.; Grand Rapids: Eerdmans, 1994).

24. S. G. F. Brandon, *Jesus and the Zealots: A Study in the Political Factor in Primitive Christianity* (Manchester: Manchester University Press, 1967); G. W. Buchanan, *Jesus: The King and His Kingdom* (Macon, Ga.: Mercer University Press, 1984). See also the more nuanced study of R. A. Horsley, *Jesus and the Spiral of Violence: Popular Jewish Resistance in Roman Palestine* (San Francisco: Harper & Row, 1987).

his religious genius in a national vision for Israel. Accordingly, it is mostly the historians who have a firmer grasp of what Jesus was really like in his ancient world. Although religious experts may have expounded his piety well, in so doing they have abstracted Jesus away from his real, Jewish world and from his national vision.[25] For Jesus, religion was a part of the nation, and it was in national terms that pious Jews expressed their allegiance to the covenants with Abraham, Moses, and David.

It follows, then, that Jesus cannot be understood if he is described exclusively, or even primarily, in the category of a spiritual master, or as one who was primarily concerned with the inner religious life and its disciplines for the individual. First and foremost, Jesus was a Jew whose vision of the proper religious life centered on the restoration of the Jewish nation and on the fulfillment of the covenants that God had made with the nation.[26] The most important context in which modern interpreters should situate Jesus is that of ancient Jewish nationalism[27] and Jesus' conviction that Israel had to repent to avoid a national disaster. Jesus' hope was not so much the "Church" as the restoration of the twelve tribes (cf. Matt. 8:11-12; 10:23; and 19:28), the fulfillment of the promises of Moses to national Israel, and the hope of God's kingdom

25. A balanced approach is that of G. B. Caird, beginning with his *Jesus and the Jewish Nation* and finishing with the sketch composed by L. D. Hurst in his *New Testament Theology*, 345-408. A fascinating study in this direction that shows considerable insight into Jesus' overall agenda is Chilton, *Temple of Jesus*. Another important study that anchors Jesus in his political world but focuses too much on apocalyptic eschatology is Sanders, *Jesus and Judaism*. Two studies that, though illuminating in their own way, focus too much on the religious element to the neglect of the political-national element, are M. Borg, *Jesus: A New Vision: Spirit, Culture, and the Life of Discipleship* (San Francisco: Harper & Row, 1988) and Crossan, *The Historical Jesus*. H. Schürmann, *Gottes Reich* (25-26), uses Zealots as a foil to dissociate Jesus from a political mission. But there is more than one sense of "political."

26. I cannot agree with the over-emphasis on the individual in the mission of Jesus that characterized the scholarship of R. Bultmann, *Theology of the New Testament* (trans. K. Grobel; 2 vols.; New York: Charles Scribner's Sons, 1951, 1955) 1.25-26. See also A. Harnack, *What is Christianity?* 60. More historically nuanced views are found in S. Schechter, *Aspects of Rabbinic Theology* (intro. N. Gilman; Woodstock, Vt.: Jewish Lights Publishing, 1993) 97-115; Caird, *Jesus and the Jewish Nation*; Becker, *Jesus von Nazaret*; Wright, *Jesus and the Victory of God*.

27. A good sketch, though limited, may be found in D. Mendels, *The Rise and Fall of Jewish Nationalism* (ABRL; New York: Doubleday, 1992; reprint, Grand Rapids: Eerdmans, 1997).

(focused on and through Israel) on earth. Thus, when Jesus sent out the Twelve (cf. Matt. 9:35–11:1), the "disciples were not evangelistic preachers sent out to save individual souls for some unearthly paradise. They were couriers proclaiming a national emergency and conducting a referendum on a question of national survival."[28]

Consistent with this national mission is another aspect of Jesus' vision: the warning Jesus announced to Israel regarding the sacking of Jerusalem. This was no simple revelation of what would happen next in God's timetable. Jesus' dire warning was founded upon personal revelation concerning the nation of Israel and his mission to that nation: Israel would either repent and accept the message of the kingdom, or it would forfeit its privileged status and become like the rest of the nations, just as happened at the hands of Assyria and Babylon, not to mention the more recent episodes with the Greeks, the Ptolemies, the Seleucids, and the Romans. Jesus' vision, for both the present and the future, concerned Israel and its place in the redemptive plan of God. His hope did not center on a universal Church but on the restoration of the twelve tribes of Israel through the fulfillment of God's promises. Jesus' vision was indeed for the world — but only because it was first for Israel. Jesus' vision was universalistic because it was particularistic.[29]

Even the much discussed title Son of Man, which in Judaism had a decidedly universalistic hope attached to it (cf. Dan. 7:13-14), became for Jesus a nationalistically based promise and threat. As G. B. Caird has said, "The Son of Man is a 'job description' for the New Israel, with Jesus inviting any and all applicants to join him in fulfilling God's full intention, *first for Israel,* and *then* for all the nations of the earth."[30] Thus, Jesus' mission was directed toward Israel in light of a coming disaster upon Jerusalem. He hoped for a national repentance movement, as did John before him, but he also envisioned a disastrous judgment on Jerusalem at the hand of Israel's enemies.

The prophecy of Jerusalem's destruction features prominently in the Gospels (Mark 13; Matt. 11:20-24; 23:37-39; Luke 19:41-44; 21:20-24; 23:27-31). As with Israel's prophets, so with Jesus the vision of the future was sometimes poetic and therefore ambiguous in particulars,

---

28. Caird, *New Testament Theology,* 361.

29. See T. W. Manson, *Only to the House of Israel? Jesus and the Non-Jews* (FBBS 9; Philadelphia: Fortress, 1955).

30. *New Testament Theology,* 380 (italics added); see pp. 369-84.

and at other times graphically historical in description; thematically, Jesus' vision of A.D. 70 concerned both redemption and judgment. We find one such prediction in Luke's Gospel:

> As he came near and saw the city, he wept over it, saying, "If you, even you, had only recognized on this day the things that make for peace! But now they are hidden from your eyes. Indeed, the days will come upon you, when your enemies will set up ramparts around you and surround you, and hem you in on every side. They will crush you to the ground, you and your children within you, and they will not leave within you one stone upon another; because you did not recognize the time of your visitation from God." (Luke 19:41-44)

In his vision of human history, Jesus saw no further than A.D. 70, and to this date he attached visions of the final salvation, the final judgment, and the consummation of the kingdom of God in all its glory. That history took another course does not at all mean that Jesus was in error; rather, like the Hebrew prophets before him, he saw the next event as the end event and predicted events accordingly.[31] This perspective was typical of Jewish prophecy from of old; the next event was seen as the end event, but that next event resulted in a series of unfolding events. Prophecy carried with it an innate poetic ambiguity. It might be argued that Jesus made a distinction between the climactic events pertaining to the nation and to Jerusalem, on the one hand, and to the final events of history, on the other; that is, that Jesus distinguished the events of A.D. 70 from the final events (judgment, kingdom, etc.). This would be very difficult to prove and need not be proved, since Jesus' method was so typical of Jewish prophecy: the next event, an event that God had enabled a prophet to see, would take shape as the last event that would wrap up God's plan for history.

In other words, Jesus emerged on the scene convinced that within a generation God would act climactically to judge Israel. His whole mission was concerned with delivering God's message to that final generation. Jesus preached impending doom, and the way to avoid that doom was to repent from sin and to adhere to his covenantal reformation. His whole ministry, then, was tied into and shaped by his insight from God

---

31. An excellent study in this regard is G. B. Caird, *The Language and Imagery of the Bible* (Philadelphia: Westminster, 1980; reprint, Grand Rapids: Eerdmans, 1997) esp. 201-71.

that a judgment was coming on Israel. Until his teachings are placed in this context, they will not be given their proper setting and therefore will be historically distorted. Jesus' view of God, his breathtaking announcement that the kingdom was drawing near, and his ethical affirmations (as seen in the Sermon on the Mount and other places) were all part of his agenda to lead Israel away from a national disaster and toward a redemption that would bring about the glorious kingdom. Even his death, so central to the Christian understanding of salvation, was connected to his preaching of impending judgment with its attendant woes. Jesus entered Jerusalem at the beginning of the last, fateful week of his life, realized the utter gravity of Israel's situation, and knew that he had to offer himself consciously and intentionally to God as a vicarious sacrifice for Israel in order to avert the national disaster, and he did so as an atoning, substitutionary sacrifice. To quote G. B. Caird once again:

> But so deeply does he love his nation, so fully is he identified with its life, so bitterly does he regret what he sees coming upon it, that only death can silence his reiterated and disturbing appeal. He goes to his death at the hands of a Roman judge on a charge of which he was innocent and his accusers, as the event proved, were guilty. And so, not only in theological truth but in historic fact, the one bore the sins of the many, confident that in him the whole Jewish nation was being nailed to the cross, only to come to life again in a better resurrection, and that the Day of the Son of Man which would see the end of the old Israel would see also the vindication of the new.[32]

God, the Christian will confess, accepted Jesus' atoning sacrifice for the nation, but the disaster came anyway. Accordingly, until we tie the surviving remnant, the Church, into Jesus' predictions about both salvation and judgment, in connection with A.D. 70, his teachings about God, ethics, and kingdom cannot be given their proper historical significance.

Seen in the context sketched above, Jesus' teaching centered on three major themes:[33] (1) *the Covenant God*, YHWH, who created the uni-

---

32. Caird, *Jesus and the Jewish Nation*, 22.

33. Wright, *Jesus and the Victory of God*, focuses the issues through the lens of kingdom helpfully but unfortunately does not devote enough space to what Jesus said about God.

verse, formed a covenant with Israel, disciplined the nation with (a still continuing) exile, and directed history to its decisive moment; (2) *the kingdom of God,* which became for Jesus the central symbol of an eschatological climax to this covenant history; and (3) *kingdom ethics,* the life that is expected by God for those who choose to be faithful to the covenant as now made known at the end of times in Jesus. In what follows, our discussion will focus on these three themes: God, kingdom, and ethics. We shall, however, limit ourselves to expounding those themes in light of this national vision of Jesus.[34]

34. A word needs to be said about my position on the Synoptic Problem: I believe Matthew and Luke both used Mark and Q; I also think they both had access to other traditions (and I will follow the scholarly custom of referring to these traditions as "M" [for Matthew] and "L" [for Luke]), but I am unconvinced that we can know much about the origin and development of these special traditions. As for Q, I am not yet persuaded that we can delineate either the composition history of the putative document or the various phases of development through which the so-called Q community passed. On this, see C. M. Tuckett, "Synoptic Problem," *ABD,* 6.263-70. On Q in particular, see J. S. Kloppenborg, *The Formation of Q: Trajectories in Ancient Wisdom Collections* (SAC; Philadelphia: Fortress, 1987); E. P. Meadors, *Jesus the Messianic Herald of Salvation* (Peabody, Mass.: Hendrickson, 1997); C. M. Tuckett, *Q and the History of Early Christianity* (Peabody, Mass.: Hendrickson, 1996); D. C. Allison, Jr., *The Jesus Tradition in Q* (Harrisburg, Penn.: Trinity Press International, 1997).

CHAPTER 2

The God of Jesus

It is strange that so little has been written in scholarship about the God of Jesus, particularly when scholars like Adolf Schlatter can say: "Jesus' primary and ultimate idea, the thought with which he began and conducted all his thinking, was the idea of God."[1] Similarly, Adolf Harnack, in his epoch-making lectures on the essence of Christianity, said of Jesus:

> He lived in religion, and it was breath to him in the fear of God; his whole life, all his thoughts and feelings, were absorbed in the relation to God, and yet he did not talk like an enthusiast and a fanatic, who sees only one red-hot spot, and so is blind to the world and all that it contains. . . . He lived in the continual consciousness of God's presence.[2]

T. W. Manson, in his exceptional study of Jesus' teaching, wrote: "The fact with which we have to reckon at all times is that in the teaching of Jesus his conception of God determines everything, including the conceptions of the kingdom and the Messiah."[3] Why, we might ask, are

---

1. A. Schlatter, *The History of the Christ: The Foundation for New Testament Theology* (trans. A. J. Köstenberger; reprint, Grand Rapids: Baker, 1997).
2. *What is Christianity?* (trans. T. B. Saunders; reprint, New York: Harper & Row, 1957) 34-35, 38.
3. T. W. Manson, *Teaching of Jesus: Studies of Its Form and Content* (Cambridge: Cambridge University Press, 1939) 211. See also W. Lowrie's introduction to A. Schweitzer, *The Mystery of the Kingdom of God: The Secret of Jesus' Messiahship and*

there so few treatments of Jesus' teachings about God if Schlatter, Harnack, and Manson are correct that both the very beginning (foundation) and the very ending (goal) of Jesus' teachings and life were about God? No answer satisfies, but a few examples should suffice.

Whatever one thinks of Rudolf Bultmann's decision to assign the teachings of Jesus to the presuppositional level of New Testament theology, Bultmann did explicate, however briefly, what he thought was "Jesus' Idea of God."[4] The section of his *New Testament Theology* bearing this heading summarizes a rather large part of his *Jesus and the Word*, which was published nearly a quarter of a century earlier. In that book, Bultmann explicated the teachings of Jesus about God in two main categories: God as remote and God as near.[5] Here Bultmann's study of Jesus is dialectical and existential; the teachings of Jesus about God are to be understood as the experience of God and not as referential language about God himself. Thus, what Jesus said is not a description of who God is, but of how God is experienced.[6] Once presented, however, Bultmann's depiction of Jesus' God turns out to be quite traditional in overall categories: God is both toweringly transcendent and lovingly present. Perhaps his best summary statement can be found in the following:

> God is God of the present, because His claim confronts man in the present moment, and He is at the same time God of the future, because He gives man freedom for the present instant of decision, and sets before him as the future which is opened to him by his decision, condemnation or mercy. God is God of the present for the sinner precisely because He casts him into remoteness from Himself, and He is at the same time God of the future because He never relinquishes His claim on the sinner and opens to him by forgiveness a new future for new obedience.[7]

Passion (trans. W. Lowrie; New York: Schocken, 1964) 40. See also J. Gnilka, *Jesus von Nazaret: Botschaft und Geschichte* (rev. ed.; Freiburg: Herder, 1993) 88.

4. R. Bultmann, *Theology of the New Testament* (2 vols.; trans. K. Grobel; New York: Charles Scribner's Sons, 1951-55) 1.22-26.

5. R. Bultmann, *Jesus and the Word* (trans. L. P. Smith; E. H. Lantero; New York: Charles Scribner's Sons, 1958) 133-219. Cf. G. Bornkamm, *Jesus of Nazareth* (trans. I. and F. McLuskey with J. M. Robinson; New York: Harper & Row, 1960) 128.

6. True to German Lutheran form, Bultmann uses "law" and "philosophy" interchangeably.

7. *Jesus*, 211.

As we will see below, Bultmann's discussion of God, though rather extensive for the history of this topic in the teachings of Jesus, is overloaded with a now-passé existentialism and is further weakened by both an inattentiveness to Judaism and a concern to present everything in Pauline (read German Lutheran) categories and logic.

Reacting to the work of Joachim Jeremias, Günther Bornkamm, a student of Bultmann, argued that Jesus' use of "Father" was not that exceptional and was to be seen as an expression of the "nearness of God."[8] Along the same lines of thought as his teacher Bultmann, Hans Conzelmann deals with Jesus' "concept of God."[9] Joachim Jeremias, justly famous for his insightful explication of Jesus' use of 'abbā', devoted but eight (out of 312) pages to Jesus' teachings about God, and here he is mostly concerned with what Jesus meant by his use of 'abbā'.[10] Leonhard Goppelt authored one of the most penetrating books ever about Jesus, but he devoted no separate section to Jesus' teachings about God.[11] Even the conservative theologian George E. Ladd, well known among evangelicals for his *New Testament Theology*,[12] presented only an abbreviated treatment of the teachings of Jesus about God.

In a rather odd combination of evangelical piety, theological acuity, linguistic subtlety, and uncritical passivity, R. A. Ward's *Royal Theology* is perhaps the closest thing to a full-scale analysis of the teachings of Jesus about God.[13] Consonant with the two themes set out by Bultmann (remoteness and nearness), Ward examines the themes of "severity" (God's judging holiness) and "kindness" (God's gracious forgiveness and love). While his book attempts to reconcile these two

8. Bornkamm, *Jesus*, 124-29.

9. H. Conzelmann, *Jesus* (trans. J. R. Lord; intro. J. Reumann; Philadelphia: Fortress, 1973) 54-59; W. G. Kümmel, *The Theology of the New Testament according to Its Major Witnesses: Jesus — Paul — John* (trans. J. E. Steely; Nashville: Abingdon, 1973).

10. J. Jeremias, *New Testament Theology: The Proclamation of Jesus* (trans. J. Bowden; New York: Charles Scribner's Sons, 1971) 61-68.

11. L. Goppelt, *Theology of the New Testament* (2 vols.; trans. J. E. Alsup; ed. J. Roloff; Grand Rapids: Eerdmans, 1981-82).

12. G. E. Ladd, *A Theology of the New Testament* (rev. ed.; ed. D. A. Hagner; Grand Rapids: Eerdmans, 1993) 79-88. See also Ladd, *The Presence of the Future: The Eschatology of Biblical Realism* (Grand Rapids: Eerdmans, 1974), a slight revision of his *Jesus and the Kingdom* (New York: Harper and Row, 1964).

13. R. A. Ward, *Royal Theology: Our Lord's Teaching about God: Studies in the Divine Severity and Kindness* (London: Marshall, Morgan & Scott, 1964).

themes in the death of Jesus as a sacrificial atonement, Ward's book often presents genuine insight into both the context of Jesus and the meaning of his practices and teachings.

Writing in the wake of Jeremias's seminal work on 'abbā' and addressing the fundamental hermeneutical and social issues raised by feminist scholarship, Robert Hamerton-Kelly examines the issue of patriarchy and God in the history of Israel as well as in the teachings of Jesus and the early Church. Hamerton-Kelly argues that Jesus is to be understood as a social revisionist who, interpreted in light of a Freudian-cum-Ricoeurian hermeneutics, advocated an egalitarianism that ultimately dismissed patriarchy. The author concludes: "If he [Jesus] did indeed speak for the reign of God, as we believe, then we must judge the passage from patriarchy to partnership to be the action of God in our history, for it conforms to the words of Jesus about the breaking and reconstituting of family ties."[14] While the central issues that drive Hamerton-Kelly are contemporary rather than historical, the book is an important contribution to the theme of God as Father in the Hebrew Bible and as seen in the activity of Jesus.

Perhaps the finest modern treatment of the teachings of Jesus is the early work of T. W. Manson in his *The Teaching of Jesus*.[15] This work not only covered the important topics (without limiting itself to the title 'abbā'), but integrated all the major teachings of Jesus (God, kingdom, ethics, eschatology, church, etc.) around his teachings about God. This groundbreaking work has not been superseded, except in its general (now passé) liberal Protestant theological orientation.[16] Manson saw God as Father as the most profound and central experience of Jesus. From this experience emerged Jesus' mission: to lead others into that same relation with God the Father (e.g., Matt. 11:25-27). Manson

---

14. R. G. Hamerton-Kelly, *God the Father: Theology and Patriarchy in the Teaching of Jesus* (Philadelphia: Fortress, 1974) 70. The book is summarized, with some slight extensions, in "God the Father in the Bible and in the Experience of Jesus: The State of the Question," in J.-B. Metz and E. Schillebeeckx, eds., *God as Father?* (New York: Seabury, 1981) 95-102.

15. T. W. Manson, *The Teaching of Jesus: Studies of Its Form and Content* (Cambridge: Cambridge University Press, 1939).

16. Manson expresses, for English readers, what began with Schleiermacher, moved to Ritschl and Harnack, and then passed into the more historically focussed efforts of G. Dalman, who influenced Manson (see N. Perrin, *The Kingdom of God in the Teaching of Jesus* [London: SCM, 1963] 13-36, 90-102).

contended that the key event in the life of Jesus was the confession of Peter; after this event, Jesus engaged only his disciples with the theme of the Fatherhood of God and with the necessity of entering the kingdom of God.

Three general observations about the scholarship on Jesus' understanding of God need to be offered. First, scholars have too often focused narrowly on the Fatherhood of God in the teachings of Jesus. In so doing, other important topics have been left untouched, undiscovered, or avoided. Thus, from Harnack to Jeremias (and his followers and critics) too much attention has been given to *'abbā'* as the key to uncovering what Jesus believed about God and what he experienced of God. The desire to find what is "new" in Jesus' teachings, in contrast to what was "traditional" in Judaism, has contributed to this overemphasis on *'abbā'*.

Second, the paucity of discussion about God in the teachings of Jesus has led to an alarming inability to integrate the three main foci of the teachings of Jesus: God, kingdom, and ethics. While it might be apparent to those who adopt Albert Schweitzer's approach to Jesus' eschatology that Jesus' ethic is thereby partly (if not wholly) explained contextually, when God reenters the picture, the theme of eschatology is altered, leaving a newer, fresher vision of the ethic of Jesus. This is not to pretend that Jesus' imminent eschatology had no impact on his ethical teaching; nor is it to suggest that reintroducing God into the picture solves all of the problems connected with Jesus' imminent eschatology. It is just that Jesus' view of God deserves its place as we attempt today to put the whole picture into some reasonable whole and unity.[17] Put simply, until we understand each of the three foci, we do not understand any of them; only when we put our hands around each of the three can we grasp what Jesus and his teaching were all about.

Third, scholarship is now recognizing that Jesus' mission was directed toward the nation of Israel. This means that his understanding of God himself must also be oriented toward an understanding of God that emerges from the covenants with Abraham, Moses, and David, which guided the history of the nation to the time of Jesus. The God of Jesus, accordingly, is the God of Israel who is now restoring the nation and renewing its people as he had promised long ago.

---

17. Jesus did not have what we now call a "systematic theology." See B. H. Young, *Jesus the Jewish Theologian* (Peabody, Mass.: Hendrickson, 1995) 269-74.

Older studies of the development of Christianity out of Judaism may have found in Jesus a great proponent of a universal God, but they did so at the expense of historical accuracy: the God of Jesus is above all the God of Israel. The tensions between Jesus and his Jewish contemporaries did not stem from devotion to a different God, or even a different perception of God, for the God Jesus trusted, obeyed, and proclaimed was the God of the Bible he had been taught to hear. This in no way means, however, that Jesus did not bring new perceptions to the age-old presentation of God. What bears emphasizing is that the God of Jesus is the God of Israel, and this God (so Jesus believed) is now active in him for the redemption of Israel. God, for Jesus, is the God who is now active in restoring Israel and not a God who has abandoned his covenants with Israel. When scholarship finds in Jesus' view of God the release from what constrained Judaism, it has failed to understand what Jesus was all about. As Jesus saw it, God was seeking through him to restore the nation, not to create a new religion.

In our discussion of Jesus' teaching about God, two themes will occupy center stage: (1) God as inflexibly holy and (2) God as relationally loving. These two themes formed the foundation for Jesus' entire life and teachings; they were the platforms on which he stood in making all his pronouncements.[18] Jesus was a theocentric prophet, and his teachings were soaked in theology proper.[19] Until his theology is expounded, neither kingdom nor ethics can make sense. As Marcus Borg has put it:

> Thus as a Jewish holy man, Jesus knew God. Out of this intimate knowing flowed his understanding of God's nature or quality, and his perception of what Israel was to be. . . . Thus, Jesus' basic "program" for the internal reform of Israel — "Be merciful as God is merciful" — flowed out of knowledge of God which he, as a holy man, was given in his own internal experience.[20]

18. Adolf Deissmann, *The Religion of Jesus and the Faith of Paul* (trans. W. E. Wilson; London: Hodder and Stoughton, 1923) 69-97, connects love with "Father" and holiness with "Lord" in the experience of Jesus with God. See also Schlatter, *History*, 117-25, esp. 118-19.

19. See, e.g., L. W. Hurtado, "God," *DJG*, 270-72; Deissmann, *Religion of Jesus*, 125-26.

20. M. Borg, *Conflict, Holiness and Politics in the Teachings of Jesus* (SBEC 5; New York: Edwin Mellen, 1984) 232-34.

Of course, behind Jesus' teachings *about* God was an experience *of* God, but these two cannot simply be equated; in particular, the latter is much more difficult to define than is sometimes imagined.[21] Although many scholars dismiss Jesus' experience of God as unapproachable or unknowable, their thoroughly modern and empirical approach too hastily denies what may be knowable, however partial and difficult that might be. And, to the degree that our own religious experience is knowable and communicable, we can by analogy know what others find in religious experience. What Adolf Deissmann called the "white-hot blazing metal" behind the iron rods of Jesus' teachings can be partly known, and the topic is therefore worthy of current discussion.[22] In part, then, we are not just looking at the external teachings of Jesus but also at the driving force of a magnetic personality and religious genius behind those teachings.

Before we begin our exposition, a word must be said about the relationship of Jesus' understanding of God to Judaism's. What Jesus said about God was consistent with what he learned in public religious gatherings and from his parents. Jesus taught no new thing about God, and his experience of God was consonant with what other Jews, in Israel's past and present, had already experienced or were experiencing. Christian attempts to contend that Jesus taught a new idea about God amount to little more than vain polemics and wishful thinking.[23] The pages of the Gospels teach nothing about God that does not have a substantial background in Jewish literature and experience. To argue that Jesus' experience of God was either unique or more intimate than that of other Israelites is to argue for something that cannot be shown. This is not to deny the intimacy of Jesus with God, but only to maintain that the people of Israel also had an intimate relation with God whenever they uttered the words

21. One of the earlier treatments of this is Deissmann, *Religion of Jesus.* The two most important modern studies on this are J. D. G. Dunn, *Jesus and the Spirit: A Study of the Religious and Charismatic Experience of Jesus and the First Christians as Reflected in the New Testament* (Philadelphia: Westminster, 1975; reprint, Grand Rapids: Eerdmans, 1997) and M. Borg, *Jesus: A New Vision: Spirit, Culture, and the Life of Discipleship* (San Francisco: Harper & Row, 1987).

22. Deissmann, *Religion of Jesus,* 25-26.

23. A good example of this can be found in W. Marxsen, *New Testament Foundations for Christian Ethics* (trans. O. C. Dean, Jr.; Minneapolis: Fortress, 1993) esp. 59-126.

of the Psalter. Jesus' God, his view of God, and his experience of God, so far as we are able to perceive the latter, are thoroughly and consistently Jewish.[24] In this regard, Deissmann had it right when he wrote: "Jesus is so great that He can dispense with the efforts of those who seek to glorify Him at the expense of His ancestors."[25] If Jesus' mission was primarily directed at the restoration of Israel, his God must have been the same as his nation's.

God as Inflexibly Holy

When Jesus spoke of God, he assumed what nearly all Jews thought about God: that he was creator (e.g., Matt. 10:29; 19:4); that he was the sovereign ruler over his created world, the universe (Matt. 5:45; 6:26-30);[26] that there was but one God, YHWH (Deut. 6:4-6; Mark 12:29), who had chosen Israel, to whom he had granted the law[27] and grace through both election and repentance; and that this God was now calling his people to be restored or else encounter the Day of YHWH. Jesus' own expressions of God's jealousy over those who were called to follow Jesus in the ordinary activities of the day can only be understood against this background. When Jesus called his fellow Israelites to single-minded righteous living, as can be seen in the Q tradition behind Luke 12:33-34; 11:34-36; 16:13; 12:22-31//Matt. 6:19-34, such a call was rooted theologically in God's unique oneness and in his jealous owner-

24. So also, e.g., G. Vermes, *The Religion of Jesus the Jew* (Minneapolis: Fortress, 1993) 173-80; J. H. Charlesworth, "A Caveat on Textual Transmission and the Meaning of *Abba*: A Study of the Lord's Prayer," in J. H. Charlesworth, M. Harding, and M. Kiley, eds., *The Lord's Prayer and Other Prayer Texts from the Greco-Roman Era* (Valley Forge, Penn.: Trinity Press International, 1994) 1-14. For two examples of those who seek to find tension, however small or great, see J. H. Klausner, *Jesus of Nazareth: His Life, Times, and Teaching* (trans. H. Danby; New York: Macmillan, 1926) 377-80; Ladd, *Presence*, 173-76.

25. Deissmann, *Religion of Jesus*, 70.

26. See Ward, *Royal Theology*, 25-30, who examines the notion of God as creator who owns and operates his creation.

27. On Jesus' view of scripture, see C. A. Evans, "Old Testament in the Gospels: 3. Jesus' Use of the OT," *DJG*, 579-83; B. D. Chilton and C. A. Evans, "Jesus and Israel's Scriptures," in B. D. Chilton and C. A. Evans, eds., *Studying the Historical Jesus: Evaluations of the State of Current Research* (Leiden: Brill, 1994) 281-335.

ship of Israel.[28] It was utterly foreign for Jesus to teach apart from this Jewish construct about God and his relation to Israel.

In speaking of God's holiness in the teachings of Jesus, the entire history of Israel can be brought forward as evidence for what "holy" (Hebrew *qādōš*) means; the reason we speak of Israel's history is that Israel's theology developed in the form of historical narrative, as opposed, say, to a philosophical treatise. God's holiness was experienced in Israel in at least two dimensions: (1) theophanic or cultic holiness and (2) instructive holiness.

Theophanic or cultic holiness speaks of the transcendence of God, of his utter majesty when he displayed his glory and presence, whether at the burning bush, on Mt. Sinai, in the parting of the Red Sea, in the conquest of Canaan, in the return to the land, or in the institution of sacrifice (e.g., Abraham in Gen. 15:1-21; the *Shekinah* attending the tabernacle or the temple of Solomon). The same applies to the directives of the Torah concerning priestly purity: God's holiness lies at the foundation of the codes to sanctify days, places, things, and relationships. This holiness, while it can be said to describe the "separateness of God," pertains equally to the encounter with God.[29]

Instructive holiness pertains to the comprehensive set of codes, commands, and ordinances that YHWH granted to Israel as its side of maintaining the covenant that God had made with Abraham and extended through Moses and David (see, e.g., Genesis 12, 15, 17; Exodus 20–24; Deuteronomy; 2 Samuel 7). In conforming to these revelatory commands, the people of Israel were to allow their character to be shaped by YHWH's and so spread YHWH's name and glory throughout his created order. These codes were not seen as onerous demands; nor were they separated from God's gracious redemption.[30] Instead, the law of God was seen as the gracious revelation of God's will to his people, for their good and for their salvation. Even the Levitical pre-

---

28. See E. P. Sanders, *Judaism: Practice and Belief (63 BCE–66 CE)* (Philadelphia: Trinity Press International, 1992) 241-78.

29. On God's holiness as his utter separation, see N. Snaith, *The Distinctive Ideas of the Old Testament* (New York: Schocken, 1964) 21-50. On holiness pertaining to encounter, see H. Seebass, "Holy, Consecrate, Sanctify, Saints, Devout," in *NIDNTT*, 2.223-28.

30. See esp. E. P. Sanders, *Paul and Palestinian Judaism: A Comparison of Patterns of Religions* (Philadelphia: Fortress, 1977); R. Brooks, *The Spirit of the Ten Commandments: Shattering the Myth of Rabbinic Legalism* (San Francisco: Harper & Row, 1990).

scriptions, which seem so strange to moderns, were seen as God's gracious revelation of his will in specific matters pertaining to such things as sexual purity and clean versus unclean animals (cf. Leviticus 11–16). All of these commands were designed to conform Israel's behavior to YHWH's essential character traits: his absolute purity and holiness. At least from the Hellenistic period onward, this foundation in holiness was also used as a basis for constructing Jewish identity among various sectarian movements, including the Hasidim, the Pharisees, and the Essenes.[31] Thus a fundamental feature of the Judaism in which Jesus was nurtured was the option of a radical pursuit of holiness. At the bottom of this pursuit, however, was the law of Moses, the precious gift of YHWH to Israel as the focus of instructive holiness.

In the history of Christian polemics with Judaism, radically developed as they were through the growth of the printing industry after Luther, grace and law have been tragically disconnected. In the Judaism of Jesus' day, God's law was never regarded as inferior to God's grace, nor was it seen to stand in competition with some nobler principle. Rather, God's law was treated by Jesus as God's will, permanent (Matt. 5:17-20) and salvific (Mark 10:17-22). Jesus' own pursuit of holiness was driven by his observance of the law and by his belief that the law was God's revealed will for Israel. In the teaching and practice of Jesus, God's holiness can be seen in at least five different areas: (1) his demand to revere God, (2) his manner of speech, (3) his call to surrender, (4) his warnings of judgment, and (5) his final words from the cross.

The Demand to Revere God

Jesus demanded that his followers revere God. Consistent with Jewish piety, known for its sometime obsessive reserve about speaking God's name (the tetragrammaton YHWH), Jesus taught his followers to honor God by sanctifying his name (Luke 11:2//Matt. 6:9) and by reserving the name "Father" for him alone (Matt. 23:9). Ancient Israelite religion may have moved, in perception or practice, from henotheism to monolatry to monotheism; by the time of Jesus, however,

---

31. See Borg, *Conflict, Holiness and Politics,* 51-72. A more nuanced presentation of this history can be seen in Sanders, *Judaism: Practice and Belief,* 1-43, 380-451.

Judaism was firmly based on a consistent monotheistic substructure.[32] This covenant God is not only a "one and only God" but a jealous God (cf. Exod. 20:5; Deut. 5:9) who demands that Israelites love and obey him with all their being (Deut. 6:5). Throughout the Bible, but especially in the Deuteronomic history recounted in Joshua through 2 Kings, Israel's misfortunes are traced back to Israel's decisions to make God less than the one and only God. Jesus' injunctions to revere God were rooted deeply in the Jewish doctrine and practice of monotheism, and especially in the need for ancient Israel to refrain from polytheistic worship, since God is God Most High (Luke 6:35). It comes as no surprise that, when Jesus called the nation to repent in the face of the coming judgment of God, he did so in terms of God's holiness.

Accordingly, Jesus taught his disciples to honor and sanctify the name of God (Matt. 6:9). But how was this to be done? Was it simply a matter of not uttering the true pronunciation of the tetragrammaton? An answer may be found in the expression "profaning the name," which occurs frequently in the prophets: to profane the name of God was to live in sin, to depart from the ways of the covenant in either sinful practices or in sinful, idolatrous worship (cf., e.g., Amos 2:6-8, where profanity is connected with mistreatment of the poor, sexual sins, and idolatrous activities; cf. Jer. 34:16; Ezek. 20:39; Mal. 1:8-10).[33] To be sure, how Israelites spoke of God was important, but profanity and sanctity had chiefly to do with ethical behavior, ceremonial concerns, and cultic matters. We are justified, then, in contending that Jesus had in mind not so much "God-talk" as covenant obedience demanded by God in the codes of the Bible and by Jesus in his call for Israel to repent (Mark 1:15 pars.; Luke 13:1-5; Matt. 5:17-48 pars.). No one who prayed for God's name to be sanctified could at the same time live in disobedience to the covenant without incurring the displeasure of God. The prayer request for God's name to be sanctified includes within it, therefore, a dominating ethical corollary.

In addition, the prayer for God's name to be sanctified should be connected with the Roman occupation of Palestine: as under Babylonian rule, YHWH's name is defiled when Israel is too weak to ward off

---

32. See J. J. Scullion, "God in the OT," *ABD*, 2.1042-43 ("Toward One God"); Sanders, *Judaism: Practice and Belief*, 242-47.

33. See W. Dommershausen, "*ḥll, chōl, chālîl*," *TDOT*, 4.409-17.

its enemies, and it becomes weak when it fails to live according to God's covenant. With Palestine under Roman rule, Jesus taught his disciples to pray for Israel's restoration, that is, to pray for God once again to honor his name by liberating his people from foreign domination.[34] This fits more adequately with the parallel requests "may your kingdom come, may your will be done *on earth* as it is in heaven." God's utter holiness, involving the sanctification of his name throughout the Roman empire, was the primary request of Jesus: he taught his followers to live holy, righteous, law-abiding lives so that God's will would be established and so that God's name would be restored as the one, true God. This "political" vision of Jesus lies at the heart of the Lord's Prayer.[35] In speaking of the resemblance of the Lord's Prayer to the Jewish *Qaddish* prayer, upon which Jesus built his community (cf. Luke 11:1-4) prayer, John P. Meier states:

> God is besought to bring about a definitive manifestation of his power, glory, and holiness by defeating the Gentiles, gathering the scattered tribes of Israel back to the holy land, and establishing his divine rule fully and forever. It is within this trajectory that Jesus' prayer that God will sanctify his name and bring in his kingly rule is to be understood.[36]

After Jesus divulged his new name for God (*'abbā'*, "Father") and taught his disciples how to address and trust such a God, he instructed his disciples to call no one upon earth "father" (cf. Acts 7:2; 22:1),[37] for there is but one Father, and he is in heaven (Matt. 23:9). While discussions of this text have focused on the dating of the terms "father" and "rabbi," and other studies have questioned Jesus' sagacity in suggesting that one's father not be addressed as "father," the general import of this text is both entirely Jewish and consistent with Jesus' use of the term *'abbā'*. The emphasis here falls on the jealousy of God (Exod. 20:5), especially for his new name *'abbā'*, and on the total focus the disciples are

---

34. Cf. Dommershausen, "ḥll, chōl, chālîl," 410-11, who summarizes the message of Ezekiel as it pertains to the Babylonian captivity and the defilement of God's name.

35. See also Hamerton-Kelly, *God the Father*, 74.

36. J. P. Meier, *A Marginal Jew: Rethinking the Historical Jesus* (ABRL; 3 vols.; New York: Doubleday, 1991-) 2.297.

37. Cf. R. S. Barbour, "Uncomfortable Words. 8: Status and Titles," *ExpTim* 82 (1970-71) 137-42.

to have in their obedience of him. The disciples of Jesus are to reserve this kind of respect, trust, and obedience for God alone, who is now called '*abbā*'; no teacher on earth and no human father are to be given this kind of honor and trust.[38] This one God, then, is jealous[39] for obedience and for how his covenanted people are to address him: in a disposition unlike any granted to human beings. To be ready for the coming kingdom of God, to be the kind of nation God wants Israel to be, the followers of Jesus must honor God completely.

Jesus also taught his disciples to live in such a way that others might see their deeds (of mercy) and be led by them to ascribe glory to God (cf. Matt. 5:16; 15:31; Mark 2:12; Luke 18:43).[40] That is, through the behavior of the disciples, including not least their righteousness, love, and deeds of power on behalf of those in need of mercy (Matt. 25:31-46; see 10:7-8; Luke 10:17-20), and because of the distinctive impress of those actions, others would confess the God of Jesus and his followers to be their God as well, and so would give him glory and honor for his goodness. In light of how the term *glory* is used eschatologically (cf. Ps. 86:9, 12; Ezek. 39:13), it might be said that the mission of Jesus was to lead Israel to repentance and restoration and, through such reform, to bring glory back to the God of Israel (cf. Mark 10:37; Matt. 16:27; 19:28; 24:30; 25:31). The coming judgment would be a time of triumph for Jesus' God, but his glory could be brought forward in time if Israel would only repent.[41]

Jesus' Manner of Speech

Jesus spoke about and to God in a special manner. Because the disciples of Jesus were to sanctify their God in both thought and deed, Jesus illustrated by his own example both a reserve and a special manner of speaking about and to this God. Jesus may well have avoided using *Elohim*; the

---

38. See Jeremias, *Proclamation of Jesus*, 67-68; idem, *Prayers of Jesus*, 41-43, 57-65.

39. See Ward, *Royal Theology*, 34.

40. See S. McKnight, *A Light Among the Gentiles: Jewish Missionary Activity in the Second Temple Period* (Minneapolis: Fortress, 1991) 67-68.

41. See Ward, *Royal Theology*, 36-47. The theme of honor/glory and shame may be behind the story in Luke 11:5-8; see K. E. Bailey, *Poet and Peasant: A Literary Cultural Approach to the Parables in Luke* (Grand Rapids: Eerdmans, 1976) 119-33.

Evangelists could easily have inserted *Theos*,[42] and, whether or not Jesus used *Adonai* or *Hashem* when citing scripture in places where YHWH was found, it is clear that Jesus practiced a measure of caution in speaking to and about God.[43] The second commandment was generally extended to prohibit uttering the tetragrammaton (Exod. 20:7; Deut. 5:11). Other safeguards attended this practice, one of which was the use of circumlocutions for God and his name: "the Highest One" (cf. Luke 6:35), "the Blessed One" (see *m. Berakot* 7:3; cf. Mark 14:61), "the Powerful One" (Mark 14:62), "the Holy One"[44] and "the Merciful One."[45] As can be seen in Matt. 5:34-35 and other Jewish texts, this practice was well established before Jesus.[46]

Jesus' occasional use of the term "kingdom *of heavens*" for "kingdom of God" (cf. Matt. 4:17) reflects the characteristic Jewish reserve in addressing God. But this favorite Matthean expression by no means exhausts the evidence.[47] When the repentant son comes to his senses, he decides to return to his father and to say these words: "Father, I have sinned *against heaven (eis ton ouranon)* and before you . . ." (Luke 15:18). Clearly, "against heaven" is a periphrase for "God" and reflects the Jewish tradition of extending the second commandment. When Jesus informs the rich young man what he needs to do to be worthy before God, he says, "You lack one thing; go, sell what you own, and give the money to the poor, and you will have treasure *in heaven*" (Mark 10:21), with *in heaven* surely a substitute for *with/before God*. This holy

---

42. See G. Dalman, *The Words of Jesus Considered in the Light of Post-Biblical Jewish Writings and the Aramaic Language* (trans. D. M. Kay; Edinburgh: T & T Clark, 1902) 196-98. Compare Matt. 10:32-33 with Luke 12:8-9 for such a development.

43. Cf. Dalman, *Words,* 182-83. The reserve of Jesus, however, did not become as compulsive as it later became for the Tannaim and Amoraim, who were consistently uneasy about use of *YHWH;* cf. Dalman, *Words,* 194-98.

44. The use of "holy" with Spirit is a surrogate for "the Spirit of God"; cf. Mark 3:29; Luke 11:13.

45. A survey of the evidence for this and the other titles can be found in Dalman, *Words,* 194-204.

46. See, e.g., Dan. 4:31, 34; 6:27; 1 Maccabees; and all the odd spellings for *YHWH* and *Elohim.* See on this Dalman, *Words,* 195-96; G. B. Caird, *The Language and Imagery of the Bible* (Philadelphia: Westminster, 1980; reprint, Grand Rapids: Eerdmans, 1997) 73-75.

47. Some have argued that "of heavens" is a Matthean redactional favorite and therefore is not to be seen as characteristic of Jesus, but in some instances Matthew may be restoring a usage that goes back to Jesus.

talk about God is also seen when Jesus asks his adversaries about John's baptism: "Did the baptism of John come *from heaven,* or was it of human origin?" (Mark 11:30). The alternative makes the case clear: either it is from humans or it is from God.[48]

A special case is the frequent use of the passive voice when used of action that seems to be performed by God (the so-called divine passive).[49] "A great many of the sayings of Jesus only make their full impression when we realize that the passive is a veiled hint at an action on the part of God."[50] Its presence in all strata and forms of the Gospel tradition, as well as its usage in Jewish apocalyptic literature contemporaneous with Jesus, demonstrates its antiquity, authenticity, and probable characteristic use by Jesus, while such concerns were normally expressed in contemporary Jewish piety with the third person plural. Thus, Luke 16:9: "And I tell you, make friends for yourselves by means of dishonest wealth so that when it is gone, *they may welcome you into the eternal homes.*" Jeremias goes so far to say, "All these 'divine passives' announce the presence of the time of salvation, albeit in a veiled way, for the consummation of the world has dawned only in a veiled form."[51] This may be overstated, but it remains the case that one of Jesus' characteristic ways of speaking of God's activity, whether in an eschatologically realized context or not, was to use the passive voice.

Thus, the Beatitudes:

Matt. 5:4: "Blessed are those who mourn, for *they will be comforted.*"

Matt. 5:6: "Blessed are those who hunger and thirst for righteousness, for *they will be filled.*"[52]

Matt. 5:7: "Blessed are the merciful, for *they will receive mercy.*"

---

48. Further examples may be found in Dalman, *Words,* 204-20, though the conclusions he draws on 233-34 are condescending and historically unjustifiable.

49. See esp. Dalman, *Words,* 224-26; Jeremias, *Proclamation of Jesus,* 10-14; M. Zerwick, *Biblical Greek, Illustrated by Examples* (ed. J. Smith; Rome: Pontifical Biblical Institute, 1963) §236 (p. 76); M. Reiser, *Jesus and Judgment: The Eschatological Proclamation in Its Jewish Context* (trans. L. M. Maloney; Minneapolis: Fortress, 1997) 266-73.

50. Jeremias, *Proclamation of Jesus,* 10.

51. Jeremias, *Proclamation of Jesus,* 14.

52. Matthew uses the third-person plural (χορτασθήσονται), whereas Luke uses the second-person plural (χορταθήσεσθε).

Matt. 5:9: "Blessed are the peacemakers, for *they will be called children of God.*"

When Jesus says "they will be comforted," he means "God will comfort them"; when he says "they will be filled," he means "God will fill them up"; when he says "they will receive mercy," he means "God will show them abundant mercy"; and when he says "they will be called 'children of God,'" he means "God will call them 'my special children.'" In each of these cases, the point about God's action is made without having to mention God. This practice of Jesus emerged from his conviction that God is inflexibly holy, and so holy that one's speaking of God should reflect one's reverence for God. As noted above, this kind of language is found on the lips of Jesus especially when he is describing the future, apocalyptic acts of the Father.

A particularly weighty example, which shows that Jesus preferred reserve in speaking about God and that such a preference was characteristic of the Jewish world in which he was raised, can be seen in Mark 14:61-62:[53]

> Again the high priest asked him, "Are you the Messiah, the Son of *the Blessed One?*" Jesus said, "I am; and 'you will see the Son of Man seated at the right hand of *the Power,*' and 'coming with *the clouds of heaven.*'"[54]

Circumlocutions for God were typical of Judaism and characteristic of Jesus' own God-talk. Such God-talk was an extension of his belief in God's holiness and in his commandment to worship him alone. Jesus directed his call to Israel, and the content of that call was repentance and moral reform. In his call, Jesus both taught and exemplified that Israel needed to revere God in its very language.

---

53. Cf. Eusebius, *Church History* 2.23.13; *Gospel of Peter* 5:19: "My power, O power, you have forsaken me!" For this, cf. R. E. Brown, *The Death of the Messiah: From Gethsemane to the Grave* (2 vols.; ABRL; New York: Doubleday, 1994) 2.1058; see also Mark 6:14; Matt. 11:21-22; Dalman, *Words*, 200-202.

54. It is highly improbable that either "Son of Man" or "I am" would be included in italics as a periphrasis for God. R. E. Brown calls all of this into question on the dubious grounds of Mark's pretense; see Brown, *The Death of the Messiah*, 2.468-70, 496-97. There is no evidence that Mark operates in this manner, as Brown himself confesses.

The Call to Surrender

Jesus demanded righteousness and obedience from his followers, and this demand itself flowed from a view of God. Jesus' characteristic God-talk was consonant with another feature of his teachings and practice: his unwavering demand to obey God by following him and his directives. The Mosaic law revealed God's will for Israel, but God's law was not Moses' law. It was not Moses who dreamed up the Decalogue, the Levitical purity system, or the Deuteronomic codification of laws. Rather, Moses was regarded as the mouthpiece of God, even if he was held in unparalleled esteem.[55] The covenant obedience demanded of the people of Israel was to flow from their relationship to YHWH: he brought them into the covenant (Genesis 12, 15, 17) and renewed that covenant with Moses (Exodus 24). God is holy and therefore unapproachable, but he is also benevolent enough to give to his people his will: the law. He commanded them to keep his ordinances, teaching them from generation to generation (Deut. 6:4-6), so that each successive generation might experience his blessing and good fortune (Deut. 28:1-14; Lev. 26:1-13). But this same God threatened Israel with extreme forms of punishment if it decided to follow other gods and to neglect to do everything written in the law (cf. Deut. 28:15-68; Lev. 26:14-39). An integral feature of the covenant with YHWH is its conditional nature: to enjoy that covenant, to maintain their relationship to this God, and to benefit from his providential care and protection, Israelites had to obey the commandments of the law. The foundation of the entire Mosaic law is a singular fact about God, his holiness: "For I am the LORD your God; sanctify yourselves therefore, and be holy, for I am holy" (Lev. 11:44).[56]

This theological foundation is the sole explanation for the sweeping commands of Jesus. When Jesus encountered hesitation, he warned of judgment for any failure to obey God and follow his eschatological demands:

55. On the place of Moses in Judaism, see D. M. Beegle, "Moses," *ABD*, 4.909-18.

56. G. Dalman is surely accurate when he contends that, though Jesus did not call God "the Holy One," the use of "holy" with "Spirit" in the Gospels may well go back to Jesus and expressly mean divinity; see *Words*, 202. Cf. Matt. 12:32; Mark 12:36. See also R. Bultmann, *Jesus*, in his emphasis on God as being the creating will (133-37, 151).

As they were going along the road, someone said to him, "I will follow you wherever you go." And Jesus said to him, "Foxes have holes, and birds of the air have nests; but the Son of Man has nowhere to lay his head." To another he said, "Follow me." But he said, "Lord, first let me go and bury my father." But Jesus said to him, "Let the dead bury their own dead; but as for you, go and proclaim the kingdom of God." Another said, "I will follow you, Lord; but let me first say farewell to those at my home." Jesus said to him, "No one who puts a hand to the plow and looks back is fit for the kingdom of God." (Luke 9:57-62)

Here in this text Jesus claims that following him, that is, announcing his kingdom's arrival to others, far outstrips any other obligation in life, even the obligation to bury one's father, to part courteously from one's family, and to care for one's physical safety. Concerning Jesus' dismissal of one's obligation to bury one's father, Martin Hengel has written, "There is hardly one logion of Jesus which more sharply runs counter to law, piety and custom than does Mt 8.22 = Lk 9.60a, the more so as here we cannot justify the overriding of these in the interests of humanitarian freedom, higher morality, greater religious intensity or even 'neighbourliness.'" Hengel proceeds to quote Adolf Schlatter: "It was a purely sacrilegious act of impiety. . . . Such sayings could easily suggest to the disciples the thought that Jesus was abolishing the Law."[57]

The harshness of these sayings requires some explanation, since they seem to contradict Jewish belief in the adequacy of Mosaic law. Hengel contends that commandments like these do not reflect the practical dimension of a sweeping humanitarian vision or a new wave of religious intensity. For his part, Hengel anchors such ethical demands in the teachings of Jesus about the imminence of the kingdom of God and Jesus' own messianic authority.[58] Although Hengel is on the right track, he has skipped one foundational feature: the concept of God's holiness as it works itself out in covenantal practice. In other words, before we ask "Who would say such a thing?" and "What would be the eschatological conditions for such demands?" we must ask, "Is this not the old covenantal demand of the Holy One working itself out

---

57. M. Hengel, *The Charismatic Leader and His Followers* (trans. J. Greig; SNTW; Edinburgh: T & T Clark, 1981) 14.

58. Cf. Hengel, *Charismatic Leader*, 15.

in light of the newness of Jesus' arrival as a call for the nation to repent?"

Jesus' commands, then, are to be explained in an old-fashioned covenantal framework: the God of the Covenant, the Holy One of Israel, is calling his people for the final time to radical covenantal obedience. The commands to follow Jesus before all else are nothing but the reaffirmation and reapplication of the first commandment: "You shall have no other gods before me" (Exod. 20:3). Once again, the foundation of this commandment, and all like it, is the holiness of Israel's God. Thus, the ethical demands of Jesus, in however radical a form, must be explained on the basis of Israel's covenant ethics, that is, on the basis of God's holiness. Only when this is appreciated can the eschatological and messianic dimensions properly be considered. The covenantal context shaped the mission of Jesus; he called the nation to repent and enjoy the blessing of God, the restoration of the nation and the land. If the nation remains in its stiff-necked ways of disobedience, understood by Jesus as a pursuit of a righteousness contrary to God's newly revealed will, they will experience God's curse, the destruction of Jerusalem.

The Warnings of Judgment

A rock-solid feature of the teachings of Jesus pertains to rewards and punishments, a theme as old as the covenant (cf. Leviticus 26; Deuteronomy 28).[59] The reason modern Jesus scholarship scoffs at the historical reliability of this theme is that it flies directly in the face of the soteriology of the Reformation and bites into the prickly surface of modern pluralism.[60] Jesus, however, should not be made subservient to the Reforma-

---

59. The bibliography here is immense: see R. Schnackenburg, *Die sittliche Botschaft des Neuen Testaments* (2 vols.; HTKNTS 1-2; Freiburg: Herder, 1986-88) 1.81-85. See also his *The Moral Teaching of the New Testament* (New York: Seabury, 1965). See also Sanders, *Paul and Palestinian Judaism*, 107-47; G. F. Moore, *Judaism in the First Centuries of the Christian Era: The Age of the Tannaim* (2 vols.; New York: Schocken, 1971) 2.89-111; E. E. Urbach, *The Sages: Their Concepts and Beliefs* (trans. I. Abrahams; Jerusalem: Magnes, 1979) 420-44; L. D. Hurst, "Ethics of Jesus," *DJG*, 214-17; S. H. Travis, *Christ and the Judgment of God: Divine Retribution in the New Testament* (Basingstoke: Marshall Pickering, 1986) 142-50.

60. See the survey of Reiser, *Jesus and Judgment*, 1-16, 197-205.

tion; his theology stands on its own in its thoroughly Jewish context. Reformation theology needs to answer to Jesus, not Jesus to it. Jesus did not talk about earning salvation; he talked about what covenant members are obligated to do (or strive to do) if they wish to be faithful. To be sure, Jesus taught about the kingdom and practiced table fellowship as a symbol of God's forgiveness, but these two features of his ministry should not be used to render the language of reward otiose. Instead, the language of reward needs to be understood as an extension of the justice of God, but in the context of kingdom and grace. Once again, it is Jesus' mission to the nation of Israel that best explains this theme: Jesus' call to Israel to repent, so that the disaster could be averted, led him inexorably to an emphasis on national judgment.

Accordingly, the God of Jesus is one who "sees in secret" (Matt. 6:1) and who rewards on the basis of what is done from the heart or what is done in private (cf. Luke 12:2-3).[61] Those who follow Jesus through times of persecution will be rewarded (Matt. 5:12 par. Luke 6:23) just as those who receive the children/messengers connected with Jesus will also be rewarded (Mark 9:37//Matt. 10:42). Reward, according to Jesus, is commensurate with how one relates to Jesus (Mark 8:38 pars.), or one's works (cf. Mark 10:29-30; Matt. 16:27//Mark 8:38;[62] Matt. 20:1-16[63]), and those who do good deeds will be ushered into eternal life (Mark 10:29-30; Matt. 6:20//Luke 12:33; Matt. 25:31-46); those who refuse to do what Jesus says will be punished eternally (Matt. 8:11-12//Luke 13:28-30; Matt. 7:13-14//Luke 13:23-24; Matt. 7:24-27//Luke 6:47-49; Matt. 25:31-46). The God of Jesus is just.[64] God watches the behavior of his people, knows why they do what they do, and knows what they do when they are in pri-

---

61. *Contra* Matt. 10:26-27. On this, see S. McKnight, "Public Declaration or Final Judgment? Matthew 10:26//Luke 12:2-3 as a Case of Creative Redaction," in C. A. Evans and B. D. Chilton, eds., *Authenticating the Words of Jesus* (NTTS; Leiden: Brill, forthcoming).

62. Matthew's words are probably redactional, but nonetheless a legitimate explication of what is implicit in the earlier tradition.

63. The parable of the workers in the vineyard has suffered much under the hands of Christian interpretation, usually with the good motive of attempting to salvage grace and eliminate any kind of merited salvation. The parable's context is Deuteronomy 28 and Leviticus 26. See S. T. Lachs, *A Rabbinic Commentary on the New Testament: The Gospels of Matthew, Mark, and Luke* (Hoboken, N.J.: Ktav, 1987) 332-34.

64. This is the appropriate theological category for understanding the place of rewards and punishments in Judaism and in Jesus' teaching; soteriology is not the appropriate category. See Sanders, *Paul and Palestinian Judaism*, 127-28.

vate, determining the final status of the people of God on the basis of that same behavior and motivation. The justice of God, then, anchored the teachings of Jesus about judgment and final status before God. Jesus and a wide spectrum of Judaism were nearly identical when it came to the matter of rewards and punishments.

The "dark side" of rewards and punishments hovers over the latter term, but Jesus was no stranger to caustic words about punishment and eternal damnation. This relentless hardness on the part of Jesus can be seen especially in another radical saying:

> Enter through the narrow gate; for the gate is wide and the road is easy that leads to destruction, and there are many who take it. For the gate is narrow and the road is hard that leads to life, and there are few who find it. (Matt. 7:13-14//Luke 13:23-24)[65]

There can be no escaping sayings like this: either they are taken in all their rugged severity, or they are trivialized through some form of reinterpretation. This saying has its origin in the same context that we sketched above: Jesus' ethical demands were rooted in the utter holiness of a God who brooks no rivals. And, as the codes of both Deuteronomy and Leviticus carried with them the threat of punishment for those who entered the covenant but became unfaithful, so also with Jesus. Those who refuse to follow the path he carves will find themselves on the wrong side of the judgment.

What would have been even stranger for an Israelite is the numerical limitation Jesus puts on his followers. He contends that only "few" find his gate and path. For the "many" there is the threat of judgment. While it has been common, in almost Marcionite fashion, to contend that the God of the Hebrew Bible is a warrior God, venting his wrath in all directions, whereas the God of Jesus is a merciful, loving, compassionate God, this fashion is a thin veneer placed over the unmistakable and penetrating words of Jesus that deal with judgment. Perhaps no one in

---

65. For a negative assessment of the authenticity of the logion, except for the first clause (and then in its Lukan form), cf. R. Parrott, "Entering the Door: Matt 7:13-14//Luke 13:22-24," *Forum* 5 (1989) 111-20; so also Reiser, *Jesus and Judgment*, 303. Recent studies of Jesus include this saying as part of the authentic Jesus tradition; cf. R. A. Horsley, *Jesus and the Spiral of Violence: Popular Jewish Resistance in Roman Palestine* (San Francisco: Harper & Row, 1987) 192; Borg, *Jesus: A New Vision*, 103-15; B. D. Chilton, *Pure Kingdom: Jesus' Vision of God* (Grand Rapids: Eerdmans, 1996) 80.

the Bible puts more emphasis on judgment than does Jesus. Consider the following judgment-threat sayings, the central theme of which can be found in nearly every form and strata of the Jesus tradition:

> Then he began to reproach the cities in which most of his deeds of power had been done, because they did not repent. "Woe to you, Chorazin! Woe to you, Bethsaida! For if the deeds of power done in you had been done in Tyre and Sidon, they would have repented long ago in sackcloth and ashes. But I tell you, on the day of judgment it will be more tolerable for Tyre and Sidon than for you. And you, Capernaum, will you be exalted to heaven? No, you will be brought down to Hades. For if the deeds of power done in you had been done in Sodom, it would have remained until this day. But I tell you that on the day of judgment it will be more tolerable for the land of Sodom than for you." (Matt. 11:20-24//Luke 10:13-15; cf. Matt. 8:11-12//Luke 13:28-29;[66] Matt. 25:31-46)

The Jesus who urges his disciples to come to God in reverential terms, who teaches his followers to speak of God in indirect ways, and who calls his followers to obey God and follow his new teachings with unwavering faithfulness also warns the same group that those who fail to obey God will be punished, even to the point of torment. How do we explain such a conclusion? The answer may be found in traditional Judaism: the God of the covenant is the one and only God, an awesome, holy God. His holiness is so jealous that he will punish his people in holy wrath if they place anything or anyone before him. Such is the logic of the holiness of God for Jesus as he called the nation to turn back and reestablish its covenant faithfulness.

This logic explains the warning Jesus gave to the nation about the destruction of Jerusalem, found now in what is sometimes called the Little Apocalypse (Mark 13:1-37; cf. also Matt. 24:1–25:46; Luke 21:5-36 and 17:22-37; 12:39-40, 42-46; 19:12-27; cf. also John 2:19).[67] This

---

66. This expression, "weeping and gnashing of teeth" is found only in Matthew: cf. 8:12; 13:42, 50; 22:13; 24:51; 25:30. While it is evidently redactional, it appears also to be entirely consistent with Judaism and with the emphasis Jesus gave to judgment and punishment.

67. An attempt to unravel the complicated tradition history behind these apocalyptic texts has been made by D. Wenham, *The Rediscovery of Jesus' Eschatological Discourse* (GP 4; Sheffield: JSOT, 1984).

warning has part of its tradition-history in the ancient warnings of Israel's prophets who predicted the sacking of Samaria in 722 B.C. and Jerusalem in 586 B.C.. This prophetic background cannot be minimized. Thus, 2 Kgs. 21:10-15:

> The LORD said by his servants the prophets, "Because King Manasseh of Judah has committed these abominations, has done things more wicked than all that the Amorites did, who were before him, and has caused Judah also to sin with his idols; therefore thus says the LORD, the God of Israel, I am bringing upon Jerusalem and Judah such evil that the ears of everyone who hears of it will tingle. I will stretch over Jerusalem the measuring line for Samaria, and the plummet for the house of Ahab; I will wipe Jerusalem as one wipes a dish, wiping it and turning it upside down. I will cast off the remnant of my heritage, and give them into the hand of their enemies; they shall become a prey and a spoil to all their enemies, because they have done what is evil in my sight and have provoked me to anger, since the day their ancestors came out of Egypt, even to this day."

The ultimate foundation for even these prophetic sayings of doom lies deeper than prophecy itself. The foundation for the prophetic warnings is clearly the warnings of both the Deuteronomic and priestly traditions. Deuteronomy 28 and Leviticus 26 both express the God of the covenant's holy demand to follow his ways or be judged. Jesus' prediction of the destruction of Jerusalem, then, especially needs to be seen as part of the Deuteronomic history: if God's covenant people faithlessly abandon his covenant ordinances, God will wreak havoc on the nation. This is the context of Jesus' warnings. His call was not individualistic but corporate and national.

The sacking of Jerusalem, however, was not the final word of Jesus about judgment and punishment, because Jesus frequently spoke about the final judgment.[68] It may be attractive to our contemporary sensitivities to historicize all of Jesus' warnings about final punishment as nothing more than graphic symbolism for the destruction of Jerusalem, but such an approach does not do justice to the evidence. It may also be attractive to mitigate these words by eliminating them from the

---

68. This topic has been treated most completely in Reiser, *Jesus and Judgment*; but see also Travis, *Christ and the Judgment*, 125-65; Ward, *Royal Theology*, 68-113.

core of authentic sayings, but once again they are found too frequently, in too many images, and in too many forms and sources to eliminate. Yet one more attempt has been to soften the blow of Jesus' words — suggesting that he taught some kind of annihilationism — but once again this appears to be inconsistent with the evidence and with much of ancient Jewish thinking. Instead, we must admit that Jesus taught the possibility and reality of an eternal, conscious punishment for Israelites.[69]

At times, then, Jesus spoke of more than a historical, national destruction; sometimes he was concerned with a final, utter destruction of everything that was an abomination to his God. Thus,

> So he said to them, "You are those who justify yourselves in the sight of others; but God knows your hearts; for what is prized by human beings is an abomination in the sight of God." (Luke 16:15)

> "Then he will say to those at his left hand, 'You that are accursed, depart from me into the eternal fire prepared for the devil and his angels; for I was hungry and you gave me no food, I was thirsty and you gave me nothing to drink, I was a stranger and you did not welcome me, naked and you did not give me clothing, sick and in prison and you did not visit me.' Then they also will answer, 'Lord, when was it that we saw you hungry or thirsty or a stranger or naked or sick or in prison, and did not take care of you?' Then he will answer them, 'Truly I tell you, just as you did not do it to one of the least of these, you did not do it to me.' And these will go away into eternal punishment, but the righteous into eternal life." (Matt. 25:41-46)

Punishment in an individual, eternal sense, then, is the inevitable corollary of belief in a holy God who has made a covenantal arrangement with his people and who warns them of punishment for disobedience.[70]

At this point it becomes theologically fitting to speak of a certain

---

69. See S. McKnight, "Eternal Consequences or Eternal Consciousness?" in W. V. Crockett and J. G. Sigountos, eds., *Through No Fault of Their Own? The Fate of Those Who Have Never Heard* (Grand Rapids: Baker, 1991) 147-57.

70. Other images are used for this final judgment: *humiliation* (cf. Matt. 23:12; Luke 14:11; 18:14), *being uprooted* (Matt. 15:13), *Gehenna/fire* (Mark 9:44, 45, 47, 48; Matt. 23:23; Luke 16:19-31); and *darkness* (Matt. 8:12).

terror before this God. To be sure, the word *fear* in the Bible is usually taken in the sense of *awe*. However, this awe turns into terror when people find themselves falling into the hands of a holy God who acts in judgment. Thus,

> "Do not fear those who kill the body but cannot kill the soul; rather *fear* him who can destroy both soul and body in hell." (Matt. 10:28; cf. Luke 12:4-5)

> "But God said to him, 'You fool! This very night your life is being demanded of you. And the things you have prepared, whose will they be?' So it is with those who store up treasures for themselves but are not rich toward God." (Luke 12:20-21)

For Jesus, God could become a God of wrath;[71] like the writer of Hebrews (10:31), Jesus believed that such an experience would incite terror and the utter undoing of human character and conscience.

This context, the threat of impending doom along with final punishment and redemption, animated the ministries of both John and Jesus; from John, Jesus received the tradition of preparing the nation of Israel for judgment. Jesus' calls to follow and his calls to obey, therefore, are extensions of the logic of the holy God's covenant with Israel. Awaking as they did to God's last call to Israel, both John and Jesus set upon a course of calling Israel to repent. Repenting for them meant reaffirming the covenant with Israel established long ago and recorded in the Torah. Repenting for them was rooted also in the new call they trumpeted throughout the land of Israel: an imminent judgment on those who refused to hear this covenant call. We misunderstand Jesus when we superficially compare his apocalyptic threats with those contemporaneous to him. Important parallels are there, but the fundamental basis for Jesus' warnings about the destruction of Jerusalem was the Bible he heard every Sabbath, especially in Leviticus and Deuteronomy.

71. On the theme of wrath, see Q: Matt 8:12; Mark: Mark 12:9; 13:19; M: Matt. 18:34; 22:7, 13. On Matt. 18:34, cf. T. W. Manson, *The Sayings of Jesus* (London: SCM, 1949) 213.

The Words from the Cross

Of the sayings of Jesus from the cross, the so-called cry of dereliction undoubtedly commands the most respect as *ipsissima verba Jesu.*[72] Fundamentally, however, these words represent yet another example of the judgment of the holy covenant God of Israel. No matter how Jesus experienced what gave rise to these words (whether he felt a real abandonment, a sense of God's judgment and his vicarious role in that punishment on sinful persons, or a sense of victory, which the opening words of Psalm 22 could be used to express), the words themselves can only mean that Jesus sensed some kind of judgment at the hand of his Father and that he cried out to him in trust, in hope, and in prayer for the cup to pass — quickly. It is a cry of pain that eludes modern description, but it is "certainly not the cry of one who has despaired of God."[73] We need to see these words, as others, in the context of the holiness of Israel's God, specifically, in the context of the covenant demand that God's people respond to him in faithful obedience or be judged, and in the context of Jesus' message that the final judgment was coming upon those who did not respond to his offer to Israel. He offered himself as an atoning, vicarious sacrifice for the "many" (Mark 10:45), that is, for those who needed atonement in preparation for the coming kingdom, and in this act of sacrifice he experienced what the holiness of God does to the victims of sacrifice: God exacts a deathly, punishing judgment.

Jesus' God is inflexibly holy: in all that he says, in all that he does, and in all the history he directs, Jesus' God manifests his holiness. In Jesus' call to Israel at its final hour, it is the God of Israel who gives shape to that call. He commands deferential speech, he demands unflagging commitment and faithful obedience, he threatens judgment and punishment on all those who choose to ignore his covenant demands, and he punishes the one who sacrificed himself vicariously for the many. But the God of Jesus reveals himself not only as demanding judge and commanding covenant God; he is also loving, merciful, and compassionate. No depiction of the God of Jesus can be adequate if it omits either the

---

72. Undoubtedly, the main reason this saying is regarded as authentic is that it is taken to express abject failure and disappointment with the Father.

73. Bornkamm, *Jesus,* 167. So also G. B. Caird, *New Testament Theology* (completed and edited by L. D. Hurst; Oxford: Clarendon, 1994) 34.

loving nature of God or the holy nature of God. The God of Jesus manifests himself in polarized extremes: both as holy and as love.[74]

God as Relationally Loving

That Jesus' God loves Israel and, through Israel, all the nations has rarely been questioned. Ever since the rise of Protestant liberalism, notably in the work of Adolf Harnack on Jesus' teachings, the focus of critical study of Jesus has centered entirely on the love of God as seen in Jesus' affirmation of the Fatherhood of God and the brotherhood of humanity.[75] But, apart from the full picture of Jesus' continued emphasis on the holiness of God, the genuine love of God becomes nothing more than wishful thinking by those who prefer to think of God in their own terms: tolerant, benevolent, pluralistic, always kind. As George E. Ladd once pointed out, for Jesus "God is seeking love; he is also *holy* love."[76] When the discerning eye turns to the surviving records about Jesus, it is clear that Jesus described God, even if indirectly at times, as one who is always holy and always loving.

Table Fellowship with Sinners

To begin with, Jesus practiced table fellowship with sinners in a manner that revealed his view of God. Among various pursuits of holiness by divergent groups within Judaism, food laws had become a central symbol for many Jews.[77] Table fellowship represented for those practicing

74. See Bultmann, *Jesus*, 138.

75. See A. Harnack, *What Is Christianity?* (trans. T. B. Saunders; New York: Harper, 1957) 19-74.

76. Ladd, *Presence*, 184.

77. Jeremias, *Proclamation of Jesus*, 114-21; N. Perrin, *Rediscovering the Teaching of Jesus* (New York: Harper & Row, 1967) 102-8; B. F. Meyer, *The Aims of Jesus* (London: SCM, 1979) 158-62; Borg, *Conflict*, 78-121; E. P. Sanders, *Jewish Law from Jesus to the Mishnah: Five Studies* (Philadelphia: Trinity Press International, 1990) 23-42; B. D. Chilton, "The Purity of the Kingdom as Conveyed in Jesus' Meals," *SBLASP* (1992) 473-88; J. D. Crossan, *The Historical Jesus: The Life of a Mediterranean Jewish Peasant* (San Francisco: HarperSanFrancisco, 1991) 341-44. For the Greco-Roman symposium, see

and for those observing the practice a particular vision for Israel and for God's will concerning Israel. This understanding has been captured well by N. T. Wright:

> He ate with "sinners", and kept company with people normally on or beyond the borders of respectable society — which of course, in his day and culture, meant not only merely social respectability but religious uprightness, proper covenant behaviour, loyalty to the traditions and hence to the aspirations of Israel.[78]

The earliest traditions about the Pharisees were preoccupied with their attention to table purity and food laws.[79] Recently it has been shown that they were concerned not so much with extending priestly purity to the general practice of all Jews as with directing it toward themselves and their vision for a holier Israel. Nonetheless, their purity practices parallel in significant ways the ordinances for priests in the Levitical codes.[80] Concern for purity at table served not only to express visibly their vision for Israel but also to uphold their honor and to shame others into consideration of their ways. Members of despised trades naturally excluded themselves from sitting with the pure ones of Israel (no matter who made the boundaries), and attention to these matters was evidently socially obvious to those concerned.[81] The Pharisees and members of other holiness movements in the land of Israel refused to eat with those who did not share their particular group's holiness concerns with food. Evidence for this may be found in the troubled questioning of the Pharisees:

> Then Pharisees and scribes came to Jesus from Jerusalem and said, "Why do your disciples break the tradition of the elders? For they do not wash their hands before they eat." (Matt. 15:1-2; cf. Mark 7:1-5)

F. Lissarrague, *The Aesthetics of the Greek Banquet: Images of Wine and Ritual (Un Flot d'Images)* (trans. A. Szegedy-Maszak; Princeton: Princeton University Press, 1990).

78. N. T. Wright, *Jesus and the Victory of God* (Christian Origins and the Question of God, vol. 2; Minneapolis: Fortress, 1996) 149.

79. See J. Neusner, *From Politics to Piety: The Emergence of Pharisaic Judaism* (Englewood Cliffs, N.J.: Prentice-Hall, 1973).

80. So Sanders, *Judaism: Practice and Belief,* 438-40.

81. On despised trades, see J. Jeremias, *Jerusalem in the Time of Jesus: An Investigation into Economic and Social Conditions during the New Testament Period* (Philadelphia: Fortress, 1969) 303-12.

Regardless of whether the incident has been cast in anachronistic terms, this group of Jews showed a squeamishness about eating with other Jews who had not practiced a special holiness rite of purifying the hands.[82]

Later rabbinic testimony confirms the evidence of the Gospels. Thus, in *m. Ṭoharot* 7:6 we read:

> If taxgatherers entered a house [all that is within it] becomes unclean; even if a gentile was with them they may be believed if they say ("We did not enter"; but they may not be believed if they say) "We entered but we touched naught". . . . What do they render unclean? Foodstuffs and liquids and open earthenware vessels; but couches and seats and earthenware vessels having a tightly stopped-up cover remain clean. If a gentile or a woman was with them all becomes unclean.

And *m. Demai* 2:3 reads:

> He that undertakes to be an Associate may not sell to an *Am-haaretz* [foodstuff that is] wet or dry, or buy from him [foodstuff that is] wet; and he may not be the guest of an *Am-haaretz* nor may he receive him as a guest in his own raiment.[83]

Finally, even later we read from *b. Berakot* 43b (baraita):

> Six things are a disgrace for the student: . . . (5) he should not recline at table with a common person . . . why [should he not recline at table with a common person]? He could feel obliged to them and so assume their practices.

Critical scholarship today is rightly wary of retrojecting the practices informing these rabbinic texts to the world of Jesus. However, these texts

---

82. The best study of the purity rite is M. Hengel, "Mk 7,3 πυγμῇ: Die Geschichte einer exegetischen Aporie und der Versuch ihrer Lösung," *ZNW* 60 (1969) 182-98; but see the studies of S. M. Reynolds, "Πυγμῇ (Mark 7,3) as 'Cupped Hand,'" *JBL* 85 (1966) 87-88; idem, "A Note on Dr. Hengel's Interpretation of Πυγμῇ in Mark 7,3," *ZNW* 62 (1971) 295-96.

83. The "raiment" is unacceptable because it is suspected of *midras*-uncleanness. See Sanders, *Judaism: Practice and Belief,* 439.

may serve simply to provide examples of general table-purity concerns that would have inevitably come up in any Jewish movement's attempts to conform to its ideal of holiness. Jesus' practice of table fellowship with sinners and tax collectors took place within a world that took great care in its choice of place, partners, and food when it came to meals. Meals and table fellowship made a social statement and reflected a worldview; they could be used to symbolize one's view of holiness and one's view of Israel.[84] Table fellowship was for all a microcosm of the whole, a small token of what God had established for the nation. In the words of Norman Perrin, Jesus' table fellowship was "an acted parable."[85]

Eating with others symbolically expressed acceptance and some kind of equality. For instance, table fellowship could symbolize the end of exile, restoration, forgiveness, and social acceptance — as can be seen in the case of Jehoiachin:

> In the thirty-seventh year of the exile of King Jehoiachin of Judah, in the twelfth month, on the twenty-seventh day of the month, King Evil-merodach of Babylon, in the year that he began to reign, released King Jehoiachin of Judah from prison; he spoke kindly to him, and gave him a seat above the other seats of the kings who were with him in Babylon. So Jehoiachin put aside his prison clothes. *Every day of his life he dined regularly in the king's presence.* For his allowance, a regular allowance was given him by the king, a portion every day, as long as he lived. (2 Kgs. 25:27-30)

Closer to the time of Jesus, and in the land of Israel, a certain Silas, who was known for boldness in speech (especially of his own talents), eventually angered Agrippa enough to get himself exiled.[86]

> But in time his [Agrippa's] anger lost its edge, and he submitted his judgement on the man to dispassionate reflection, taking into consideration all the hardships that the man had borne for his sake. In consequence, when he was celebrating his birthday and all his subjects were participating in the joyous festivities, he recalled Silas at a moment's notice to share his table.

84. See D. E. Smith, "Table Fellowship," *ABD*, 6.302-304.
85. *Rediscovering the Teaching of Jesus*, 102.
86. Josephus, *Ant.* 19.317-25.

Consistent in character, Silas obstinately refused the king's offer, and so Agrippa left him in prison. Nonetheless, the story reveals the social import of table fellowship. The act in and of itself revealed friendship, acceptance, and some measure of equality. One did not eat with a person who was incompatible with one's vision for Israel.[87] For Jews of the first century, then, inclusion in a meal setting symbolized acceptance of another person, including that person's social status, moral practices, and attitude toward Israel's covenant with God.

If we recognize the religious, covenantal associations that Jews would have seen in meals, we can fathom more accurately the significance of Jesus' persistent and provocative practice of table fellowship with tax collectors and sinners. Prayers would have been offered; conversations revolving around Israel, the covenant, and ethics would have taken place; and religious ideals of purity would have governed the entire affair. Many of the teachings of Jesus now preserved for us in the Gospel records likely had their origin in Jesus' regular evening table fellowship with his disciples and others who cared to join.[88] Jesus' mission, then, was embodied, incarnated as it were, in his meal practice: he envisioned a God of forgiving, restoring love; a society of obedient, restored Israelites following his teachings and praying for God's kingdom to erupt into history soon; and a kingdom now operative in the land.

In various passages and in all strands of the Gospel tradition, Jesus sits on a regular basis at table with sinners, or tax collectors, or the unlikely characters of the land of Israel. Following his call of Levi/Matthew (cf. Mark 2:13-17 pars.), Jesus sits at table with some tax collectors and sinners, but the "scribes of the Pharisees" complain about such behavior. Jesus legitimates his behavior by appealing to the need for mercy on those who have been restricted from kosher meals. The story of Zacchaeus, known more for his size than his profession (Luke 19:1-10), provides yet another example. The words of the text are socially realistic and revealing:

> When Jesus came to the place, he looked up and said to him, "Zacchaeus, hurry and come down; for I must stay at your house today." So he hurried down and was happy to welcome him. All who

87. See M. Douglas, "Deciphering a Meal," *Daedelus* 101 (1972) 61-81.
88. See Perrin, *Rediscovering*, 107-8; Wright, *Jesus and the Victory of God*, 264-74.

saw it began to grumble and said, "He has gone to be the guest of one who is a sinner." (Luke 19:5-7)

The key expressions are "stay at your house," "welcome him," and "the guest of one who is a sinner." The fundamental problem for the grumblers is not that Zacchaeus, the chief tax collector, is a quisling; Jews in the surrounding area might have been glad to see Zacchaeus won over to the Jewish side. Rather, the problem is that Jesus is willing to behave contrary to the holiness codes of others. Jesus' eating with defiled persons defiles him, his followers, and the nation. It is out of order for Jesus to do this — according to some.

The stories of the lost sheep, the lost coin, and the prodigal son are all well known. Less known is the socioreligious context into which Luke (probably accurately) places them:[89] table fellowship with sinners and the opposition Jesus provoked for such behavior (Luke 15:1-2). Such a context is entirely typical of the Jesus tradition and other sources: eating with sinners is both typical of and consistent with the stories of a God who searches for lost sheep, who sweeps for lost coins, and who waits eagerly for repentant sinners. So also is the pregnant epitaph placed upon Jesus by his opponents:

> "The Son of Man came eating and drinking, and they say, 'Look, a glutton and a drunkard, a friend of tax collectors and sinners!'" (Matt. 11:19)

Unlike John, who was known for his abstemiousness, harshness, and asceticism (and who was labeled "demonic"; cf. Matt. 11:18), Jesus joyfully celebrated the arrival of the kingdom (11:19). But he, too, was rejected and considered beyond the pale for his decision to pursue another course for Israel. He partied with outcasts, warned them of the coming catastrophe, taught them about God's kingdom and covenant forgiveness, and led them down the road to repentance; but his path was considered contrary to the accepted pattern of holy living. No one can question that Jesus knew what he was doing in eating with sinners,

---

89. One unfortunate result of form criticism is that scholars have become totally skeptical about the historical usefulness of the contexts into which the Evangelists have placed events and sayings of Jesus. It is, however, highly unlikely that the social contexts of the Evangelists were so different from that of Jesus that sweeping changes in the tradition had to be made.

nor that he knew what would happen when he did so. Jesus consistently, intentionally, and provocatively ate with sinners.[90] Why did Jesus eat with the unlikely? Why did he choose to act in a way that was contrary to established patterns of holiness and covenant faithfulness?

The answer is clear: because he thought that he was God's agent and that in so doing he was acting in harmony with God's loving grace. More fundamentally, if we recognize that in his table fellowship Jesus contravened the practice of other holiness movements, like that of the Essenes (cf., e.g., 1QSa 2:3-10; 4QCD[b]; 11QTemple 45:12-14) and the Pharisees, we will also have to contend that Jesus constructed an alternative vision for Israel, because the Israel Jesus had in view was all-inclusive (cf. Luke 14:13, 21).[91] This vision for a more inclusive, forgiven Israel implies a view of God: the God of Jesus, the one who fellowships with sinners, is a God who graciously forgives, invites sinners to his table, and dispenses his grace through the open fellowship established around Jesus.[92] Marcus Borg is certainly right when he says of Jesus' practice of table fellowship:

> In short, Jesus' practice of table fellowship and his teaching concerning issues related to table fellowship contravened the understanding of Israel as a holy, separated community. In this context, table fellowship cannot be described simply as festive celebration and acceptance, but *as a political act of national significance:* to advocate and practice a different form of table fellowship was to protest against the present structures of Israel. Moreover, there was more than protest — an alternative program was advocated for the people of God in their historical existence.[93]

Along with this national vision for a restored holiness in Israel, there are two features that emerge from Jesus' regular fellowship with

90. Other evidence supporting the practice of Jesus includes Matt. 20:1-16; 21:28-32; Luke 7:41-43. Borg points to the following as generally supporting Jesus' attack on a Pharisaic construction of the holy community: Luke 6:39; 10:29-37; 11:44; 18:10-14; Matt. 21:28-32; 23:13; 25:14-30. See Borg, *Conflict*, 102-21.

91. See J. D. G. Dunn, "Jesus, Table-Fellowship, and Qumran," in J. H. Charlesworth, ed., *Jesus and the Dead Sea Scrolls* (ABRL; New York: Doubleday, 1992) 254-72.

92. Meyer, *Aims of Jesus*, 161-62.

93. Borg, *Conflict, Holiness and Politics*, 120-21.

sinners. The first is that in his table fellowship Jesus anticipated and made clear *the arrival of the kingdom and its inclusive, gracious nature.* Thus, Jesus described the final day as one of fellowship:

> "I tell you, many will come from east and west and will eat with Abraham and Isaac and Jacob in the kingdom of heaven, while the heirs of the kingdom will be thrown into the outer darkness, where there will be weeping and gnashing of teeth." (Matt. 8:11-12)

Commenting on this verse, Norman Perrin states that "the parallel between the situation envisaged in the saying and that providing its point of departure in the ministry of Jesus is such that we must see the table-fellowship of that ministry as a table-fellowship 'of the kingdom' and as anticipating a table-fellowship 'in the kingdom.'"[94] Furthermore, if we connect this idea to the Lord's Supper and to Jesus' anticipation of never enjoying a meal with the disciples until the Final Day (cf. Mark 14:25), then it becomes clear that Jesus saw in his practice of eating with sinners an acted parable of the final constitution of God's kingdom and its forgiveness. The practice symbolized Jesus' entire vision for the kingdom, which was an inclusive vision of a restored, forgiven, and celebratory community.[95]

But the practice is not only eschatological; the action of the table reveals the God whom Jesus worships, follows, and proclaims in his kingdom message. The God of Jesus is a God who calls Israel to repent but who dearly loves sinners, who invites them to table with Jesus and his community, who forgives their sins through inclusion in this new vision for the nation and its holiness, and who reveals to them, through Jesus, his covenant pattern of obedience. The opposition that Jesus provoked in his table practices is surely to be understood in this context; he provoked the Pharisees and other holiness movements because he had a different vision for the nation, because he understood holiness in different categories, and because he had a different perception of how the God of Israel was now at work among his people. It might be said that these other holiness movements had a different *ordo salutis,* in which

---

94. *Rediscovering,* 106-7.

95. The vision of Jesus for the future was one of celebration, glory, joy, love, and fellowship. See Matt. 22:1-10//Luke 14:15-24; Matt. 22:29-30; Mark 4:30-32; 9:1. See Wright, *Jesus and the Victory of God,* 398-403.

repentance leads to holiness, which permits fellowship. Jesus affirmed, rather, that fellowship leads to both repentance and holiness. In so doing, Jesus had to sit lightly with respect to some of the laws pertaining to periods for establishing purity. Norman Perrin may well be right when he says that it "is hard to imagine anything more offensive to Jewish sensibilities."[96] One need not resort to the now discredited Lutheran reinterpretation of Jesus, which has Jesus affirming grace over against Judaism's scheme of works righteousness. Both Jesus and his opponents believed in God's grace, but Jesus emphasized a fellowship with God and fellow humans in which the codes of holiness were not to be obstacles to that fellowship. In true Levitical fashion, the opponents of Jesus believed that God's law taught that people had to be holy or they would defile the meal and the fellowship and then the nation. Jesus, by simply reordering the items, rushed the process and in so doing constructed an alternative vision for how Israel was to prepare itself for the coming judgment.

In preparing themselves for this judgment, the followers of Jesus were supposed to learn that God was ready to forgive their sins if they would repent and join in fellowship with Jesus, and they were to realize that this God was loving in his tender relationship with this new people that he was formalizing around the table.[97] Thus, the God Jesus embodied in his table fellowship is a God like the father in the story of the prodigal son; God waits in anxious love for his children to turn to him in repentance and delights to invite them to his table for a festive occasion, an occasion that richly symbolizes a forgiven fellowship. In Jesus' context this actualized the hope of an end to exile and a reversal of Israel's fortunes.

'abbā' as the Address to Israel's God

In addition to his praxis of table fellowship with sinners, Jesus taught his followers to call God *'abbā'*, "Father," in both conversation about him and in prayer. Jesus' insistence on calling God *'abbā'*[98] lies on the

---

96. *Rediscovering*, 103.

97. On forgiveness, see Bultmann, *Jesus*, 194-219.

98. On the philology of the Aramaic term, see J. Barr, "Abba Isn't Daddy," *JTS* 39 (1988) 28-47, here 29-35.

cutting edge of a vision for Israel. Although older scholarship was guilty of overstatements about the significance of Jesus' calling God *'abbā'*,[99] the fundamental insight that Jesus' use of this term revealed his understanding of God remains valid.[100] While Gustaf Dalman, George F. Moore, and T. W. Manson could speak of this term reflecting the piety in which Jesus was raised, others have argued that "the discrepancy between the Testaments is so great that we can only conclude that Jesus himself chose to give the symbol [Father] a special importance. In doing so he expressed his own peculiar experience of God. . . ."[101] Behind disagreements over both the innovativeness and the meaning of *'abbā'* on the lips of Jesus stands the work of Joachim Jeremias.[102] He made two major claims: (1) that the term *'abbā'* as an address to God in prayer was unique to Jesus, expressing his special sense of God; and (2) that the term connoted a deep, familial intimacy that was unknown in Judaism. To test the theses of Jeremias, we need to begin with a brief survey of the ancient evidence in Judaism. Because this issue has been so hotly debated in New Testament scholarship, it deserves more complete analysis than others bearing on Jesus' perception of God.

'abbā' in Judaism

With minor exceptions, the evidence indicates that Jews, as discerned from their literary deposits in the Hebrew Bible and various other

---

99. Heading this list is J. Barr, "Abba"; J. Fitzmyer, "Abba and Jesus' Relation to God," in F. Refoulé, ed., *À cause de L'Évangile: Etudes sur les Synoptiques et les Actes offertes au P. Jacques Dupont* (LD 123; Paris: Cerf, 1985) 16-38; Charlesworth, "Caveat"; Vermes, *Religion,* 152-83; J. D. G. Dunn, *Christology in the Making: A New Testament Inquiry into the Origins of the Doctrine of the Incarnation* (2d ed.; London: SCM, 1989; Grand Rapids: Eerdmans, 1996) 26-27.

100. Jeremias, *Prayers of Jesus,* 11-65; idem, *Proclamation of Jesus,* 61-68; Dunn, *Jesus and the Spirit,* 15-40, esp. 22-26; R. H. Stein, *The Method and Message of Jesus' Teachings* (rev. ed.; Louisville, Ky.: Westminster John Knox, 1994) 82-89; Fitzmyer, "Abba," 16-20. Critical of Jeremias's research are: J. Barr, "Abba"; idem, "'Abba, Father' and the Familiarity of Jesus' Speech," *Theology* 91 (1988) 173-79; M. R. D'Angelo, "*Abba* and 'Father': Imperial Theology and the Jesus Traditions," *JBL* 111 (1992) 611-30. See also E. M. Schuller, "The Psalm of 4Q372 1 within the Context of Second Temple Prayer," *CBQ* 54 (1992) 67-79.

101. Hamerton-Kelly, *God the Father,* 20.

102. Jeremias, *Prayers of Jesus,* 11-65.

sources, did address God as *'abbā'* in prayer.[103] A suitable place to begin is Jewish prayers. For instance, if one lifts a few of the terms for God found in the *Shemoneh 'Esreh*, the traditional Jewish prayer which many Jews recited three times a day at the set hours of prayer,[104] one finds the following titles:[105]

> Lord, God of our fathers, God of Abraham, etc.
> The Holy God
> Our Father

The *Ahabah Rabah*, a part of the morning *Shema*, says:

> Our Father, our King (*'ābînû malkēnû*),
>> for the sake of our fathers,
>> who trusted upon thee
>> and whom thou taughtest the statutes of life —
> have mercy upon us and teach us.[106]

And the *Litany for the New Year* says,

> Our Father, our king,
>> we have no other king but thee;
> our father, our king,
>> for thine own sake have mercy upon us.[107]

Here we have three prayers, all ancient (but perhaps not as early as Jesus), which prescribe addressing God as *'abbā'* in supplication. Prayers reflect a group's customary theology. If these prayers are at all ancient or contemporary with Jesus, we would have to conclude that Jesus did find *'abbā'* in the diction of his day and simply adapted it. However, in their use of

---

103. In addition to Jeremias, the best studies of the background of *'abbā'* are: G. Schrenk, "πατήρ," *TDNT,* 5.945-59, 974-81; G. Quell, "πατήρ," *TDNT,* 5.959-74 (OT); D'Angelo, "*Abba* and 'Father'"; Schuller, "The Psalm of 4Q372 1."

104. On this, see Jeremias, *Prayers of Jesus,* 66-72.

105. I quote here from the Palestinian recension as translated in E. Schürer, *The History of the Jewish People in the Age of Jesus Christ (175 B.C.–A.D. 135)* (3 vols.; rev. and ed. G. Vermes, F. Millar, M. Black, et al.; Edinburgh: T & T Clark, 1973-87) 2.460-61.

106. The text is from Jeremias, *Prayers of Jesus,* 25.

107. Text from Jeremias, *Prayers of Jesus,* 25.

'abbā', these prayers stand out from prayers in the Bible and from others that have been discovered. That Jesus used the title 'abbā' for God and that it was probably not a central aspect of Jewish practice need no longer be seriously questioned. But to say that Judaism did not know of the Fatherhood of God fundamentally misrepresents Judaism,[108] especially since Judaism was patriarchal and patriarchy was used to explain God.[109]

Neither the Psalms nor the prayers of the Hebrew Bible show any emphasis on praying to God as Father, though the term is clearly used.[110] Thus, God the Father is Creator (Mal. 2:10)[111] and therefore Lord (Mal. 1:6); the fatherliness of God evokes his tender mercy and love (Pss. 68:5; 103:13-14; Hos. 11:3, 8; Jer. 3:22; 31:9, 20); it was God as Father who elected Israel and made Israel his chosen possession through the Exodus (Exod. 4:22; Deut. 14:1-2; Hos 11:1) and who is therefore uniquely God, the Father of Israel (Jer. 31:9). Due to Israel's rejection of God the Father (Jer. 3:4-5, 19-20; Mal. 1:6), Israel needs to come to God as Father, in prayer, and plead for his forgiveness and restoration (Isa. 63:15-16; 64:8-9). When Israel repents, God forgives and restores like a father (cf. Jer. 31:20). While the evidence is not abundant, the Hebrew Bible does associate the Fatherhood of God with nearly everything fundamental to its life: creation, exodus, God's love, God's lordship, God's election of Israel, the return from exile, restoration of the nation, and a way of approaching God in prayer.

We are thus driven to ask: How can modern scholars contend for a uniqueness on the part of Jesus when the Bible Jesus heard and read regularly said things like the following?

> "Then you shall say to Pharaoh, 'Thus says the LORD: Israel is my firstborn son.'" (Exod. 4:22)

> As a father has compassion for his children,
>   so the LORD has compassion for those who fear him. (Ps. 103:13)

---

108. Here is the extrabiblical evidence: *Jub.* 1:25, 28; 19:29; Tobit 13:4; Sir. 23:1; 51:10 (Heb.); 3 Macc. 2:21; 5:7; 6:3, 8; 7:6; Wis. 2:16; 11:10; 14:3; *Jos. and Asen.* 12:8, 14-15; Josephus, *Ant.* 2.158; *Apoc. Ezek.* frg. 2; 1QH 9:35; 4Q 371; 4Q 372; 4Q 460; *Tg. Ps.* 89:27. On the rabbinic evidence, see Jeremias, *Prayers of Jesus,* 16-18.

109. See Hamerton-Kelly, *God the Father,* 21-38.

110. See Jeremias, *Prayers of Jesus,* p. 12, n. 4; Vermes, *Religion,* 173-75.

111. "Creation" and "Father" are natural connections; cf. Deut. 32:6; Isa. 64:8; see esp. J. Becker, *Jesus von Nazaret* (New York: Walter de Gruyter, 1996) 331-33.

With weeping they shall come,
    and with consolations I will lead them back,
I will let them walk by brooks of water,
    in a straight path in which they shall not stumble;
for I have become a father to Israel,
    and Ephraim is my firstborn. . . .
  Is Ephraim my dear son?
    Is he the child I delight in?
As often as I speak against him,
    I still remember him.
Therefore I am deeply moved for him;
    I will surely have mercy on him,
        says the LORD. (Jer. 31:9, 20)

Look down from heaven and see,
    from your holy and glorious habitation.
Where are your zeal and your might?
    The yearning of your heart and your compassion?
    They are withheld from me.
For you are our father,
    though Abraham does not know us
    and Israel does not acknowledge us;
you, O LORD, are our father;
    our Redeemer from of old is your name. (Isa. 63:15-16; cf. 64:8-9)

Is anything more graphically loving than the depiction of God in Hos. 11:1-4?

When Israel was a child, I loved him,
    and out of Egypt I called my son.

The more I called them,
    the more they went from me;
they kept sacrificing to the Baals,
    and offering incense to idols.

Yet it was I who taught Ephraim to walk,
    I took them up in my arms;
    but they did not know that I healed them.

I led them with cords of human kindness,
    with bands of love.
I was to them like those
    who lift infants to their cheeks.
I bent down to them and fed them.

Thus Fatherhood was a part of ancient Israel's perception of God and was woven into the fabric of its Bible. The two notions connected to God as Father are his authoritative lordship (e.g., 2 Kgs. 16:7; Deut. 14:1; Jer. 18:6-7) and his covenantal forgiveness, care, and love (Deut. 32:6, 18-19; Ps. 103:13; Hos. 11:1-4). However, in the interests of balance, we do need to emphasize that those who are represented in the Hebrew Bible preferred other forms of addressing God in prayer. But this picture would almost certainly be significantly increased if we were to include what R. G. Hamerton-Kelly calls "indirect symbolization," that is, passages in which God behaves like a father or parent-like figure.[112]

The rarity of addressing God in prayer as Father along with the occasional use of Father as a title for God as seen in the Hebrew Bible is extended significantly in the evidence from postcanonical Jewish texts. Here also God is occasionally referred to, or described, as Father. Perhaps one of the more notable instances is that of Johanan b. Zakkai (fl. A.D. 50-80), who evidently called God "our heavenly Father" on a regular basis.[113] As noted above, there are only a dozen or so examples of this term for God in the evidence of the Apocrypha, Pseudepigrapha, and Dead Sea Scrolls, though there is a rather steep increase in the later rabbinic writings.[114] Thus, while known and not at all unusual for describing a personal relationship to God (cf., e.g., Sir. 51:10; *Mekilta Exodus* on 20:6; *T. Levi* 17:2), "Father" occurs only occasionally in the evidence that survives from Second Temple Judaism. Once again, the same connections are made: as Father, God is authoritative and lordly, as well as caring, forgiving, restoring, and loving.

---

112. See his *God as Father*, 21-38.

113. Jeremias aptly draws a parallel to Matthew's penchant for this expression and maintains that Matthew and Johanan emerged from the same environment (*Prayers of Jesus*, 16-17).

114. See Schechter, *Aspects of Rabbinic Theology*, 21-56; Moore, *Judaism*, 2.201-11; Str-B, 1.392-96.

'abbā' in the Gospels

Even though God is addressed in prayer as Father in the Hebrew Bible and in early Jewish literature, there is a singular difference in the case of Jesus. Jesus taught his disciples to pray, as a matter of routine address, "Our Father" (Matt. 6:9; Luke 11:2). It is not so much form and content as *emphasis* that distinguishes Jesus; as we saw with Jesus' teachings about God as inflexibly holy, so also here: there is nothing in Jesus' use of *'abbā'* that was not also known in Judaism. Use of the term *'abbā'* was certainly characteristic of Jesus. What he meant by *'abbā'* is what it meant in Judaism. The centrality he gave it, however, reserved for it a special significance among his followers.[115] Here we may draw together the evidence that shows this distinctive emphasis of Jesus.[116]

We can be sure that Jesus addressed God as Father and encouraged his followers to do so when they prayed; behind "Father" is the Aramaic word *'abbā'*.[117] The evidence also clearly suggests a significant development in the growth of the traditions about Jesus: namely, the numbers change from a relative paucity of references to God as Father in the earliest traditions to a rather striking contrast in the Gospel of John, where the term is used ubiquitously.[118] However, a nuanced understanding of the Jesus traditions will show that, while some of the evidence for God as Father has been inserted by the Evangelists in their redactional activity, such evidence is not to be construed as "creative" or "unhistorical." Rather, as T. W. Manson said so eloquently: "Matthew and John do not introduce, so far as the Fatherhood of God is concerned, a new doctrine; they rather proclaim from the housetops what, in the more primitive documents, is

115. Charlesworth, "Caveat," 11.

116. It is not possible here to examine the issue of the psycho-social origins of Jesus' use of *Abba*. On this, see J. Miller, *Jesus at Thirty* (Minneapolis: Fortress, 1997).

117. The precise terms, with only a few references, are: "The Father" (Mark 13:32//Matt. 24:36; Matt. 11:27//Luke 10:22; Luke 11:13; Matt. 28:19); "Your Father" (Mark 11:25; Matt. 6:32//Luke 12:30; Luke 12:32; Matt. 6:1); and "My Father" (Mark 8:38//Matt. 16:27; Matt. 11:27//Luke 10:22; Luke 22:29; Matt. 10:32-33). On other Jewish evidence for "My Father," see Str-B, 2.49-50.

118. See Dalman, *Words*, 189-94; Jeremias, *Prayers of Jesus*, 29-54; Manson, *Teaching of Jesus*, 94-99. That "heavenly Father" was used rather often by the rabbis could indicate (1) Matthean redaction, (2) a Jewish milieu, or (3) a solid anchor in the Jesus tradition. See Jeremias, *Prayers of Jesus*, 16-18; Moore, *Judaism*, 2.205; Charlesworth, "Caveat," 1-5.

whispered in the ear."[119] One is, therefore, probably justified in speaking of a certain reserve on the part of Jesus in using the term "Father" for God, and this is precisely the way the term was used in Judaism.

Furthermore, apart from the cry of dereliction (Mark 15:34),[120] every prayer of Jesus recorded in the canonical Gospels begins with *'abbā'*/"Father." For example,

> "Pray then in this way:
> Our Father in heaven,
>   hallowed be your name." (Matt. 6:9)[121]

> At that time Jesus said, "I thank you, Father, Lord of heaven and earth, because you have hidden these things from the wise and the intelligent and have revealed them to infants; yes, Father, for such was your gracious will. All things have been handed over to me by my Father; and no one knows the Son except the Father, and no one knows the Father except the Son and anyone to whom the Son chooses to reveal him." (Matt. 11:25-27; cf. Mark 14:36; Luke 23:34, 46; John 17:1)

We can infer, then, that Jesus typically prayed like this and that this form of address was at the heart of Jesus' prayer life.[122] "Thus where Jesus prayed in his own words the testimony remains unshaken that his emotions and faith found clearest expression in the word 'Abba'. When we 'listen in' on Jesus' prayers *the distinctive word we hear is 'Abba.'* "[123] This

---

119. *Teaching of Jesus,* 100. See also H. F. D. Sparks, "The Doctrine of the Divine Fatherhood in the Gospels," in D. E. Nineham, ed., *Studies in the Gospels: Essays in Memory of R. H. Lightfoot* (Oxford: Basil Blackwell, 1955) 241-62.

120. It may be that addressing God as Father would be inappropriate here because of the sense of abandonment. However, several occurrences in early Jewish texts of God being called "Father" are in the context of abandonment; see, e.g., Sir. 23:1; 51:10; 4Q460 5 6 (see Schuller, "Psalm," 79).

121. For bibliography on the Lord's Prayer, see J. H. Charlesworth, M. Harding, and M. Kiley, eds., *The Lord's Prayer and Other Prayer Texts from the Greco-Roman Era* (Valley Forge, Penn.: Trinity Press International, 1994) 186-201.

122. This practice is evidenced in all strands of the Gospel tradition: cf. Mark 14:36; Matt. 6:9//Luke 11:2; Luke 23:34, 46; Matt. 26:42; John 11:41.

123. Dunn, *Jesus and the Spirit,* 21. See also C. Geffré, "'Father' as the Proper Name of God," in J.-B. Metz and E. Schillebeeckx, eds., *God as Father?* (New York: Seabury, 1981) 43-50, esp. 44-47.

best explains the survival of an Aramaic term for addressing God in early, non-Palestinian churches (cf. Gal. 4:6; Rom. 8:15-16). In addition to this, Jesus calls God *"Father"/'abbā'* frequently in the Gospel tradition:

> "But about that day or hour no one knows, neither the angels in heaven, nor the Son, but only the Father." (Mark 13:32)

> "For it is the nations of the world that strive after all these things, and your Father knows that you need them." (Luke 12:30//Matt. 6:32)

> "Not everyone who says to me, 'Lord, Lord,' will enter the kingdom of heaven, but only the one who does the will of my Father in heaven." (Matt. 7:21)

> ". . . and I confer on you, just as my Father has conferred on me, a kingdom, so that you may eat and drink at my table in my kingdom, and you will sit on thrones judging the twelve tribes of Israel." (Luke 22:29-30)

> Then they said to him, "Where is your Father?" Jesus answered, "You know neither me nor my Father. If you knew me, you would know my Father also." (John 8:19)

In other words, Jesus' use of "Father" was distinctive to his approach to God, his experience of God, and his beliefs about God. When he thought and taught about God, the term he preferred was "Father," and this in simple analogical terms. "We must suppose that Jesus used it [the term "Father"], by choice, because it is the appropriate way of speaking about the personal life with God which was his concern, but, even more, because it was the only possible way of speaking of God as he himself knew him."[124]

We now need to explore the various dimensions of Jesus' use of the term *'abbā'*. First, there is the covenantal dimension, which emerged from Judaism. When Joachim Jeremias entered the discussion about *'abbā'*, the term was taken in scholarship to refer to God's benevolent care and loving relationship with his people.[125] Jeremias's contribution

---

124. C. H. Dodd, *The Founder of Christianity* (New York: Macmillan, 1970) 61-62.
125. E.g., Harnack, *What Is Christianity?* 63-70; Klausner, *Jesus*, 378.

was to emphasize *'abbā'* as a childlike and familial address. This further led him to argue for a special, even unique, intimacy as the distinctive connotation of the address. Such scholarship conceptualized Jesus' teachings about the Father in terms of love and a universal Fatherhood of God, who treats all people with infinite worth, dignity, and freedom because they are part of God's good created order.[126] However, an important challenge in this regard was made by H. F. D. Sparks when he argued that, if one follows the growth of the Jesus tradition carefully, one is led to see that Jesus himself called God *'abbā'* out of his special sense of sonship and led others to address God as *'abbā'* as they were related to Jesus.[127] In other words, for Sparks (and many have followed him here[128]), Jesus taught that God's Fatherhood is a relationship reserved only for himself and for those who follow Jesus. God's Fatherhood is not universal; rather, like the Fatherhood of YHWH in the Hebrew Bible, it is confined to the covenantal relationship with Israel.

Second, in Judaism the term *'abbā'* always denoted respect and authority. Rabbi Eleazar b. Azariah was said to have taught:

> "Do not say: 'I have no desire to wear (clothing made of different sorts of stuff), to eat pork, to have intercourse with a woman within the prohibited degrees (because of incest, Lev. 18.6-18)', but (say): 'I do (indeed) desire these things, (but) what shall I do, seeing that my heavenly Father has prohibited them?'" (*Sipra Leviticus* on 20:26)

Those who are truly of Israel, who have been called by God out of Egypt into the wilderness to receive his commands, are those who obey God. Consistent with the ancient Israelite custom of unbounded respect for one's father (cf. Gen. 3:16; Exod. 20:12; Luke 2:41-51, esp. 51), when Jesus taught his followers to call God *'abbā'*, implicit in that instruction was a call to obey that Father. Thus, the one who taught them to pray "hallowed be your name" and "your kingdom come" also taught them to pray "your will be done, on earth as it is in heaven" and to "forgive us our debts, as we also have forgiven our debtors" (Matt.

---

126. See also H. W. Montefiore, "God as Father in the Synoptic Gospels," *NTS* 3 (1956-57) 31-46.

127. Sparks, "Divine Fatherhood."

128. So also Jeremias, *Prayers of Jesus*, 43; Ladd, *Presence*, 179, 181; Dunn, *Jesus and the Spirit*, 24; R. Bauckham, "Sonship," 248-249; Caird, *New Testament Theology*, 398-99.

6:9-12). That is, those who address God as *'abbā'* are those who sanctify God's name through covenant obedience, seek God's kingdom (cf. Matt. 6:33),[129] seek God's will on earth, and forgive others — eschatological signs of repentance. When Jesus faced public humiliation and death, he connected both authority and love with the Fatherhood of God: "Abba, Father, for you all things are possible; remove this cup from me; yet, not what I want, but what you want" (Mark 14:36). The Johannine evidence, which probably reflects a different setting, is still entirely consistent with both Judaism and what can be more securely known about Jesus: obedience to the Father is the responsibility of the Son of God (John 6:38; 12:49-50; 14:31). All John has done here is to tease out of the Jesus traditions what was a minor theme: "Father" means authority and implies obedience.[130]

This is exactly how the term *'abbā'* was used in Judaism, and the evidence deserves a brief survey here. In the Hebrew Bible it is only those who are faithful to the terms of the covenant who are called "sons," and they are the ones who can call God "Father" (e.g., Ps. 103:13; Mal. 3:17; cf. *Psalms of Solomon* 13:8-9; 18:4). Further, when the prayer in 4Q372 1 calls God "My father and my God" (line 16), it also describes God as "great, holy, mighty and majestic, awesome and marvelous" (line 29). Also, Judah b. Tema is reported to have taught:

> Be strong as a leopard, fast as an eagle, fleet as a gazelle, and brave as a lion, *to carry out the will of your Father who is in heaven.* (*m. Abot* 5:20; emphasis added)

In Jesus' day, then, calling God *'abbā'* did not stem from some sentimental religiosity but from a rigorous commitment to the God of Israel who had revealed his will in the Torah and now also in Jesus as he carries out God's mission to Israel: "To the Jew the first connotation of the Fatherhood of God is the right to obedience."[131] Thus, Mary Rose D'Angelo, after summarizing a wide range of evidence, says, "Rather, wherever the word is used, even when it is used as a challenge to imperial claims or to the patriarchal family, it evokes the image of God as the

129. "Father" and "King" are frequently connected in Judaism. See Moore, *Judaism*, 2.209-10; Ladd, *Presence*, 178-84; Caird, *New Testament Theology*, 404.
130. See L. W. Hurtado, "God," *DJG*, 274-75; M. M. Thompson, "John, Gospel of," *DJG*, 377-78.
131. Caird, *New Testament Theology*, 401.

pater whose *potestas* exceeds and so affirms, limits, or challenges the power of every other *pater.*"[132] This explains why, for Jesus, only God is to be called *'abbā'* (Matt. 23:9): because only he is to be obeyed and loved. Thus, the historical context of the address "Father" illuminates a saying of this sort and places it in the context of the Decalogue: "you are to have no other gods before me" (Exod. 20:3).

Third, to call God *'abbā'* involves an intimate, familial trust and love.[133] While this dimension of *'abbā'* has surely been overdone, this term was nevertheless special to Jews of the ancient world. A classic example, though from a later age, of the loving tenderness of a father can be found in *Mekilta Beshallah* 5 (on Exod. 14:19). This passage functions well as an analogy to what Jesus taught:

> *And the Angel of God . . . Removed,* etc. R. Judah says: This is a verse rich in content, being echoed in many places. To give a parable, to what is this like? To a man who is walking on the road with his son walking in front of him. If robbers who might seek to capture the son come from in front, he takes him from before himself and puts him behind himself. If a wolf comes from behind, he takes his son from behind and puts him in front. If robbers come from in front and wolves from behind he takes the son up in his arms. When the son begins to suffer from the sun, his father spreads his cloak over him. When he is hungry he feeds him, when he is thirsty he gives him to drink. [At this point, the writer appeals to Hos. 11:3; Ps. 105:39; Exod. 16:4; Ps. 78:16; Cant. 4:15; and Prov. 5:15.][134]

The parable describes the kind of behavior characteristic of a loving father: tenderness, protection, and sacrifice.

Because Jewish children grew up calling their fathers *'abbā'* (and their mothers *'imma'*),[135] this term probably recalled for them the

---

132. D'Angelo is disputing Hamerton-Kelly's notion that Jesus subverted patriarchy; see *"Abba,"* 629. See also Barr, "Abba," esp. 34-46.

133. See Schechter, *Aspects of Rabbinic Theology,* 50-56; Jeremias, *Prayers of Jesus,* 59-60; Dunn, "Prayer," *DJG,* 619.

134. The translation is from the edition of J. Z. Lauterbach, *Mekilta de-Rabbi Ishmael* (Philadelphia: Jewish Publication Society of America, 1976) 224-25.

135. See *b. Ber.* 40a: "One rabbi said, 'When a child experiences the taste of wheat (i.e. when it is weaned), it learns to say *abba* and *imma* (i.e. these are the first sounds that it prattles)." See J. Barr, "Abba," 32-35.

days of their youth. The language of childhood, however, extended over the course of a lifetime.[136] While modern Americans may move from "Daddy" to "Dad" in their psycho-social development, and in so doing shed their former childhood language, this was not the case with ancient Jews. They continued to address their fathers as 'abbā', and this shows the fundamental connotations of the term: *both respectful authority and love*. It is highly unlikely that Jesus or other Jews of his time would have addressed God or described God with childish or overly familiar terms; the evidence shows a massive consistency in speaking of God in reverent terms and even refusing to use his name.

The special appeal of 'abbā', however, was neither its loving dimension nor its authority dimension but its ability to shoulder both. Jesus probably used the term more for its connotations of familial and trusting love than for its authoritative connotations, but the latter remains a significant aspect of the term. Jesus frequently described God as one who loves, who forgives, who restores, and who cares, but also as one who expects his kingdom to be pursued wholeheartedly, his name to be held in honor, and who expects to have no rival. Accordingly, Jesus is thankful to the Father, because in his mercy God has granted his revelation to the unlikely (Matt. 11:25-27);[137] in utter pain and torment, Jesus cries out to God in the most intimate of terms that the Father God might find a way of deliverance (Mark 14:36); and Jesus prays to the Father that, in his mercy, he will find a place to forgive his persecutors (Luke 23:34). All of these usages express the loving mercy of God and his caring protection.[138]

Fourth, 'abbā' for Jesus was not just a title for God or a description of God; for Jesus, 'abbā' revealed his innermost relation to God and the secret to his heart for God. That is, 'abbā' best represented for Jesus the experience he had of God and the only way he could express

---

136. James Barr points out that neither the diminutive πατρίδιον (surely the language of a child) nor the obviously familiar πάππας was used by the Gospel tradents ("Abba," 35-39). 'Abbā', as it turns out, may be more of an adult term than the language of a child. See also Charlesworth, "Caveat," 5-10.

137. See R. H. Fuller, *The Mission and Achievement of Jesus: An Examination of the Presuppositions of New Testament Theology* (SBT 12; London: SCM, 1954) 89-95; Jeremias, *Prayers of Jesus*, 45-52; Dunn, *Jesus and the Spirit*, 26-34; R. Bauckham, "Sonship," 251-52.

138. See Vermes, *Religion*, 180.

that relationship.[139] Jesus' experience of God was the experience of a person with his or her father, and the term reflects an "intense reality and deep sacredness of the experience itself."[140] Again, "the point can bear reiteration, that for Jesus himself, his sonship was primarily an existential conviction and relationship, not a merely intellectual belief nor something fully metaphysical."[141] Jesus did not come to teach about God; he came to experience God, to dwell in that experience with God, and out of that experience to point others to the kingdom. In the words of G. B. Caird, "For Jesus the Fatherhood of God has become a profoundly personal religious experience, long before it became a doctrine to be communicated to others."[142] It is probably this experience (not the teachings about 'abbā'), and the effects it had on his disciples, that led to the use of 'abbā' in early Christian worship.[143]

Fifth, as Jesus learned from John the Baptist, those who are destined to be part of God's eschatological people are not so on the basis of heredity; rather, the new people of God are those who have turned from idolatry, sinfulness, and unfaithfulness to the God John proclaimed in his prophetic protest against Israel (Matt. 3:7-10//Luke 3:7-9; cf. 3:10-14). Jesus learned from John that God was forming a new people, and Jesus extended this concept (cf. Mark 1:16-20; 3:13-19; Matt. 19:28). However, the God of this new people, this eschatological Israel, is to be called 'abbā' because he relates to them as a father does to his children and they, as a new community, are to be brothers and sisters in a new family (Mark 3:31-35). In predicting the future restoration of Israel, the author of *Jubilees*, an expansionistic paraphrase of the book of Genesis from the second century B.C., speaks in language strikingly similar to that of Jesus:

> And after this they will turn to me in all uprightness and with all their heart and soul. And I will circumcise the foreskin of their heart and the foreskin of the heart of their sons, and I will create in them a holy spirit, and I will cleanse them so that they shall not turn away from me again, from that day till eternity. And they will hold fast to me and to all my commandments, and fulfill my commandments;

139. At perhaps no point in the evidence about Jesus is the appeal to experience made more than here.

140. Manson, *Teaching of Jesus*, 108.

141. Dunn, *Jesus and the Spirit*, 39.

142. Caird, *New Testament Theology*, 401.

143. See Hamerton-Kelly, *God the Father*, 83-91, 96-97.

and I will be their father, and they shall be my children. And they all shall be called children of the living God; and every angel and spirit shall know (they shall know indeed) that these are my children and that I am truly and genuinely their father, and that I love them. (*Jub.* 1:23-25; trans. R. H. Charles; rev. C. Rabin)

Here we observe the important connections of eschatology, restoration, and God as Father with Israelites as his children.

The God of Jesus, *'abbā'*, generates a mission in which Jesus passes on special knowledge (Matt. 11:25-27) and spreads experience of God as Father.[144] No text is more instructive here than Luke 12:32:

"Do not be afraid, little flock, for it is your Father's good pleasure to give you the kingdom."

This significant text coheres with everything we have seen thus far about Jesus' view of God: loving care, kingly authority, and new community. This communal aspect explains why Jesus, when asked by his disciples if they were to have a prayer among themselves as John's disciples were marked off by a prayer, taught them the "Our *'abbā'*" (Luke 11:1-4). The Lord's Prayer, in its historical sense, is not a prayer for the closet of the individual but a prayer to be recited and repeated on a constant basis in the presence of others who have made the same commitment to follow Jesus as the one who can bring an end to Israel's exile: fundamentally, it is a community prayer. And the community of Jesus, when it addresses God, calls him *'abbā'* as a continuation of the experience of Jesus.

Finally, the God of Jesus, who is revealed especially as *'abbā'*, is the God of Israel who is forming a new Israel. The term *'abbā'* itself entails a national vision; the experience of Jesus generated a vision for Israel as a community. Readers of the Hebrew Bible will know that the term "son of God" sometimes refers to the nation of Israel (Exod. 4:22; Hos. 11:1). Jesus extended this relation not only to himself but also to his followers. Thus, Luke 22:29-30 reads:

"and I confer on you, just as my Father has conferred on me, a kingdom, so that you may eat and drink at my table in my kingdom, and you will sit on thrones judging the twelve tribes of Israel."

144. Dunn, *Jesus and the Spirit*, 24-26, 39.

The vision of Jesus for Israel, for the Israel who calls God *'abbā'*, who trusts and obeys this *'abbā'*, centered on Israel's restoration. Throughout the Hebrew Bible, the image of Father is evoked to remind Israel of God's electing liberation from bondage and therefore forms the basis for restoration (e.g., Deut. 32; Hos. 11:1-4). In the words of James H. Charlesworth,

> Rather than proving unparalleled communion between himself and God, Jesus' use of *'abbā'* probably reminded the Jews who heard him of some familiar and ancient traditions. His *'abbā'* probably evoked in them an awareness of God the Father, who had been active on their behalf in history. According to Sacred Scriptures God had called his people "son" when he freed them from Egyptian slavery (Exod. 4:22-23) and he had adopted Israel's king as his special son during the enthronement ceremony (Ps. 2).[145]

Jesus arrived on the scene to announce the impending judgment and the arrival of the kingdom, which was surely the promised restoration for Israel. Those from Israel who choose to repent and turn to the gospel of the kingdom are those who will either sit on the twelve thrones or enjoy their beneficent rule over God's new family. This *'abbā'*, this loving and demanding God, is a Father to Israel and for Israel's salvation. The vision of Jesus about *'abbā'* God did not concern the universal Fatherhood of God and the brotherhood of humanity; rather, it had Israel at its very center and no doubt intended to displace Rome.[146] Jesus contended that, if Israel would turn to *'abbā'* in repentance, it would avoid the impending destruction of Jerusalem and would experience the glorious kingdom of God.

In summary, the God of Jesus is to be called *'abbā'* when Jesus' followers pray to God and when they speak of God. Why? Because the God Jesus experienced, talked about, and revealed is a God who is holy and compassionate, loving and demanding. Jesus chose this term because he thought it best described what the God of Israel had called him to announce to his people in the last hour and what he himself experi-

---

145. Charlesworth, "Caveat," 10-11. This tradition of the Hebrew Bible is continued in Judaism; see *Deut. Rab.* 2:24 (cited in Young, *Jesus the Jewish Theologian*, 152).
146. So M. R. D'Angelo, "Abba," 628-30.

enced of God. This Holy *'abbā'* is a God who can be trusted the way children trust their father, who loves Israel as a father loves his children, who can be talked to the way children talk to their father, and who wants Israel to respect him and obey him in the same way a father deserves respect and obedience.

Compassionate Deeds

The God of Jesus also manifests his nature in the acts of compassion Jesus performed. On several occasions the Gospel writers remark that Jesus was perceived, in some action of his, to be "full of compassion."[147] The same term is used throughout the Hebrew Bible and Septuagint for God's special electing love of Israel: as a result of God's election and covenant, his "compassion" continues with Israel, bringing especially the forgiveness of sins (cf. Exod. 33:19; 34:6; Deut. 4:31; Isa. 30:18; 49:10, 13, 15; 54:8, 10; see also 1QS 1:22; 2:1; 11:13), but when Israel acts disobediently, God withdraws his "compassion" as an act of judgment against Israel (Isa. 13:18; 27:11; 63:15; Jer. 6:23; 13:14; see also 1QH 11:18); however, if Israel repents, God will again have "compassion" on Israel (Deut. 13:18; 30:3; 1 Kgs. 8:50; Isa. 55:7; Prov. 28:13; see also 1QS 2:7; *T. Zeb.* 9:7, 9; *T. Naph.* 4:5; *T. Levi* 4:4). The "compassion" of God is seen as the basis for the eschatological renewal of the covenant and restoration of the people (cf. Deut. 13:18; Isa. 14:1; 49:10, 13; 54:8, 10; 60:10; Jer. 12:15; 33:26; Ezek. 39:25; Micah 7:19; Hab. 3:2; Zech. 10:6). Thus, there is a significant biblical context that leads us to expect a *national-political focus — the restoration of Israel —* for the description of Jesus as one who was "full of compassion." We can turn now to sketch the contours and the significance of Jesus' being described as one who acted in compassion.

When the Gospels describe Jesus as one who had "compassion," a clear pattern emerges. First, a situation of serious need emerges: someone with leprosy (Mark 1:41), crowds of people in need of care (Mark 6:34; Matt. 9:36), people in need of sustenance but too far from a vil-

---

147. The Greek term is σπλαγχνίζομαι *(splanchnizomai);* behind this term is the Hebrew רחם *(rḥm).* In the classical world σπλάγχνον denoted the entrails. On the terms, see esp. H. Koester, "σπλάγχνον," *TDNT,* 7.548-35; H.-H. Esser, "σπλάγχνα," *NIDNTT,* 2.599-601; H. J. Stoebe, "רחם," *THAT,* 2.5761-68.

lage for immediate relief (Mark 8:2), someone with epilepsy (Mark 9:22), a person suffering from blindness (Matt. 20:34), and the death of a person (Luke 7:13). Second, Jesus is filled with compassion:[148] typically, the texts say that "Jesus was moved with compassion" (cf. Matt. 9:36; 14:14; 15:32; 18:27; 20:34). Third, and often overlooked, a contrast is made with someone or some group that does not show the needed compassion: disciples (Mark 9:22; cf. Matt. 11:5-6), Pharisees (Matt. 9:36; cf. 9:32-34), or the crowds (Matt. 20:34; cf. 20:31). Finally, the compassion of Jesus leads him to alleviate the need: he cleanses a leper (Mark 1:41), teaches/feeds (Mark 6:34), heals an epileptic (Mark 9:22), sends out the disciples (Matt. 10:1-8), and gives sight (Matt. 20:34).

In light of this Jewish context and this sketch of the Jesus traditions, it becomes obvious that Jesus was a man of compassion who, in meeting others' needs, responded with vivid emotion and helpful action. Jesus performed these actions in order to present his vision of a pure Israel, of what God wanted done on earth, of what God was doing through Jesus in actualizing the kingdom, and of what God wanted Israel to see as it faced judgment. What Jesus wanted Israel to see was that God responds in joy and celebration when his children turn to him as Father (cf. Luke 15:20-24); that God cares for his people so much that he is acting in Jesus to help and heal; and that the true Israel is composed of all kinds of people who find in Jesus the solution to their needs. Jesus' actions, then, were national acts; he acted in compassion and worked to alleviate human need in order to show to Israel what God was doing for it.

In the Gospels, no one but Jesus is described as having "compassion," except the characters of Jesus' parables of the good Samaritan (Luke 10:29-37) and the prodigal son (Luke 15:11-32). The good Samaritan functions as Jesus' alter ego, visibly demonstrating in story form what Jesus did in constant action: he accepted, he sat at table with, and he healed those whom the various holiness movements had rejected. In the parable of the prodigal son, the father represents God's action on behalf of Israelites whom the holiness movements have spurned as unworthy of God's special grace; his love prompts

---

148. I assume that Jesus experienced this emotionally; it could, less probably, be a description of Jesus that coincides simply with the bare fact that he acted to help.

the action that Jesus himself performed in table fellowship (cf. Luke 15:1-2).

Jesus' compassion was a national-political act through which he visibly demonstrated his vision of an Israel that would finally conform to God's will and express his designs as it experienced his eschatological compassion. His compassion was as much socially and eschatologically motivated as spiritually energized. It is entirely reasonable to see in Jesus' acts of compassion emotional actions that conformed to his regular practice of table fellowship with sinners. In his compassion, Jesus revealed what he thought God was like and what he thought God wanted for Israel: a loving act of restoration that would lead Israel to repentance and away from the coming disaster, which had dominated Jesus' vision of the future ever since his days with John the Baptist.[149] The God who calls Israel to this momentous decision is a God who is compassionate enough to loosen the bonds of sin and suffering, but who is also powerful enough to shackle demonic forces, shatter the powers of sin, and re-create a new people who accomplish his will.

Jesus' God, then, loves Israel and has acted at the end of days to restore his people and end its exile. His holiness does not overshadow his mercy, nor does his mercy hide his holiness. For Jesus, God is both holy and loving. He is a God who is perfectly good. God can, without denying his absolute control of history, lay aside his holiness with perfect integrity and justice, his holy zeal, and overlook the sins of the nation as he seeks its fellowship in calling Israel to turn to him once again. This God desires table fellowship with his people, he yearns for Israel to call him 'abbā' (thereby both obeying and loving him), and he showers his power and love on them by acts of the kingdom that restore Israelites to society and health by fulfilling expectations about the final kingdom of God.

Jesus' view of God is nowhere more amply illustrated than in his parable of the prodigal son (Luke 15:1-2, 11-32). In this parable, surely a story about Israel's relationship to God and not simply about an individual Israelite, we have a father whom Jesus uses to describe what he means by 'abbā'. This 'abbā' permits the audacity of a younger son to go unpunished as the younger boy demands (or at least presumptu-

---

149. The *Testaments of the Twelve Patriarchs* associate the idea of "compassion" with the end-time messianic salvation and restoration of his people: cf. *T. Zeb.* 8:2; *T. Naph.* 4:5; *T. Asher* 7:7.

ously requests) his inheritance early; to this son the 'abbā' grants freedom to choose to go "into exile" (he goes to a far country).[150] When the younger son realizes his foolishness in abandoning his homeland and his family, this 'abbā' is anxiously awaiting his return from exile. When the younger son does repent and return to the father, the 'abbā' is quick and eager to forgive, to restore the boy to his former status in the family, and to share an 'abbā''s joy with his friends. But for this boy to be restored, forgiven, he must repent because this 'abbā', though loving, has a heart of justice and integrity; until his son repents, he cannot be restored to his former status and enjoy the love of his 'abbā'. While this 'abbā' surely represents the Father of all Israel, only those who repent can enjoy the table of the 'abbā'. The older son is still a son, but he cannot enjoy his 'abbā''s love until he, too, repents and comes inside to sit at table.

As has often been noted, this parable is not about a prodigal son but an 'abbā' who has a prodigal love for his son.[151] This is Israel's 'abbā'; this is Israel's history; and it is now time for this 'abbā' and this nation to make peace, because the God of Israel is now acting to bring in the kingdom by sitting down at table with a forgiven, restored, and now obedient son. It is no surprise that this kind of son gets the ring and robe!

Conclusion

In Jesus' view, Israel had persisted in its sinful disobedience to the covenant that God had made with the nation. Over and over God had called Israel to repentance and restoration. Now he was calling one more time before disaster struck the nation. Jesus, following John, stepped into Israel's history of covenantal election and disobedience and was compelled to warn Israel of impending judgment. His God called him to warn Israel of the judgment. God is so holy that those who follow Jesus

150. Cf. Ward, *Royal Theology*, 125-29, on God's restraint, a consistent theme of the prophets; this has been explored from a Freudian view in Hamerton-Kelly, *God the Father*, 27, 28-34, 50-51.

151. The best studies of this parable are Jeremias, *Parables*, 128-39; Bailey, *Poet and Peasant*, 158-206; Young, *Jesus the Jewish Theologian*, 143-54; Wright, *Jesus and the Victory of God*, 125-31, 133-37.

in preparation for that judgment must learn to honor him in all that they say and do; he is so holy that Jesus must warn of judgment; he is so holy that nothing but absolute commitment to God's will (as revealed by Jesus) is acceptable, beginning with repentance; he is so holy that even Jesus experiences the wrath of God when he offers himself for his people. This same God is warning his people of the coming judgment; but this judgment is not an inevitable, predetermined fate for Israel. This God, one more time, offers to Israel the chance to be restored and forgiven, and this people need only listen to God's messenger, Jesus, and repent (like the prodigal son). They need only to learn how good God's love is by relating to him as *'abbā'*, by sitting at table with Jesus, and by watching him act in compassion as he demonstrates to all Israel just what vision God has in mind for those who will return to the covenant.

The God of Jesus, then, is a God of inflexible holiness, but he is also a God of intense love who mercifully gives his people time to respond to his acts of love and grace. For those who do not respond, Jesus warns of the judgment; for those who do respond in repentance and return to the covenant, Jesus offers forgiveness, restoration, and a new community of pure Israelites who can now participate in the vision of Jesus for the kingdom of God.

Thus, Jesus' God is the national God of Israel, not some abstract, universal deity. He is the God of Abraham, Isaac, and Jacob; he is the God of David and of the prophets; he is the God of the Maccabees and of John the Baptist. From the time of John, this God has been forming a new Israel that will turn away from its disobedience and toward the kingdom whose dawning Jesus is now proclaiming.

CHAPTER 3

The Kingdom Now Present

Jesus stepped into history with the mission of warning Israel of a coming disaster upon the nation. His warning also contained a call to repent and, for those who did repent, a promise of escape from judgment. Undergirding Jesus' call to Israel was his vision of the kingdom of God, the term he chose to express the end of Israel's self-imposed exile and the fulfillment of Israel's hopes. Behind the impending judgment stood the kingdom; beyond the judgment loomed the kingdom for those who turned to God as Jesus called them. No one questions *that* Jesus spoke of the kingdom,[1] but questions abound about what Jesus meant by the kingdom.

Because of the complexity of this topic, we must begin with a brief survey of scholarship on the meaning of the kingdom of God in the teachings of Jesus. I shall present only the barest outline of the history of this hotly disputed aspect of Jesus' ministry and conclude with a few summary points.[2] Following this I shall expound the meaning of both the presence and the future of the kingdom. The discussion will center on what Jesus meant by the formulations he used in his context; I am not concerned here with the systematic exploration of the Chris-

---

1. On the centrality of the kingdom in the teaching of Jesus, see H. Schürmann, *Gottes Reich — Jesu Geschick: Jesu ureigener Tod im Licht seiner Basileia-Verkündigung* (Freiburg: Herder, 1983); O. Camponovo, *Königtum, Königsherrschaft und Reich Gottes in den frühjudischen Schriften* (OBO 58; Göttingen: Vandenhoeck & Ruprecht, 1984).

2. On the history of discussion, see esp. W. Willis, ed., *The Kingdom of God in 20th-Century Interpretation* (Peabody, Mass.: Hendrickson, 1987); Camponovo, *Königtum*, esp. 11-71.

tian view of either salvation or eschatology, though our study may indirectly shed some light on how those items of theology might be explained if one were to begin with Jesus' teachings.

The Kingdom of God in Scholarship

The most pervasive academic perception of Jesus' view of the kingdom has undoubtedly been that of *consistent eschatology*. Though championed by Albert Schweitzer, this view actually has its origins in the work of Johannes Weiß,[3] who, in an atmosphere conducive to historicism, was the first to wrest the concept of the kingdom away from Protestant liberalism's moralistic equation of it with the highest good, social reconstruction, and the saving community.[4] The most notable proponent of the liberal view of the kingdom was Weiß's teacher and father-in-law, Albrecht Ritschl, the famous systematic theologian.[5] For Weiß, Jesus was to be understood within the context of Jewish eschatology; Jesus' own vision of the kingdom was not to be equated with moral improvement, as Ritschl maintained,[6] but rather with the miracle of God's supernatural intervention in this world. Furthermore, for Jesus the kingdom was imminent, not present.[7] While it

3. J. Weiß, *Jesus' Proclamation of the Kingdom of God* (trans. R. H. Hiers and D. L. Holland; Philadelphia: Fortress, 1971). This translates the first edition of Weiß, *Die Predigt Jesu vom Reiche Gottes* (1892). Significant changes were made in his second edition of 1900. A third edition, edited by F. Hahn and with an introduction by R. Bultmann, was published in 1964; references in this study are to this third edition.

4. See the trenchant comments of A. Schweitzer, *The Quest for the Historical Jesus: A Critical Study of Its Progress from Reimarus to Wrede* (trans. W. Montgomery; intro. J. M. Robinson; New York: Macmillan, 1968) 398.

5. The work of Leo Tolstoy reveals a similar perception of the kingdom of God: humans, yearning for the kingdom on earth, need to act upon the truth of love and peace to bring about moral order and justice. See his *The Kingdom of God Is within You: Christianity Not as a Mystic Religion but as a New Theory of Life* (trans. C. Garnett; foreword by M. Green; Lincoln, Nebr.: University of Nebraska Press, 1984) 208-35, 264-368. Though later, and from the United States, one thinks of S. Mathews, *Jesus on Social Institutions* (ed. K. Cauthen; reprint, Philadelphia: Fortress, 1971) esp. 29-42. See, e.g., the analysis of Weiß, *Predigt*, 73-85.

6. In his later, more systematic work (*Die Idee des Reiches Gottes in der Theologie*; Giessen: Ricker, 1901), Weiß permits a separation of the historical task (what Jesus meant) from the theological task (what it means to the church).

7. For Johannes Weiß, the logia of presence (e.g., Luke 17:20-21 or Matt. 12:28) are

would be inaccurate to speak of Weiß as anchoring the message of Jesus about the kingdom in Jewish apocalypticism, he nevertheless laid the foundation for the work of Schweitzer.

For Schweitzer,[8] however, the message of Jesus was too deeply rooted in apocalyptic soil. He argued that Jesus' kingdom teaching represented an intense manifestation of the Jewish apocalyptic spirit. Jesus expected the end of history to come imminently, within his own lifetime, and he believed that it would involve a moral revolution.[9] Hence, he sent out the Twelve (Matt. 10:1-16), expecting them not to return before the Son of Man came (Matt. 10:23). When they did return, Jesus had to reevaluate his entire program and eventually, upon realizing that he could bring in the eschatological conditions by suffering, threw himself into the turbulence of Jerusalem at a critical point and was crucified in his attempt to force God's hand in bringing about the kingdom. Weiß was outdone by Schweitzer, not because of the latter's genius, but because, even though Weiß was more accurate and balanced, Schweitzer's rhetoric was unsurpassed, and remains so. One example of his eloquence will suffice:

> There is silence all around. The Baptist appears, and cries: "Repent, for the Kingdom of Heaven is at hand." Soon after that comes Jesus, and in the knowledge that He is the coming Son of Man lays hold of the wheel of the world to set it moving on that last revolution which is to bring all ordinary history to a close. It refused to turn, and He throws Himself upon it. Then it does turn; and crushes Him. Instead of bringing in the eschatological conditions, He has destroyed them. The wheel rolls onward, and the mangled body of the one immeasurably great Man, who was strong enough to think of Himself as the

---

not statements of fact but high moments of Jesus' consciousness (*Predigt*, 95). But he does think that in some exorcisms Jesus saw the kingdom as beginning to break into history.

8. The fundamental books for understanding Schweitzer's thought, besides his famous *Quest*, are: *The Mystery of the Kingdom of God: The Secret of Jesus' Messiahship and Passion* (trans. W. Lowrie; New York: Schocken, 1964; originally published in 1901); idem, *The Kingdom of God and Primitive Christianity* (New York: Seabury, 1968; originally published in 1967).

9. Perhaps the most trenchant critiques of Schweitzer are those of T. F. Glasson. Among others, see esp. Glasson, "Schweitzer's Influence — Blessing or Bane?" *JTS* 28 (1977) 289-302; reprinted in B. D. Chilton, ed., *The Kingdom of God* (IRT 5; Philadelphia: Fortress, 1984) 107-20.

spiritual ruler of mankind and to bend history to His purpose, is hanging upon it still. That is His victory and His reign.[10]

The position of consistent eschatology as articulated by Weiß and Schweitzer contends that, for Jesus, (1) the kingdom was entirely future, (2) the future was in some sense imminent, and (3) his eschatological framework completely controlled everything about him. This view has dominated discussion about Jesus from the time of Schweitzer; it has been propounded by countless scholars from Weiß's student, Rudolf Bultmann,[11] to contemporary scholars like E. P. Sanders and N. T. Wright.[12] For these scholars, Mark 1:15 would be translated: "the kingdom of God has drawn (very) near." In the view of these scholars, then, Jesus expected an immediate fulfillment of his vision of the kingdom.[13]

Dissatisfied with the emerging consensus that the kingdom was future for Jesus, C. H. Dodd argued for the opposite:[14] with messianic authority, Jesus believed that the kingdom was *fully realized* in his person and ministry, as seen in his exorcisms and acts of power, but most especially in the obedience of his followers. Arguing from the now discredited idea that both *ēngiken* ("has drawn near"; cf. Mark 1:15) and *ephthasen* ("has come"; cf. Matt. 12:28//Luke 11:20) speak of the presence, rather than future, of the kingdom, Dodd maintained that Jesus believed the kingdom to be present and that the language of the future is a sort of code for the "ulti-

---

10. Schweitzer, *Quest,* 370-71.

11. See his *Jesus and the Word* (trans. L. P. Smith and E. H. Lantero; New York: Charles Scribner's Sons, 1958) 35-56. The acceptance of linear time, in the form of a tension between the "now and not yet," characterized the work of O. Cullmann (*Christ and Time: The Primitive Christian Conception of Time and History* [rev. ed.; trans. F. V. Filson; Philadelphia: Westminster, 1964]) and led to heated debate in the decade immediately following World War II.

12. E. P. Sanders, *Jesus and Judaism* (Philadelphia: Fortress, 1985); N. T. Wright, *Jesus and the Victory of God* (Christian Origins and the Question of God, vol. 2; Minneapolis: Fortress, 1996). Another recent study close to this viewpoint is C. C. Caragounis, "Kingdom of God/Kingdom of Heaven," *DJG,* 417-30.

13. An incredibly patronizing comment about Jesus' view of the future can be found in A. E. Harvey, *Jesus and the Constraints of History* (Philadelphia: Westminster, 1982) 66.

14. See Dodd, *The Parables of the Kingdom* (London: Nisbet, 1936) esp. 34-80. An excellent survey of Dodd's full, and changing, viewpoint can be found in N. Perrin, *The Kingdom of God in the Teaching of Jesus* (London: SCM, 1963) 58-78. For the fuller perspective on Dodd's life, including the influence of Harnack rather than Schweitzer, see F. W. Dillistone, *C. H. Dodd: Interpreter of the New Testament* (Grand Rapids: Eerdmans, 1977).

mate," the "eternal order," or the "transcendent" being experienced in time. This kingdom, Dodd argued, is realized through the human obedience that emerges from the crisis of decision.[15] For Dodd, Mark 1:15 should be translated: "the kingdom of God has (already) arrived."[16]

Several important concerns find a home in Dodd's view. Notably, his approach to the issue of time recalls the noneschatological reinterpretation of Jesus' imminent expectation offered by Bultmann, even though Dodd himself was not an existentialist interpreter. Further, Dodd's position proved compatible with the then dominant Protestant liberalism: "religious experience" in the liberal tradition became, in Dodd's terminology, the "presence of the ultimate or the eternal." At the same time, Dodd's viewpoint permitted an escape for those who were embarrassed by the imminent expectation of Jesus.[17] Dodd also gave younger scholars an opportunity to shift the focus away from imminence in an exclusively temporal sense, and to pastors he provided an interpretation of Jesus' teaching that could be easily grasped and used in parish ministries.

In line with the themes mentioned above, Protestant liberalism continued to exercise an important influence on kingdom scholarship, both influencing Dodd and being influenced by him with his presentation of a realized kingdom. For Protestant liberalism the kingdom was an ethic, or the ideal for society, expressed both in the social gospel of the Church and in its many attempts at social and cultural reformation.[18] This tendency to equate the kingdom of God with various social, cultural, or political agendas has continued into the late twentieth century, especially in liberation theology, though it owes much of its impetus to earlier European theologians.[19]

Alongside this emphasis on a realized kingdom on earth, at least as seen in the view of the kingdom as social vision, we might consider recent studies of Jesus that emphasize the (present) experience of Jesus,

---

15. Dodd, *Parables*, 197-98.

16. A recent case for a modified realized eschatology can be seen in L. D. Hurst, "Ethics of Jesus," *DJG*, 210-22 (esp. 210-14). Less nuanced, but heavily dependent upon Dodd, is G. Vermes, *The Religion of Jesus the Jew* (Minneapolis: Fortress, 1993) 146-48.

17. Cf. W. G. Kümmel, *Promise and Fulfillment: The Eschatological Message of Jesus* (trans. D. M. Barton; London: SCM, 1957) 141-55.

18. C. A. Briggs, *The Ethical Teaching of Jesus* (New York: Charles Scribner's Sons, 1904) 59-67.

19. See the incisive critique of E. Gräßer, "Zum Verständnis der Gottesherrschaft," *ZNW* 65 (1974) 3-26; translated and reprinted in Chilton, ed., *Kingdom*, 52-71.

or his religious genius, as the essential aspect of his vision of the kingdom of God.[20] Perhaps no scholar today has done more for this perception of the kingdom than Marcus Borg.[21] Borg has defined the kingdom of God as follows:[22]

> The phrase kingdom of God is thus a symbol for the presence and power of God as known in mystical experience. It is Jesus' name for what is experienced in the primordial religious experience, and his name for the power from that realm which flows through him as holy man.

The vast majority of scholars today recognizes that Jesus spoke of both the presence and the future of the kingdom. Though they may disagree on particulars, most scholars agree in general that Jesus thought he was *inaugurating* the kingdom through his words and deeds but believed that a *consummation* of the kingdom was yet future. There is within Jesus' teachings clear evidence for both the present reality of the kingdom (Matt. 12:28; Luke 17:20-21) and its future consummation (Mark 1:15; Matt. 8:11-12). While Mark 1:15 might be translated "the kingdom of God has drawn near (but is not yet here)," Matt. 12:28 would be understood as "the kingdom of God has (already) come upon you." Two of the most important representatives of this view are Reginald H. Fuller and Werner G. Kümmel.[23]

20. An older example is E. von Dobschütz, *The Eschatology of the Gospels* (London: Hodder and Stoughton, 1910) 164-69; see also A. Deissmann, *The Religion of Jesus and the Faith of Paul* (trans. W. E. Wilson; London: Hodder and Stoughton, 1923). Another influential study was T. W. Manson, *The Teaching of Jesus: Studies of Its Form and Content* (Cambridge: Cambridge University Press, 1939) 160-70, 191, 195, 234. His later study *The Sayings of Jesus* (London: SCM, 1949) opted for more of a tension between present and future.

21. M. Borg, *Jesus: A New Vision: Spirit, Culture, and the Life of Discipleship* (San Francisco: Harper & Row, 1988) 197-99.

22. M. Borg, *Conflict, Holiness and Politics in the Teachings of Jesus* (SBEC 5; New York: Edwin Mellen, 1984) 254. Though from a more hermeneutically oriented angle, see also the substantive conclusions of N. Perrin, *Rediscovering the Teaching of Jesus* (New York: Harper & Row, 1967); idem, *Jesus and the Language of the Kingdom: Symbol and Metaphor in New Testament Interpretation* (Philadelphia: Fortress, 1976); also cf. B. B. Scott, *Jesus, Symbol-Maker for the Kingdom* (Philadelphia: Fortress, 1981).

23. Too often neglected is R. H. Fuller, *The Mission and Achievement of Jesus: An Examination of the Presuppositions of New Testament Theology* (SBT 12; London: SCM, 1954); W. G. Kümmel, *Promise*.

In his study *The Mission and Achievement of Jesus,* Fuller argues that the kingdom is imminent but that it is also operative in advance through Jesus' works. In contrast to the vast majority of scholars, Fuller deals directly with how Jesus envisioned his own death as part of the kingdom he thought himself to be inaugurating. However, as Fuller sees it, the decisive event for Jesus still lay in the future: "God is already at work in him in a way which is organically related to the future event. The powers of the kingdom are proleptically operative in advance in Jesus, although its coming remains a decisive act of the future."[24] In his study *Promise and Fulfillment,* Kümmel argues that the kingdom was a future reality that was beginning to be felt already in and through Jesus' ministry. His book has made a decisive contribution; no study of the subject has put together the whole picture with such a mastery of critical sifting, careful exegesis, and theological synthesis. Together, Fuller and Kümmel have modified the consistent eschatology of Weiß and Schweitzer and have provided a bridge for those who see the kingdom as both present and future.

The issue of the imminence or futurity of the kingdom has proven central to the position staked out by Fuller and Kümmel. While Kümmel maintained that Jesus believed the kingdom to be present in his ministry, he also held that Jesus thought, mistakenly, that the consummation of the kingdom was imminent.[25] On the other hand, Fuller, while maintaining that the kingdom for Jesus was imminent, also thought that Jesus regarded it as so near that its presence was being felt. For Fuller, the death of Jesus inaugurated the kingdom, but there would be a clear interval between his death and the Parousia. The issue of when Jesus thought the kingdom would be fully realized marks the most crucial dividing line in the history of scholarship on the kingdom.

In summary, scholarship has proposed four interpretations of the kingdom of God in the teaching of Jesus: (1) it is *imminent* (Weiß, Schweitzer), (2) it is *existential* (Bultmann), (3) it is an *eternal order* (Dodd), or (4) it is *inaugurated* (Fuller, Kümmel). While the first and fourth interpretations emphasize the *content* of the Gospel texts, the second and third emphasize the *form* of the expressions in the Gospel traditions. Of course, scholarship cannot be rigidly divided into camps. There is a continuum of emphases; positions range from present realization to

---

24. Fuller, *Mission,* 50.
25. See Kümmel, *Promise,* 149.

future consummation, with scholars taking their stance on the spectrum at different points. Fuller, for instance, takes a more consistently future orientation than does Kümmel, but both see some kind of present realization and make it a clear mark of emphasis. Weiß, on the other hand, lays heavy emphasis on the imminent future but does concede that, in certain moments, Jesus seemed to think that the kingdom was in some sense present. Dodd, though he has been severely criticized for thinking that everything in Jesus' teaching about the kingdom was present, actually provides some grounds for seeing certain elements of Jesus' vision taking place in the (imminent) future. It is not a question of either-or but of how much emphasis is given to which elements.

Several key lines of thought have emerged from the history of scholarship. Before charting them, we ought to observe the fundamental influence that Jesus' Jewish context has had on the scholarly understanding of what he meant. Jesus needs to be situated in first-century Judaism, and the safest point at which to do this is his view of the kingdom.[26] A number of studies have attempted to relate Jesus to his Jewish world, and those that have sought to understand his view of the kingdom in that context have made significance contributions. Today, more than ever, scholars recognize that Jesus' mission was a national undertaking. His mission involved a belief that God's long-awaited era of salvation was now at work in Israel, bringing an end to the exile and restoring the nation, but that the fullest realization of the kingdom was yet future, awaiting the judgment and complete restoration.

Among the important findings of scholarship, the following deserve special attention. First, it has become clear that the kingdom of God in the teaching of Jesus is both a *dynamic reign,* the sovereignty or rule of God (an abstract substantive), and a *static realm* (a national, political entity). Kingdom language describes both a *place,* whether a celestial city with a throne or a national boundary with subjects, and a *relationship* to the king in which the human subjects willingly submit to him. It is God's action as king, his ruling power at work, his saving work now manifest.[27] This conclusion does not dissolve kingdom lan-

26. See B. D. Chilton, "Jesus within Judaism," in J. Neusner, ed., *Judaism in Late Antiquity. II: Historical Syntheses* (HO 17; Leiden: Brill, 1994) 262-84.

27. See esp. B. D. Chilton, *God in Strength: Jesus' Announcement of the Kingdom* (SNTSU B:1; Freistadt: Plöchl, 1979) 283-88.

guage into nothing more than experience or existential encounter; nor does it yield a national or moral order quietly established through legislation and social reformation. On the other hand, the experience or relationship of God as king cannot be divorced from what Jesus meant when he said that the kingdom was present. To the degree that the kingdom is a relationship, it can be experienced; but to the degree that it is a political arrangement, it is also a realm over which God is king. Too much of scholarship has placed its emphasis on the present, experiential aspect with the effect that the many scholars who attribute some sort of political vision to Jesus forget to adjust their understanding of the dynamic nature of the kingdom in accord with this political vision. When God's kingdom is also seen as some sort of earthly arrangement of God, the kingdom is also a realm and not just a dynamic relationship.[28] Amid the various forms of Judaism that he encountered, it is unlikely that Jesus would have understood the kingdom of God in a strictly relational sense; his mission was to Israel and for Israel, and this means that he must have had some national, political concept in mind when he thought of the kingdom of God.

Second, for Jesus the kingdom was fundamentally *theocentric* and not *christocentric*.[29] To be sure, Jesus thought that he was the agent of the kingdom (cf. Mark 4:11), but he was still the proclaimer and not the proclaimed.[30] For Jesus, the kingdom of God was *God's* (read: *the Father's*) kingdom, so it is only logical that he taught his disciples to pray "May *your* kingdom come!" (Matt. 6:10). As we have seen, Jesus' teachings begin and end with his religious experience and view of God; a consistent explication of his teachings about the kingdom will demonstrate that for him the kingdom was fundamentally about God and his final activity on behalf of Israel. God was at the center of Jesus' vision.[31]

---

28. See G. B. Caird, *New Testament Theology* (completed and edited by L. D. Hurst; Oxford: Clarendon, 1994) 368.

29. See A. Schlatter, *The History of the Christ: The Foundation for New Testament Theology* (trans. A. J. Köstenberger; Grand Rapids: Baker, 1997) 117-25; H. Ridderbos, *The Coming of the Kingdom* (trans. H. de Jongste; ed. R. O. Zorn; St. Catharines, Ont.: Paideia, 1962) 18-24; G. E. Ladd, *The Presence of the Future: The Eschatology of Biblical Realism* (Grand Rapids: Eerdmans, 1974) 171-94; Chilton, *God in Strength*, 287. Cf. also J. Schlosser, *Le Régne de Dieu dans les dits de Jésus* (Paris: Gabalda, 1988).

30. See Fuller, *Mission*, 109.

31. See L. Goppelt, *Theology of the New Testament* (2 vols.; trans. J. E. Alsup; ed. J. Roloff; Grand Rapids: Eerdmans, 1981-82) 1.69.

"The kingdom of God" was not a mere abstract formula for Jesus but connected with his own experience. As Ben F. Meyer has observed, this "pithy phrase, which might easily be mistaken for a trite technical formula in Jesus' usage, was inevitably charged with his own religious intentionality: his existential understanding of God (i.e., of how he himself related to God) and his understanding of God's will for the world and activity in it at this moment."[32] In this sense, then, the kingdom of God is wholly supernatural and is not a human reconstruction of social norms. Jesus set out to make God king one more time on Mount Zion (Psalm 2; *Jubilees* 1:28; 11QPs[a] 22).[33] This is where the famous line of Rudolf Otto makes most sense:

> It is not Jesus who brings the kingdom — a conception which was completely foreign to Jesus himself; on the contrary, the kingdom brings him with it. Moreover, it was not he but rather God himself who achieved the first great divine victory over Satan. His own activity lies in, and is carried forward by, the tidal wave of the divine victory.[34]

Third, scholarship has demonstrated that the term "kingdom of God" evokes myriad images and does so intentionally.[35] Jesus intended the term to provoke in his hearers a series of images (tensive symbol) and not just one idea (steno-symbol).[36] What was the background for this usage? Cases have been made for rabbinic Judaism (especially in its use of "taking on the yoke of the kingdom of heaven"; e.g., Dalman) and for apocalyptic Judaism (with its graphic image of God's mighty interven-

32. B. F. Meyer, *The Aims of Jesus* (London: SCM, 1979) 136.

33. K. H. Tan, *The Zion Traditions and the Aims of Jesus* (SNTSMS 91; Cambridge: Cambridge University Press, 1997).

34. R. Otto, *The Kingdom of God and the Son of Man* (London: Lutterworth, 1938), reprinted in Chilton, ed., *Kingdom*, 31.

35. So, e.g., A. Wilder, *Early Christian Rhetoric: The Language of the Gospel* (Cambridge, Mass.: Harvard University Press, 1971); Perrin, *Language*, 32-56. See the excellent summary in W. Emory Elmore, "Linguistic Approaches to the Kingdom: Amos Wilder and Norman Perrin," in Willis, ed., *Kingdom of God*, 53-65.

36. However, I cannot go as far as Perrin in his nonreferential approach. Cf. Sanders, *Jesus and Judaism*, 152; J. P. Meier, *A Marginal Jew: Rethinking the Historical Jesus* (ABRL; 3 vols.; New York: Doubleday, 1991-) 2.240-42; G. R. Beasley-Murray, *Jesus and the Kingdom of God* (Grand Rapids: Eerdmans, 1986) 338-44. Schürmann, *Gottes Reich*, calls it an "Assoziationskomplex" (22).

tion in history; e.g., Weiß and Schweitzer). Others have argued that the Psalms and the *Targum of Isaiah* form the appropriate background (with their emphasis on the kingdom as God's acting in strength and power; e.g., Chilton). Most interpreters, however, would look no further than the Hebrew Bible as filtered through various interpretive traditions (e.g., Wright). The very diversity of proposals highlights an important point: the background varies from item to item in what Jesus said. While the phrase "kingdom *of heaven*" surely owes its origins to Jewish usage that was to become rabbinic, the eschatological dimensions of the term "kingdom" find their appropriate background in apocalyptic material, beginning with the poetic visions of the major prophets and Daniel and continuing through a host of Jewish apocalypses.

It is wrong to insist on one single background, as if Jesus must have obtained his ideas from only one source.[37] And it is even more mistaken to find the background to what Jesus said about the kingdom only when the expression occurs in earlier or contemporary material. At times, the background for what Jesus said about the kingdom can best be seen when we focus on larger concepts like covenant, salvation, liberation, deliverance from exile, or theophany. For Jesus, the term "kingdom" was intentionally polyvalent; the language itself was meant to evoke a multitude of ideas associated with the Jewish concept of, and belief in, God's activity for the salvation and judgment of his people at the end of history. This tensive symbol deserves to be viewed against as rich a background as scholarship can uncover; limiting its background leads only to forced interpretations and narrow exegesis. Furthermore, limiting its meaning to what can be learned from background is inadequate; it is reasonable to think that Jesus took a multivalent term and added to it some of his own evocations. The wry question of G. B. Caird grasps the nettle without injury: "But if the Synoptic Gospels are right to insist that Jesus spent much of his time explaining what *he* meant by the kingdom, would it not follow that he did not mean what everybody else meant by it?"[38]

Fourth, time per se is not the issue. The evidence itself clearly raises a temporal issue: is the kingdom present, future, or both? But this

---

37. See the wise comments of B. D. Chilton, *Pure Kingdom: Jesus' Vision of God* (Grand Rapids: Eerdmans, 1996) 23-31.

38. Caird, *New Testament Theology,* 367. See also Schürmann, *Gottes Reich,* 31; Camponovo, *Königtum,* 443-46.

temporal issue is not the heart of the matter.[39] Too often the matter has been treated as if it were settled.[40] The more fundamental issue is this: in what sense is the kingdom present, and in what sense is it future? What did Jesus mean when he said that the kingdom was present? Did he mean only that he could exorcise demons and do deeds of wonder? Or did he intend to evoke much more, on the order of the gift of salvation? And the same applies to Jesus' vision for a future, more glorious manifestation of the kingdom: what did he intend to evoke when he spoke of the future kingdom? The defeat of Rome? The judgment of Israel? A world where peace and justice perfectly obtained? It was precisely because T. W. Manson eschewed the debate about time that he was able to penetrate more deeply into the significance of the kingdom for Jesus.[41] Apart from a few tidy definitions, C. H. Dodd, because he was so preoccupied with arguing that the kingdom was present, hardly explicated in what sense the kingdom was present.[42]

Two recent studies have advanced the discussion. Jürgen Becker argues, in ways reminiscent of Oscar Cullmann, that the temporal issue can be approached from another angle: was the decisive turning point for Jesus the one that turns the past to the present or the one that turns the present to the future? Those who opt for the first position emphasize a realized eschatology, while those who opt for the second emphasize a futuristic eschatology.[43] Put differently, was Jesus primarily the herald of an imminent kingdom (like John the Baptist) or of the dawn of salvation? Joachim Gnilka prefers that we ask about the relationship of the present and the future rather than focus on one or the other. We ought to avoid the simplistic addition of one (the kingdom is present) to the other (*and* future).[44] Becker and Gnilka have thus asked the temporal question with more nuance than most are doing today. In addition, Bruce D. Chilton, with his mapping of the kingdom along various axes, has furthered the discussion about time by seeking to correlate it with other features of kingdom theology.[45]

39. See Chilton, *Pure Kingdom*, 21.

40. See Weiß, *Predigt*, 69.

41. See his *Teaching*.

42. See, e.g., Dodd, *Parables*, 38, 50, 108, 198-202.

43. J. Becker, *Jesus von Nazaret* (New York: de Gruyter, 1996) 126.

44. J. Gnilka, *Jesus von Nazaret: Botschaft und Geschichte* (rev. ed.; Freiburg: Herder, 1993) 153-56.

45. See his *Pure Kingdom*.

Finally, it is becoming increasingly obvious that the kingdom Jesus preached is intimately connected with his *national vision* and *political hope*. A foundational text for this hope is Isa. 52:7-9:

> How beautiful upon the mountains
> > are the feet of the messenger who announces peace,
> who brings good news,
> > who announces salvation,
> > who says to Zion, "Your God reigns."
> Listen! Your sentinels lift up their voices,
> > together they sing for joy;
> for in plain sight they see
> > the return of the LORD to Zion.
> Break forth together into singing,
> > you ruins of Jerusalem;
> for the LORD has comforted his people,
> > he has redeemed Jerusalem.

Here we find the old vision of the prophets: one day God will act to redeem Jerusalem (not the world, not all peoples, but Israel). One day he will come to Zion, stretch forth his hand throughout the land, and bring his people back to worship in a pure temple with pure sacrifices offered by a pure nation.[46] Accordingly, the vision Jesus articulated concerns Israel: God is about to intervene, for good and bad, and if Israel will but respond a disaster can be averted and new conditions can prevail. How could he think otherwise?[47]

When Jesus taught his disciples to pray for the kingdom to come (Matt. 6:10), he surely had in mind more than an existential encounter with the living God that would give his followers authentic existence. While a personal encounter with God must have been part of what he meant in using kingdom language, that very language and its historical

---

46. See the helpful exposition of Zion theology by Becker, *Jesus von Nazaret*, 100-121; see also Tan, *Zion Traditions*.

47. Many scholars have argued that Jesus universalized the promises to Israel (e.g., J. Weiß, G. Dalman, C. H. Dodd, T. W. Manson, J. Jeremias, E. Lohse, J. Becker, and H. Merklein). This approach seeks to demonstrate that Jesus was into pure religion and individualism. But this position is taken at the expense of historical nuance. The early church's universal mission must be seen as an outworking of Jesus' vision for Israel.

context meant that the kingdom Jesus proclaimed had political and national connections. It follows that Jesus envisioned a kingdom that had, at its head, his chosen twelve on the thrones judging the twelve tribes of Israel (Matt. 19:28), with the focus being once again on the major institutions of Judaism: temple, law, and land.[48] As we have seen, the God of Jesus was the God of Israel, and the kingdom of Jesus was a kingdom for Israel. Thus, Jesus' vision was not an abstract religious feeling but a concrete, realistic vision for God's chosen nation, Israel.[49] In the words of Ben F. Meyer,

> In the biblical perspective salvation was always and everywhere understood as destined precisely for Israel. 'Salvation' and 'Israel' were utterly inseparable. There was never a Saviour apart from a saved Israel, nor would there be a Messiah apart from a messianic Israel. . . . Israel, in short, understood salvation in ecclesial terms. Where the salvation of the nations was promised or announced, this was conceived as an assimilation to saved Israel.[50]

And, again, from N. T. Wright:

> But at least we can be sure of this: anyone who was heard talking about the reign of Israel's god would be assumed to be referring to the fulfillment of Israel's long-held hope. The covenant god would act to reconstitute his people, to end their exile, to forgive their sins. When that happened, Israel would no longer be dominated by the pagans. She would be free. The means of liberation were no doubt open to debate. *The goal was not.*[51]

---

48. See the exposition of J. D. G. Dunn, *The Partings of the Ways between Christianity and Judaism and Their Significance for the Character of Christianity* (Philadelphia: Trinity Press International, 1991).

49. Many scholars have noted this in recent study. See, e.g., R. A. Horsley, *Jesus and the Spiral of Violence: Popular Jewish Resistance in Roman Palestine* (San Francisco: Harper & Row, 1987) 149-208; and now especially Wright, *Jesus and the Victory of God.*

50. Meyer, *Aims of Jesus,* 133-34.

51. *Jesus and the Victory of God,* 151 (italics added). It might be asked why, if it was so important to Jesus, he did not use "exile" terms. I would contend that he did. Kingdom language is "end of exile" language; "end of exile" is the negative to the positive "kingdom."

The God of Jesus is king. He is king of creation and king of Israel. When Jesus used the language of the kingdom and its God, he was surely recalling the days before the kings of Israel when Israel was ruled by God alone. This theocratic history formed for Jesus the sure foundation upon which he built his vision for Israel. And this God, who called Abraham from Ur and who gave the law to Moses, who also guided his people through priests, kings, and prophets, and who exiled Israel, was now making himself known once again through Jesus for the redemption of Israel. When Jesus began to preach, he proclaimed that the kingdom was about to arrive (Mark 1:15), but he also announced that the kingdom was present. The future kingdom was now operative in advance of its full arrival.

Kingdom as Present

With the word "kingdom," Jesus chose a term possessed of an unusually dynamic ability to relate to his society and crystallize his vision for Israel. The genius of every Jewish prophet applies in no small measure to Jesus: an ability to capture the dreams of a generation (in light of its past and its expectations) with graphic, concrete, and evocative images.[52] Jesus did this with respect to both the present fulfillment of hope and the future consummation of promise, but our concern here is the former. The presence of the kingdom[53] involves several features: (1) God's reign among Israel fulfills Jewish hopes; (2) God's reign is operative solely through Jesus; (3) God's reign manifests itself inauspiciously but also (4) displays itself in strength; (5) God's reign calls for an ethical response of covenant faithfulness; and (6) God's reign is actualized in Jesus' final actions, culminating in his suffering and death.

52. See Becker, *Jesus von Nazaret*, 101.
53. I cannot emphasize enough the value of Beasley-Murray, *Jesus and the Kingdom*, for here one finds a comprehensive cataloguing of views and scholarship.

The Kingdom as the Fulfillment of Jewish Hope

The newness of the message of Jesus was that the kingdom of God, the long-cherished hope of Israel, was now immediately present.[54] If we ask what aspect of Jesus' teaching is most distinctive, surely it is to be placed here: Jesus' claim that the long-awaited kingdom of God was operative and was no longer a hope for Israel.[55] The pious stories of Simeon and Anna (Luke 2:25-35, 36-38) illustrate the eschatology not only of Luke but also of Jesus: "Master, now you are dismissing your servant in peace . . . for my eyes have seen your salvation" (2:29-30). The end-time restoration of Israel, Jesus claimed, was happening.

Jesus announced, in true prophetic fashion, that God's kingdom is now operative. Whether as a redactional summary of Mark or as a virtual quotation of Jesus, Mark 1:14-15 is generally taken as a reliable précis of Jesus' teaching:[56]

> Now after John was arrested, Jesus came to Galilee, proclaiming the good news of God, and saying, "The time is fulfilled, and the kingdom of God has come near;[57] repent, and believe in the good news."

In Jesus' world, the arrival of the kingdom involved a cluster of events: the end of the exile, the defeat of Rome, the return of the scattered tribes to the promised land, the restoration of pure worship in the temple, and the coming of God in full glory to Zion. Fundamental for understanding Jesus' view of the kingdom is the recognition that this kingdom is none other than what was anticipated and expected by Jews for millennia: it was the fulfillment of prophetic, and at times apocalyptic, visions. These expectations stretch back at least to Isaiah and in-

---

54. The notion of the present operation of the Kingdom is historically sound; it is found in all the sources [Mark, Q, M, L] and in various forms, including apocalyptic sayings (e.g., Matt. 13:16-17), parables (Mark 2:18-22), pronouncements (Luke 17:20-21), and historical stories (Luke 4:16-30). Cf. Becker, *Jesus von Nazaret*, 131.

55. See Dodd, *Parables*, 49; Ladd, *Presence*, 105-14.

56. Many, for instance, would argue that Mark 1:14-15 is a Markan redactional summary and that it accurately depicts the historical Jesus' message. My concern here is only with its accuracy for describing what Jesus taught. For a technical defense of the authenticity of this logion, cf. Chilton, *God in Strength*, 27-95.

57. The Greek word behind "has come near" is *ēngiken*, which is to be understood as a "drawing so near that its impact is already being felt."

clude the notion of the theophanic coming of YHWH to earth to deliver Israel, to judge with equity, and to punish evil in accordance with the covenant that God had established with Abraham. This salvation would usher the people of God into a new era of jubilee, peace, justice, and righteousness. In particular, this hope meant liberation for Israel from its enemies, including Rome. Jesus was a child of his people, and his people were children of their history. To think of the kingdom apart from national deliverance was an impossibility for Jews of Jesus' day and for Jesus himself.[58] The startling thing about Jesus is that he declared that this kingdom was now operative. Several lines of evidence support this point.

That Jesus believed the kingdom to be presently operative in himself is seen in his parable of the sower:[59] here the kingdom of God is being sown (in the present), and already both rejection and fruitfulness are evident (Mark 4:1-9). The rather surprising theme of opposition is found especially in the early rendition of a Q logion by Matthew (11:12), where we find that the kingdom of God is present and is experiencing opposition:[60]

> "From the days of John the Baptist until now the kingdom of heaven has suffered violence, and the violent take it by force."

Jesus hereby describes the effects of his ministry: he brings the kingdom to bear on present life, but the present world opposes it with force.[61] This theme of opposition, so frequent in the early traditions about Jesus, is

58. See M. Lattke, "Zur jüdischen Vorgeschichte des synoptischen Begriffs der 'Königsherrschaft Gottes,'" in P. Fiedler and D. Zeller, eds., *Gegenwart und kommender Reich* (Stuttgart: Katholisches Bibelwerk, 1975) 9-25, reprinted and translated in Chilton, *Kingdom*, 72-91; Chilton, *God in Strength*; idem, *Pure Kingdom*; Meier, *A Marginal Jew*, 2.243-70; Becker, *Jesus von Nazaret*, 100-121; C. L. Holman, *Till Jesus Comes: Origins of Christian Apocalyptic Expectation* (Peabody, Mass.: Hendrickson, 1996) 9-99; and esp. Camponovo, *Königtum*, 437-46.

59. On the importance of parables in Jesus' teaching on the kingdom, see Dodd, *Parables*; Becker, *Jesus von Nazaret*, 176-94; Wright, *Jesus and the Victory of God*, 198-369.

60. On the importance of the theme of rejection for understanding the kingdom, see Schürmann, *Gottes Reich*, 48-50.

61. Some translate "is advancing by storm" and see here the powerful attack by the kingdom. See Beasley-Murray, *Jesus and the Kingdom*, 91-96; Kümmel, *Promise*, 121-24; Ladd, *Presence*, 158-64; Meier, *A Marginal Jew*, 2.399-404.

surely to be connected with the theme of tribulation, of the long-predicted trouble for Israel that would climax in the war of YHWH against the enemies of God (e.g., *Psalms of Solomon* 17-18; *T. Dan* 5:10-13; 1QM). "What is envisaged is an aeon of conflict, of victory and defeat, of achievement and disappointment, of success and failure."[62]

Somewhat like the cry of jubilation (Matt. 11:25-27), another Q logion reveals that Jesus thought that his disciples were experiencing the eschatological blessing of God because they were hearing his words and witnessing his powerful works (Matt. 13:16-17):[63]

> "But blessed[64] are your eyes, for they see, and your ears, for they hear. Truly I tell you, many prophets and righteous people longed to see what you see, but did not see it, and to hear what you hear, but did not hear it."

As T. W. Manson once said: "The point of the saying is that what for all former generations lay still in the future is now a present reality. What was for the best men of the past only an object of faith and hope is now a matter of present experience."[65]

This eschatological blessing of God comes to those who recognize the kingdom in Jesus, as Luke 17:20-21 suggests:[66]

> Once Jesus was asked by the Pharisees when the kingdom of God was coming, and he answered, "The kingdom of God is not coming with things that can be observed; nor will they say, 'Look, here it is!' or 'There it is!' For, in fact, the kingdom of God is among you."

Jesus here rejects the apocalyptic approach to historical prognosis. Scholars, however, have intensely debated the meaning and import of the words "is among you." Two interpretations seem most probable:[67]

---

62. Perrin, *Rediscovering*, 77. See also Meier, *A Marginal Jew*, 2.404.

63. See the useful analysis of Meier, *A Marginal Jew*, 2.434-39.

64. On blessing as an eschatological term, cf. Matt. 11:6; 16:17; see also *Pss. Sol.* 17:50; 18:7; 1 Pet. 1:10-12.

65. Manson, *Sayings of Jesus*, 80.

66. See Meier, *A Marginal Jew*, 2.423-30.

67. The older Protestant liberal view, that Jesus here describes an inner, religious experience or condition of the soul, is now universally denied. For an early, but lethal, critique of this view, see Weiß, *Predigt*, 73-78, 85-88.

they mean either (1) "in your midst," in the sense that Jesus himself is inaugurating that kingdom through his mission,[68] or (2) "within your grasp," in the sense that Jesus' call to decision permits one to enter into the kingdom now.[69] Thus, one might paraphrase this saying as: "The kingdom does not come according to your calculations; rather, the kingdom is within your grasp if you have eyes to see and a heart to believe." On the other hand, one might follow a more christological rendering, along the lines of Matt. 11:6, and paraphrase thus: "The kingdom does not come according to your calculations; rather, the kingdom is here (in me and my ministry) if you would recognize the national significance of what I am doing." Taken either christologically or volitionally, the saying describes the kingdom as present and capable of being experienced.[70]

Matthew 11:2-6 should be discussed in this context. When asked by the followers of John if he was the "one to come" or not, Jesus, instead of answering the question with a direct "Yes" or "No," pointed to the *works* he had done, which would indicate that the joyous days of Isaiah were now coming to pass (Isa. 29:18-19; 35:5-6; 61:1). The deeds of Jesus were the very actions that God had promised would take place when he visited his people for final deliverance. Such an understanding reveals once again the national direction of Jesus' ministry: his acts are signs from God to the nation.

When Jesus stood up in Nazareth (cf. Luke 4:16-30; Mark 6:1-6; Matt. 13:54-58) to speak his mind about his own identity and his own mission, he declared the rather scandalous notion that God's kingdom is now operative: it has, in some sense, arrived. It is to be seen in his works, including his acts of mercy to heal, his offering forgiveness at table, and his powerful announcements of God's will. This kingdom, the long-awaited theophanic revelation of God, is now set in motion in direct fulfillment of Israel's hopes. Those who turn in repentance toward Jesus' prophetic announcements will escape the judgment of God and

68. So Kümmel, *Promise*, 32-36; Schlosser, *Le Régne*, 1.179-215; Becker, *Jesus von Nazaret*, 147-48; Meier, *A Marginal Jew*, 2.426-28.

69. See J. Fitzmyer, *The Gospel according to Luke* (AB 28-28A; 2 vols.; Garden City, N.Y.: Doubleday, 1981-85) 2.1160-62; see also Perrin, *Rediscovering*, 74. *Contra* Jeremias, *Proclamation of Jesus*, 100-101, who makes the logion futuristic by rendering it "will (suddenly) be in your midst."

70. Cf. Chilton, *Pure Kingdom*, 71-73.

enter into the kingdom when it is fully consummated. This promise of Jesus goes beyond what he learned in the circle of John the Baptist.

The Kingdom Operative Only through Jesus

The egocentric claim that the kingdom was operative only through himself lay at the heart of Jesus' mission.[71] He believed that he was the end-time agent of salvation, a prophetic spokesperson for God, and that only he, along with John before him, could discern the true will of God for Israel. This can be seen in four separate pieces of evidence: the question about fasting (Mark 2:18-22 pars.); the parable of the sower, with its attachment, the mystery of parables (Mark 4:1-9, 11 pars.); the response to John the Baptist (Matt. 11:2-6 par.); and the confession of Peter (Mark 8:27-33). Each of these traditions reveals that Jesus thought he was the one through whom the kingdom was being manifested. In the words of Rudolf Otto,

> He does not bring the kingdom, but he himself, according to the most certain of his utterances, is in his actions the personal manifestation of the inbreaking divine power. . . . rather his person and work were part of a comprehensive redemptive event, which broke in with him and which he called the coming and actual arrival of the kingdom of God.[72]

In the question about fasting (Mark 2:18-22//Matt. 9:14-17//Luke 5:33-39) is buried a logion with a solid claim to authenticity:[73]

> "No one sews a piece of unshrunk cloth on an old cloak; otherwise, the patch pulls away from it, the new from the old, and a worse tear is made. And no one puts new wine into old wineskins; otherwise, the wine will burst the skins, and the wine is lost, and so are the skins; but one puts new wine into fresh wineskins." (Mark 2:21-22)

71. This is an emphasis of Kümmel, *Promise,* 105-40. See also Becker, *Jesus von Nazaret,* 234-75; Chilton, *Pure Kingdom,* 134-38.

72. R. Otto, "Kingdom of God," 32 (in Chilton, ed., *Kingdom*). See further R. Bultmann, *Theology of the New Testament* (2 vols.; trans. K. Grobel; New York: Charles Scribner's Sons, 1951-55) 1.7, 9; Schürmann, *Gottes Reich,* 41-44.

73. See Perrin, *Rediscovering,* 77-82; Meier, *A Marginal Jew,* 2.439-50.

From this logion one can infer that Jesus believed that a new day had arrived with an explosive power that could not be contained by old forms. In his typical poetic style, Jesus also affirmed that the new day was a time for feasting and celebrating, activities that cohere with his habitual practice of table fellowship with sinners (Matt. 11:19; Mark 2:13-17).[74]

When Jesus associated his festive celebrations with the image of a bridegroom, he made a significant enhancement of Jewish hope:

> "The wedding guests cannot fast while the bridegroom is with them, can they? As long as they have the bridegroom with them, they cannot fast." (Mark 2:19)

Jesus associated the new day, his table fellowship, and the image of the bridegroom; from this constellation we can reasonably infer that he saw himself, albeit obliquely, as the bridegroom. If this be the case, then Jesus believed that the bridegroom's arrival was a day that transcended others and permitted his followers to venture onto a new path of discipleship, away from custom and tradition and toward celebration. But the day of celebration is possible only because the bridegroom, Jesus, is present.[75] Such poetical language fits the picture of a Jesus who thinks he is inaugurating the last days. Jesus is not yet the proclaimed, but he is indeed the proclaimer.

Scholars are divided on the exact significance and background of Jesus' talk of the "mystery of the kingdom of God" (Mark 4:11), but it is clear that Jesus believed that he held the key to this mystery and that it was being made known in his person and activity.[76] If Jesus saw his own person and activity in the sower of the seed (Mark 4:1-9), then it is only a small step to think that he possessed, as did all the prophets before him, secrets revealed to him by God (cf., e.g., Matt. 11:25-27//Luke 10:21-22; Matt. 11:28-30; Mark 13). It is also likely that, at some point, someone asked him why he taught in such a cryptic manner. Jesus' reply is consistent with his other teachings and responses:

74. See Meier, *A Marginal Jew*, 2.450.
75. See Ridderbos, *Coming*, 51.
76. E.g., Jeremias, *The Parables of Jesus* (2d ed.; New York: Charles Scribner's, 1972) 13-18, 152-53; Beasley-Murray, *Jesus and the Kingdom*, 103-7; Ladd, *Presence*, 218-42; idem, *Theology*, 89-102; R. E. Brown, *The Semitic Background of the Term "Mystery" in the New Testament* (FBBS; Philadelphia: Fortress, 1968).

"To you has been given the mystery of the kingdom of God, but for those outside, everything comes in parables." (Mark 4:11)

Thus Jesus believed that he had special things to say to Israel (not just to individuals), and he sensed that his message was not being well received (thus: "to *you*" and "but for *them*").[77]

Once again we can appeal to the response of Jesus to John's disciples. Jesus' own identity, and therefore his relationship to John, can be inferred from his actions. These actions include deeds of mercy done to those who have been exiled from normal relations in Jewish society; they are accomplished for those who are tormented by evil spirits and who have been driven to poverty and begging; they deeply benefit those who are most deeply in need; they are drawn into the visions of Isaiah (29:18-19; 35:5-6; 61:1); and they reveal what Jesus is accomplishing for Israel. However Jesus defined "Israel," it is clear that he viewed himself as the one who initiated actions connected with the arrival of the kingdom.[78] Jesus' form of ministry, including his association with sinners, led others to think that he could not be the one about whom the prophets spoke. To this estimation Jesus responded: "And blessed is anyone who takes no offense *at me*" (Matt. 11:6). To be sure, this is less than a direct claim to a messianic vision and status, but it is surely a personal claim to be the one whom God sent to end Israel's exile.

Though I cannot develop the theme here in any depth, Jesus' table fellowship (e.g., Mark 2:13-17; Matt. 11:19) reveals not only his perception of the arrival of the kingdom in his own ministry, but three features of that arrival, namely, forgiveness of sins, a reassembly of the true Israel of God, and a renewed communal fellowship. Jesus' regular practice of sitting down at table with sinful people, and anyone else who cared to dine with his cadre, was a social reconstruction of Israel in which he dispensed forgiveness (through social acceptance, prayers, and distribution of God's provisions; cf. Matt. 6:11, 14-15; Mark 2:3-10; Luke 7:36-50)[79] and re-created a society in which God's kingdom had the exclusive claim on life. In this new group the Deuteronomic

---

77. See Wright, *Jesus and the Victory of God*, 235.

78. See Kümmel, *Promise*, 109-11.

79. Forgiveness in Judaism is as much, if not more, a national act as an individual one. The prophetic hope is that God would forgive his covenant people of their sins and so end their exile and restore their nation. Exile is a sign of standing outside of fellowship with God; forgiveness initiates renewal of fellowship and end of exile.

principle of justice was being jettisoned in favor of a newly formulated principle of equality by grace (Matt. 20:1-16).[80] In this fellowship (Luke 15:1-2), it is the younger, rebellious son who experiences the goodness of God's kingdom while the older son (who represents a Pharisaic perception of God's covenant) fumes outside about the father's generosity (15:11-32). Such forgiveness, however extreme (Matt. 18:23-35), finds humans in need (John 7:53–8:11) and resocializes them.[81] Table fellowship functioned distinctively in Jesus' ministry; by it he summoned people to experience the good news of what God was now doing for Israel, bringing the end of exile and the dawn of the long-cherished kingdom of God.[82]

We can now unwrap what is implicit in a previous passage (Matt. 11:2-6) by looking at another: Peter's confession of Jesus as the Messiah (Mark 8:27-33 pars.). Matthew attaches to this a revelatory remark by Jesus which, though disputed by many scholars, coheres with the theme under discussion: Jesus' conviction that he is the one through whom God is operating for the redemption of Israel:

> "I will give you the keys of the kingdom of heaven, and whatever you bind on earth will be bound in heaven, and whatever you loose on earth will be loosed in heaven." (Matt. 16:19)

Critical for our point here is only the notion that Jesus has keys and that he is capable of handing those keys on to his chosen follower, Peter (cf. also Matt. 18:15-20). As with the Pharisees, who thought they held the secrets to God's knowledge (Matt. 23:13), so with Jesus: he believed he knew what was on God's mind, and his mission was to pass that on to others. In this sense, "keys," "mysteries" (Mark 4:11), and "new garment/ new wine" ought to be tied directly to Jesus' "actions" (Matt. 11:2-6), which liberate humans from bondage, decay, and demonization. The mystery is far more than esoteric knowledge; it is that God's kingdom is

---

80. See the helpful exposition of Gnilka, *Jesus,* 89-94.

81. Though perhaps a later tradition, the pericope about the adulterer has been hard to discount because of its coherence with Jesus' typical behavior. A recent defense of its essential historicity (though not as part of any of the original Gospels) can be found in G. R. Beasley-Murray, *John* (WBC 36; Waco, Tex.: Word, 1987) 143-47.

82. See the studies of Horsley, *Jesus and the Spiral of Violence,* 178-80; Becker, *Jesus von Nazaret,* 168-76, 194-211; Chilton, *Pure Kingdom,* 85-90; Gnilka, *Jesus,* 108-18.

now operating in and through God's messenger, Jesus the prophet from Galilee. The long-anticipated salvation is now here, and Jesus knows that he is so blessed that he is the one through whom God is both making it known and demonstrating its strength. "In the final analysis, the question about the present coming of the kingdom is, as can be seen in Mt. 12:28, a question about the person of Jesus."[83]

While Luke's choice to relocate Jesus' inaugural sermon in Nazareth has theological, rather than historical, motivations (Luke 4:16-30; cf. Mark 6:1-6; Matt. 13:53-58), there is nothing here that is inconsistent with what we have seen above. Jesus stands to read from Isaiah and in so doing declares that God has anointed him to be the one who brings the jubilee to the land of Israel. The "favorable year of the Lord," Jesus claims, will be known through his ministry, felt through his touch, and actualized in his community. Once again, in conformity to Matt. 11:6, 19 and Mark 4:11, Jesus' very form of ministry is scandalous, falling well below the mark of what the Jews of his hometown expect. His declaration therefore meets with opposition: the proclaimer announces the kingdom, but his audience rejects both the proclaimer and the proclamation. Jesus' connection of himself with Elijah and the widow of Zarephath (Luke 4:26), as well as with Elisha and Naaman the Syrian (4:27), is true to form; he is sent to the nation, but only the lost sheep of the house of Israel find in him the agent of God.

The day of the bridegroom is surely a new day in Israel's history, but for Jesus the present operation of the kingdom was in continuity with Jewish, especially prophetic, expectation, though there are clear traces of discontinuity as well.[84] To begin with, the very things Jesus did in his ministry, the healing and inclusion of the downtrodden, were the very things expected of the age of salvation by the Isaianic tradition (cf. Isa. 29:18-19; 35:5-6; 61:1):

> "the blind receive their sight, the lame walk, the lepers are cleansed, the deaf hear, the dead are raised, and the poor have good news brought to them." (Matt. 11:5)

83. Goppelt, *Theology*, 1.63.

84. The issue of Jesus' teachings and Jewish tradition is complex. See the new angle on the issue in B. D. Chilton, *The Temple of Jesus: His Sacrificial Program within a Cultural History of Sacrifice* (University Park, Penn.: Pennsylvania State University Press, 1992) 163-72. Cf. also C. A. Evans, "Old Testament in the Gospels," *DJG*, 579-590, with extensive bibliography.

This is not a new hope but an old hope now being fulfilled for Israel.

When the disciples were considered by Jesus to be especially blessed, it was not because what they were experiencing was something altogether new but, once again, because what they saw, heard, and experienced was precisely what the Jewish saints had hoped to see come to pass for Israel (Matt. 13:16-17). Jesus, then, saw himself bringing about just what the Hebrew prophets anticipated and predicted. In accord with such expectation, joy was a consistent theme of Jesus' perception of the kingdom (Matt. 13:44-46).[85]

This note of fulfillment, however, arrived with some surprises. To begin with, Jesus stated that John the Baptist, though greater than all of the prophets before him (because of his chance to declare the imminent arrival of the kingdom), was still less than the followers of Jesus:

> "Truly I tell you, among those born of women no one has arisen greater than John the Baptist; yet the least in the kingdom of heaven is greater than he." (Matt. 11:11)

Just what this greatness consists of is not spelled out here; nor can it be inferred. Jesus' statement is much less a reflective observation about John the Baptist than a comment about the kingdom and its fortunate participants. A similar point is made by Jesus when he answers the question about fasting (Mark 2:18-22): though the old wine and the old garment were good for their day, the new day of the bridegroom has come, and that means new threads and a robust, sparkling wine. But once again, what that new wine amounts to is not altogether clear. Certainly it involves the celebration and joy that come through the forgiveness connected with Jesus at table. Alongside this logion may be placed Matt. 13:52:

> "Therefore every scribe who has been trained for the kingdom of heaven is like the master of a household who brings out of his treasure what is new and what is old."

Even if the authenticity of this saying is subject to debate, it coheres with what has been said above: Jesus' kingdom is what the prophets anticipated, but this kingdom brings some surprises for Israel. There is

---

85. See Perrin, *Rediscovering*, 87-90.

continuity here: "what is old"; and there is discontinuity: "what is new." But once again, what the newness consists of and how it is to be understood remain unclear. For an example, Jesus calls disciples to follow him, and they form a movement around him, but he numbers them at twelve (Mark 3:13-19), signifying a new Israel with a new beginning.[86]

Perhaps more clarity can be gained from a few other pieces of evidence. When Jesus calls the disciples "blessed," it is because of what they "see" and "hear" (Matt. 13:16-17); what brings the followers of Jesus a special blessedness is that they see, hear, and experience the signs associated with the new day of the bridegroom (Matt. 11:5). The newness consists in the power of the new day Jesus brings, in the knowledge of the kingdom he reveals, and in the fellowship they experience around his table. One might say then that what is new is the fullness of the salvation that was anticipated by the prophetic visions. The discontinuity is one of privilege for those who are associated with Jesus. They get to see the kingdom in strength; they also get to hear the good news about the kingdom of God. The nation of Israel is now witnessing the dawn of God's salvation and the final restoration of his people.

The Inauspicious Presence of the Kingdom

However definitive in fulfilling the hopes and expectations of Israel, the kingdom's arrival is nonetheless inauspicious.[87] To be sure, the kingdom is at times both powerful and effective, but it is neither obtrusive nor forceful in its manifestations. This feature coheres with a long-standing tradition in Israel of God choosing unlikely means to accomplish his purposes: Abraham was called out of Ur of the Chaldees to become the father of many nations (Genesis 12); David was a Cinderella-like figure, one thought most unlikely to be anointed (1 Samuel 16);

---

86. See Meyer, *Aims of Jesus*, 153-54; Sanders, *Jesus and Judaism*, 98-106.

87. See G. Bornkamm, *Jesus of Nazareth* (trans. I. and F. McLuskey with J. M. Robinson; New York: Harper & Row, 1960) 71-75; Chilton, *Pure Kingdom*, 70-73; Wright, *Jesus and the Victory of God*, 239-43. Schürmann, *Gottes Reich*, throughout his book unravels this theme of the inauspiciousness of Jesus' ministry and teaching about the kingdom to show that the death of Jesus, as sacrificial (surely an inauspicious act), was fundamental to Jesus' own perception of his mission (what he calls his *Geschick*).

Elijah heard God in a whispering voice (1 Kings 19); and the liberating redeemer for Israel would be a suffering servant (Isaiah 52–53).

One notable feature of the Judaism in which Jesus was fostered that may well have driven him to speak of the kingdom's arrival as a humble act of God was the patriotic, nationalistic spirit of Jewish hopes. Although the prospect of war was not necessarily on the mind of every Jew in Jesus' day, the heroic images associated with the Maccabean revolt led at least some to think in terms of a mighty assault by God, no doubt with Israelites leading God's army, as the final act in bringing the kingdom to Israel (cf. 1, 2 Maccabees; 1QM).[88] Many have argued that Jesus was forced to subdue his own messianic convictions and vision for Israel. Whatever one thinks of Jesus' messianic consciousness, it is quite likely that his view of the kingdom took shape in response to the volatile political climate of his day.[89] The emergence of violence and the constant threat of revolt in the land of Israel (including Galilee) surely led Jesus to speak of the kingdom and to understand the kingdom in other than violent and insurgent categories. Nonetheless, to speak of kingdom was to speak about revolution. The challenge for Jesus, then, was to speak of God's present action without subscribing to violence and political revolution.

Various facets of Jesus' own ministry cohered with the inauspicious character of the history of God's redemptive activity in Israel. Thus, Jesus was baptized into the work of John the Baptist, having joined an inauspicious renewal movement (Mark 1:1-11; cf. Matt. 11:7-10 par.; Luke 7:31-35 par.). Jesus centered his mission not in big-city Jerusalem, but in the hillsides of lowly Galilee, where he called inauspicious people to join his personal expansion of John's call to renewal (Mark 1:16-20). When crowds clamored after him, he secretly with-

---

88. For good studies, see M. Hengel, *The Zealots: Investigations into the Jewish Freedom Movement in the Period from Herod I until 70 A.D.* (trans. D. Smith; Edinburgh: T & T Clark, 1988); R. A. Horsley and J. S. Hanson, *Bandits, Prophets and Messiahs: Popular Movements in the Time of Jesus* (Minneapolis: Winston, 1985); M. Goodman, *The Ruling Class of Judaea: The Origins of the Jewish Revolt against Rome, A.D. 66-70* (Cambridge: Cambridge University Press, 1987). For a brief survey of the evidence, see W. J. Heard, "Revolutionary Movements," *DJG*, 688-698.

89. This is especially the case with respect to Galilee; see the insightful study of R. A. Horsley, *Galilee: History, Politics, People* (Valley Forge, Penn.: Trinity Press International, 1995).

drew because for him the kingdom was not some mighty act of glory and fame (cf. Luke 4:16-30; Mark 1:35-38 par.; 6:30-33 pars.; John 6:14-15). Few would doubt that Jesus staged the event of his entry into Jerusalem or that his choice to ride a donkey was an intentional statement of humility and rejection (Mark 11:1-10 pars.). And, though many dispute the veracity of Jesus' predictions of his own death — especially some of the particulars that emerge in the passion predictions (Mark 8:31 pars.; 9:30-32 pars.; 10:32-34 pars.; cf. Matt. 26:2) — many still do contend that Jesus divined his own death.[90] He dared to believe that, in spite of his impending rejection and death, the kingdom was nonetheless imminent. He believed that it was through his death that God would achieve a decisive victory for Israel, because he saw his own death as a sacrifice for an unresponsive nation (Mark 10:45). Thus, Jesus' heritage and practice together reveal the inauspicious character of the kingdom.

There are four lines of evidence connected with this dimension of Jesus' kingdom teaching. First, there are those teachings that focus on the humble beginnings of the kingdom. A good place to start is the parable of the mustard seed (Mark 4:30-32 pars.):

> He also said, "With what can we compare the kingdom of God, or what parable will we use for it? It is like a mustard seed, which, when sown upon the ground, is the smallest of all the seeds on earth; yet when it is sown it grows up and becomes the greatest of all shrubs, and puts forth large branches, so that the birds of the air can make nests in its shade."

Scholars have debated whether this parable teaches the inexorable growth of the kingdom into a universal, world-encompassing religion, or a radical contrast between humble beginnings and glorious endings.[91] Others have focused on the birds of the air, contending that the image may recall the vision of Ezek. 17:23:

> On the mountain height of Israel
>   I will plant it,

---

90. See Wright, *Jesus and the Victory of God*, 540-611; Schürmann, *Gottes Reich*.

91. Weiß, *Predigt*, 48-49, 82-84; Bultmann, *Theology*, 1.8-9; Jeremias, *Parables*, 146-53.

in order that it may produce boughs and bear fruit,
    and become a noble cedar.
Under it every kind of bird will live;
    in the shade of its branches will nest
    winged creatures of every kind.

Most interpreters would contend that this background points the parable in the direction of universalism and that Jesus therefore envisioned a kingdom that would eventually include Gentiles. Such an allusion is cryptic at best. The central analogy of the parable seems rather to be that, even though deriving from the smallest of seeds, the mustard tree, when done growing, transcends its small beginnings by far. The kingdom has inauspicious and insignificant beginnings — since it is now composed of but a small band of Galilean artisans — but it will eventually embrace the whole nation.[92]

The same point is made in a Q parable, the parable of the leaven (Luke 13:20-21; Matt. 13:33). Here again, something small and insignificant is transformed into something large and imposing:

And again he said, "To what should I compare the kingdom of God? It is like yeast that a woman took and mixed in with three measures of flour until all of it was leavened."

To be sure, "three measures of flour" would be adequate for 100 people, and perhaps Jesus is emphasizing dramatically different results as compared with beginnings. More likely, an alarming contrast is the only point: the kingdom has insignificant beginnings, but it will become a significant movement of God. For Jesus, then, the kingdom's beginnings are much like those of mustard trees and bread; if one were to look only at the beginnings of these items (a small seed, yeast in a batch of dough), one would not normally predict the outcome.

A second line of evidence for the inauspiciousness of the kingdom concerns the kinds of people Jesus envisioned participating in the renewal of Israel and, therefore, joined in table fellowship.[93] Be-

---

92. So also Chilton, *Pure Kingdom*, 15: "the point is beginning and result rather than process."

93. See esp. Bornkamm, *Jesus*, 75-81; Goppelt, *Theology*, 1.127-38; Jeremias, *Proclamation of Jesus*, 108-21.

sides calling together a bunch of fishermen (Mark 1:16-20; Luke 5:1-11), a tax collector (Mark 2:13-17), and others of the same sort, Jesus taught that the kingdom itself is populated by the unlikely. Thus, when he sees how the disciples try to keep the little children away, Jesus is furious:

> But when Jesus saw this, he was indignant and said to them, "Let the little children come to me; do not stop them; for it is to such as these that the kingdom of God belongs. Truly I tell you, whoever does not receive the kingdom of God as a little child will never enter it." And he took them up in his arms, laid his hands on them, and blessed them. (Mark 10:14-15)

Contemporary church practices (such as the ceremonial baptism of infants, often accompanied by smartly dressed but distracted siblings) prevent many from understanding this logion of Jesus in its historical context. In a world where children were neither totally relegated to the margins nor treated as worthy of full acceptance, Jesus offered the kingdom to those who would be like children.[94] The disciples themselves were neither priestly nor educated, nor were other followers of Jesus graced with royal manners or with opportunities to exercise authoritative power. The kingdom, then, is composed of the most unlikely of people, people who humbly shoulder the yoke of the kingdom (cf. Matt. 18:3).

In another Q saying, Jesus thanks God that he has revealed his royal rule not to the "wise and the intelligent" but to "infants" (Matt. 11:25//Luke 10:21). Here Jesus is speaking not of children per se but of those with the kind of trust that God wants: people of childlike faith who believe that God is now bringing the kingdom through his messenger, Jesus (cf. Mark 10:15). If Jeremias's view of the meaning of "becoming a child" is accurate, and the phrase describes those who have learned to call God "Abba," then we have here a standard definition for those who populate the kingdom of Jesus: Abba's children.[95]

From an M tradition we find a parable that coheres with this picture of those who are to populate God's kingdom:

---

94. See S. C. Barton, "Child, Children," *DJG*, 100-104.
95. Jeremias, *Proclamation of Jesus*, 155-56.

"Again, the kingdom of heaven is like a net that was thrown into the sea and caught fish of every kind; when it was full, they drew it ashore, sat down, and put the good into baskets but threw out the bad. So it will be at the end of the age. The angels will come out and separate the evil from the righteous and throw them into the furnace of fire, where there will be weeping and gnashing of teeth." (Matt. 13:47-50)

From this parable other points might be made about the kingdom (especially about the future judgment), but here the words "every kind" deserve attention. After the casting of the nets and the pulling in of those nets are both completed, the separation will take place, *but for now* no such discrimination occurs. Jesus invites "every kind" to his banquet because the kingdom is itself all-inclusive. It is not comprised just of the holy or of the established but of all Israel, because through Jesus a new purity is formed. And the very type of people whom Jesus "catches" clearly indicates an inauspicious beginning for the kingdom. Surely Jesus' practice and associations raised the following questions imagined by Günther Bornkamm:

An unknown rabbi of Nazareth in a remote corner of Palestine? A handful of disciples, who, when it came to the show-down, left him in the lurch? A doubtful mob following him — publicans, loose women, sinners, and a few women and children and folk who got help from him? On his cross the sport of passers-by? Is this the kingdom of God? The shift in the ages? Why doesn't he authenticate himself in a different way?[96]

A third line of evidence for the kingdom's inauspicious nature is seen in its peaceful coexistence with members outside the kingdom. The parable of the weeds and wheat (Matt. 13:24-30, 36-43) has been interpreted in two mutually exclusive ways: it either portrays the kingdom as a *corpus mixtum,* that is, a place where both followers and non-followers are mixed together (in the land of Israel? the church?), or distinguishes two different groups: those in the kingdom and those outside the kingdom. The first interpretation fails on historical grounds: (1) the practice of expelling covenant breakers was common in Juda-

96. Bornkamm, *Jesus,* 72-73.

ism;[97] it had its roots in the Bible (e.g., Exod. 12:15; 22:19; Ezra 10:8; Isa. 66:5) and was carried out, for example, at Qumran (cf. 1QS 5:25–6:1); to some degree, it was probably used against the followers of Jesus (Luke 6:22; John 9:22; 16:2), and it was practiced in earliest Christianity (e.g., 1 Cor. 5:3-5; 2 Cor. 6:10; 2 John; 3 John; Ignatius, *Smyrn.* 4:1). (2) Jesus himself, or at least his earliest followers, taught that expulsion, or excommunication, may have to be practiced (cf. Matt. 16:19; 18:15-18).[98] On historical grounds, then, it seems unlikely that Jesus would have offered a blanket endorsement of all sorts of religious life or tolerated an indiscriminate mixture of faith and unfaith in the renewal movement he was establishing. Jesus' mission was to call Israel to repentance; it seems fundamentally contradictory that he would have envisioned no discrimination until the end of the age.

Thus, Jesus likely envisioned not a *corpus mixtum*, a mixed kingdom of the repentant and the impenitent, but a kingdom that inauspiciously coexists in the land of Israel alongside those who would not follow him as the herald of the kingdom.[99] That is, Jesus offered salvation for those would turn from their ways and avoid the disaster by heeding his kingdom announcement. He announced that the kingdom was coming now and the judgment later. In the words of Leonhard Goppelt, "Jesus ushered in salvation, which is followed by the *krisis*, the condemnation — in Johannine terminology — and not salvation as the consequence of *krisis*."[100] To be completely fair to the evidence, however, there is a sense in which the future kingdom as the glorious display of God's strength would occur after the judgment. The scenario thus runs: (1) the inauspicious arrival of kingdom in Jesus, followed by (2) judgment on the disobedient, and then (3) the arrival of kingdom in consummated form.

Jesus wanted his disciples to reject the way of violence in seeking to enlarge the kingdom; he renounced the way of the Maccabees and the Zealots and called his followers to an inauspicious, but peaceful, coexistence with all Israelites. Thus, as G. R. Beasley-Murray has said, the parable of the weeds and wheat "signifies a rejection of the impatience

---

97. For a technical study, see G. Forkman, *The Limits of the Religious Community: Expulsion from the Religious Community within the Qumran Sect, within Rabbinic Judaism, and within Primitive Christianity* (Lund: Gleerup, 1972).

98. See Beasley-Murray, *Jesus and the Kingdom,* 134-35.

99. See Ladd, *Presence,* 231-34.

100. Goppelt, *Theology,* 1.66; see also Jeremias, *Proclamation of Jesus,* 177-78.

of the righteous and a call for the patience of God."[101] So also George E. Ladd: "The message of the parable has nothing to do with the nature of the church but teaches that the kingdom of God has invaded history without disrupting the present structure of society."[102]

The fourth line of evidence for the kingdom's inauspicious nature can be seen in one of the more notable sayings of Jesus which we have already looked at briefly:

> Once Jesus was asked by the Pharisees when the kingdom of God was coming, and he answered, "The kingdom of God is not coming with things that can be observed; nor will they say, 'Look, here it is!' or 'There it is!' For, in fact, the kingdom of God is among you." (Luke 17:20-21)

Two points are worthy of note here. First, the kingdom of God does not come "with things that can be observed." Jesus seems to be responding to the view of so many of his contemporaries that the kingdom's arrival could be charted on some apocalyptic timetable by watching events in history to determine the final days. Jesus counters this view. Instead of this approach to the discovery or realization of the kingdom, Jesus states, second, that it is "among you" in the sense that it is within your reach to find it by realizing that God has chosen to bring it into opera-tion — now![103] Some scholars have argued that the words "among you" are to be understood as "within you" and that they describe the experi-ence of surrendering to God; others maintain that the phrase refers to Jesus' presence, and therefore the kingdom's presence "among you."[104] However, better arguments have been offered by G. R. Beasley-Murray for understanding this expression to describe the opportunity the audi-ence has of finding the kingdom now in Jesus. Thus, "the kingdom is *within their reach* — which is to say that it lies in their power to enter it

101. Beasley-Murray, *Jesus and the Kingdom*, 134.

102. Ladd, *Presence*, 263. See the discussion in Meyer, *Aims of Jesus*, 210-19, esp. 214-15. Similarly, Fuller, *Mission*, 44-45, sees the parable of the seed growing secretly (Mark 4:26-29) with the same substantive point.

103. Perhaps in the sense that Jesus is the kind of sign they are seeking — only he baffles them in his humility. See Fuller, *Mission*, 29.

104. G. Dalman, *The Words of Jesus Considered in the Light of Post-Biblical Jewish Writings and the Aramaic Language* (trans. D. M. Kay; Edinburgh: T & T Clark, 1902) 143-47.

and secure its blessings."[105] But that kingdom, so goes the saying, is not so obvious that it can be easily entered or divined. Rather, the kingdom of God is by nature inauspicious, and one must have faith to see its presence and experience its power.

The Kingdom Displayed in Strength[106]

If the kingdom is inauspicious, at times it nevertheless displays itself in strength. Jesus' miracles, exorcisms, and conflicts with evil forces evince this theme.[107] However, for Jesus the kingdom's power could not be simply equated with the kingdom. To be sure, the kingdom dramatically materializes in those situations when God displays his redemption in strength, but those situations are not the whole picture. For Jesus these displays of God in strength were but occasional reminders, signs and present tokens of the future, yet imminent, kingdom of God. To equate kingdom and power would be to turn Jesus into nothing more than a thaumaturge.

To understand Jesus' acts of power, we must learn to bracket the notion that Jesus did these acts in order to prove that he was Son of God or Messiah. Whatever one makes of the apologetic value of Jesus' miracles, his primary purpose was not to witness to himself (though his deeds did do that) but to God and to God's kingdom. Jesus' view of the kingdom was *theocentric* and, at the same time, *national:* it was God's redemption for Israel. We need to examine these acts in which God acted in strength within the scope of Jewish expectations for the kingdom and the age to come.[108] One sure feature that helps explain Jesus' association of the kingdom with acts of power was the ancient Jewish idea of the final day being the day of God's theophany. When that day came, it would be a day of stupendous power and displays of might. The final day would be marked by the transformation of the world — physical reformation and deliverance (e.g., Isa. 65:17). Consistent with a new world would be a transformation of physical life, so

---

105. Beasley-Murray, *Jesus and the Kingdom,* 102-3.

106. See Chilton, *Pure Kingdom,* 66-73, 90-97.

107. See the lucid analysis of Meier, *A Marginal Jew,* 2.509-873; see also Gnilka, *Jesus,* 118-41; E. Schweizer, *Jesus* (trans. D. E. Green; London: SCM, 1971) 23.

108. A broad survey of healing can be found in M. L. Brown, *Israel's Divine Healer* (SOTBT; Grand Rapids: Zondervan, 1995).

that neither sickness nor death would infect God's people and God's land.

Part of this theme is the Day of YHWH — the time when God would act in judgment and salvation. An integral feature of Jesus' deeds of power was his sense that in them one saw both God's saving work and God's judgment on sin and sickness. If Jesus can deliver from Satan (Luke 11:20), he can also curse a fig tree (Mark 11:12-14) and forecast the destruction of Jerusalem (Mark 13:1-32). Jesus' acts of power, then, need to be understood as theophanic demonstrations of the transforming power of God as he actualizes his reign among Israelites for the purpose of salvation and judgment in the last hour of national history. The inauguration of the kingdom in Jesus unleashes in part the powers of God's eternal reign.[109] This can be seen in at least four kinds of evidence about God's acting in strength.

First, Jesus told a parable about a seed growing secretly:

> "The kingdom of God is as if someone would scatter seed on the ground, and would sleep and rise night and day, and the seed would sprout and grow, he does not know how. The earth produces of itself, first the stalk, then the head, then the full grain in the head. But when the grain is ripe, at once he goes in with his sickle, because the harvest has come." (Mark 4:26-29)

The seed grows automatically, with no attendant watering, weeding, fertilizing, or worrying if enough bumper crop might be acquired to pay the taxes.[110] For Jesus, the kingdom was like this seed because it, too, had been sown (through Jesus' announcements and actions), and God would harvest in the end. In the meantime, the kingdom grows invisibly and inevitably toward the great harvest, and the growth itself reveals God's strength.[111] An implication to be drawn from the growth of the kingdom is that nothing can stop it; it will happen. And nothing can bring it in — neither human efforts at reformation nor forceful agitation. It happens because the power of God is at work in the process of growth. While this parable might suggest the patience or confidence of the farmer, or even the secrecy of growth, it func-

---

109. See the survey of Wright, *Jesus and the Victory of God*, 191-96.
110. See Horsley, *Galilee*, 216-19.
111. Cf. Weiß, *Predigt*, 84-85; Kümmel, *Promise*, 127-29.

tions primarily to show that no matter what happens, the power of the kingdom is at work and God is waiting for the harvest to gather in his people.[112] The kingdom's growth is spontaneous (the farmer has no power to make it grow), invisible (he does not see it grow), irresistible (he can sleep because he knows it will grow), and inevitable (the harvest is coming).

Second, the kingdom is noted for its *radical power*. Once again, the parable of the mustard seed has a lesson to teach (Mark 4:30-32 pars.). Though the kingdom begins in an inauspicious manner, it has results that far outstrip its humble origins. God's power is at work in a mustard-seed-like activity of transforming the nation. The parable drives home the shocking contrast of beginning and ending: small seed, big tree.[113] The same can be said of the parable of leaven (Luke 13:20-21): the smallness of yeast is contrasted with the largeness of the food for the feast. It is a powerful and miraculous act of God, not the result of accumulated human effort.

It is more difficult to substantiate on historical grounds that Jesus' parable of the weeds and wheat (Matt. 13:24-30, 36-43) as well as the parable of the dragnet (Matt. 13:47-50) was intended to teach a universal extension of the kingdom.[114] The decisive clue for universalism in the first parable (13:38: "world") derives, according to most scholars, from Matthean redaction and therefore is much less secure on historical grounds. But the use of "every kind" in 13:47 lends credence to the view that Jesus anticipated a universal kingdom. Not only would this be consistent with Judaism, where the idea of Israel's election led to universalism, but Jesus' own ministry occasionally reached Gentiles (cf. Luke 7:1-10 par.;[115] Mark 7:24-30 par.; Mark 13:10; John 12:20-26[116]). Thus, Jesus' understanding of the power of God's kingdom may have included the idea that the kingdom had universal implications (e.g.,

112. For a survey of interpretations, see Beasley-Murray, *Jesus and the Kingdom,* 125-27.

113. See Kümmel, *Promise,* 129-32.

114. A good survey can be found in Wright, *Jesus and the Victory of God,* 308-10.

115. That Matt. 8:11-12 ought not to be taken in simplistic universal categories has been clearly shown by Chilton, *Pure Kingdom,* 81-82.

116. I find it unlikely that "nation" in Matt. 21:43 refers exclusively to "Gentile conversions." On this logion, see esp. K. Snodgrass, *The Parable of the Wicked Tenants* (WUNT 27; Tübingen: Mohr Siebeck, 1983) 90-95. On "take away," see Dalman, *Words,* 133.

Mark 4:30-32). In early Jewish tradition, we find the expectation that on the final day the nations would flock to Zion to worship the God of Israel (compare, e.g., Isa. 2:1-4 or 49:1-6 with *1 Enoch* 48:4-5; 50:1-5; 62:9-13; 90:30-33; 91:14). This notion reflects not early Christian missionary outreach but Jewish monotheism and election theology. It would be shortsighted to think that Jesus had in mind only Israel. His vision for Israel likely included Gentiles streaming to Zion, because he envisioned a nation fully performing the task that God had given to it.[117]

Jesus clearly taught that the kingdom of God exhibits its strength in an invisible but irresistible influence grossly out of proportion to its humble beginnings. Just what this power consists of, other than its obvious covenantal dimension, remains unclear. However, a third line of evidence reveals that Jesus sometimes had in mind *the power of healing and restoring persons to health and society*.[118] In one saying Jesus declares that this power has been at work since the days of John:

> "The law and the prophets were in effect until John came; since then the good news of the kingdom of God is proclaimed, and everyone tries to enter it by force." (Luke 16:16)[119]

But here again one can only surmise the substantive content of the kingdom's manifestation. It surely entails Jesus' preaching of liberation, but of what does this consist? Once again, Luke's use of a Q logion effectively reveals what Jesus had in mind:

> Jesus had just then cured many people of diseases, plagues, and evil spirits, and had given sight to many who were blind. And he answered them, "Go and tell John what you have seen and heard: the blind receive their sight, the lame walk, the lepers are cleansed, the

---

117. See S. McKnight, *A Light among the Gentiles: Jewish Missionary Activity in the Second Temple Period* (Minneapolis: Fortress, 1991) 11-29, 50-51.

118. See Goppelt, *Theology*, 1.139-57; Horsley, *Jesus and the Spiral of Violence*, 181-84; Becker, *Jesus von Nazaret*, 211-33; Fuller, *Mission*, 35-43; Brown, *Israel's Divine Healer*.

119. If *biazetai* is a true middle and means "advance by storm" (Luke has "is proclaimed"; Matthew could be "advance by storm"), then the emphasis upon God at work in strength is even more apparent; see Ladd, *Presence*, 158-64; Chilton, *God in Strength*, 205-30.

deaf hear, the dead are raised, the poor have good news brought to them. And blessed is anyone who takes no offense at me." (Luke 7:21-23; cf. Matt. 11:4-6)

Here we have an intentional reflection by Jesus on how it is that the kingdom manifests its power and of what it consists. It consists of physical healings, of restoring people to equal covenant relationships with others, and of social equalization through inclusion of the poor.[120] These are not just signs of the kingdom, as if the kingdom were something more fundamental or other than physical deliverance; nor are they merely symbols of some spiritual work that manifests itself in physical deliverance. Rather, the kingdom means physical restoration of God's good land; it involves social integration and restoration of the nation; and it brings in its wake a reordering of society so that all Israel can enjoy the covenant on an equal basis. To be sure, these mighty deeds fulfill Isaianic hopes (cf. Isa. 26:19; 29:18-19; 35:5-6; 42:18; 61:1) and so indicate that God's promises and Israel's hopes are now materializing — after all, Jesus says this to inform John about who he is. In this sense, then, they are signs, but they must not be reduced to mere signs, for Judaism knows no sharp separation of the spiritual and the physical. The kingdom hope is an earthly, physical hope of deliverance and liberation, of restoration and perfection; but that hope is to materialize in the land of Israel. Thus, Jesus' mighty deeds are not just tokens of the kingdom but signal the arrival of the kingdom itself. For this reason the Gospels are full of stories of physical deliverance and social rehabilitation, not to mention other miracles that evince the power of God's deliverance now available to Israel in its final days (cf. Mark 4:35-41; 6:35-44, 45-52; cf. Matthew 8–9). These mighty acts of Jesus fulfill Jewish expectations for the final days of deliverance, and that deliverance has physical and social dimensions.

God's power reveals itself in a fourth aspect: *cosmic conflict*.[121] The ancient Jewish worldview entailed belief in Satan and the demonic forces. Many contemporaries of Jesus therefore saw evidence of the ar-

---

120. A good exposition can be found in J. D. G. Dunn, *Jesus' Call to Discipleship* (Cambridge: Cambridge University Press, 1992) 32-61.

121. On this, see esp. G. H. Twelftree, *Jesus the Exorcist: A Contribution to the Study of the Historical Jesus* (Peabody, Mass.: Hendrickson, 1993); see also his essay "Demon, Devil, Satan," *DJG*, 163-72.

rival of the kingdom in his exorcisms.[122] "Hence, however disconcerting it may be to modern sensibilities, it is fairly certain that Jesus was, among other things, a 1st-century Jewish exorcist and probably won not a little of his fame and following by practicing exorcisms (along with the claim of performing other types of miracles)."[123]

A leading theme of this conflict can be found in the bedrock logion of Mark 3:27:[124]

> "But no one can enter a strong man's house and plunder his property without first tying up the strong man; then indeed the house can be plundered."

Jesus believed that the kingdom had already arrived; its arrival had conquered the forces of evil by binding up the strong man. The same point is made in Luke 10:18:

> He said to them, "I watched Satan fall from heaven like a flash of lightning."

In both of these authentic logia of Jesus, we see the same theme, though from two different angles (one is a wisdom saying, while the other is a prophetic interpretation of his exorcisms): Satan has already been captured, and his powers have been stripped.[125] Such powerful action by God enables Jesus to announce the arrival of the kingdom and its benefits of liberation for those who have been demonized.

When is Satan's downfall understood to have occurred? Scholars have debated this point vigorously. The best options are (1) at Jesus' temptation in the wilderness, (2) during Jesus' ministry in general, or (3) in the exorcisms performed through Jesus' disciples.[126] But even this list is incomplete. In light of the continued Satanic and demonic

---

122. See Meier, *A Marginal Jew*, 2.398-506; Horsley, *Jesus and the Spiral of Violence*, 184-90, though he essentially demythologizes the evil supernatural world, showing the socio-political significance of the demonic construct.

123. Meier, *A Marginal Jew*, 2.406.

124. See R. Bultmann, *The History of the Synoptic Tradition* (rev. ed.; trans. J. Marsh; New York: Harper & Row, 1963) 105.

125. Kümmel, *Promise*, 114.

126. Beasley-Murray, *Jesus and the Kingdom*, 109-11, concludes that it refers to the entirety of Jesus' ministry.

opposition (cf., e.g., Matt. 13:24-30), it is best to turn to the Jewish notion that Satan's defeat would take place in two stages: a binding (which takes place in Jesus' ministry of exorcisms) and a final, eschatological triumph (cf. Isa. 24:21-22; *1 Enoch* 10:4-6).

Another relevant logion is Luke 11:20:[127]

"But if it is by the finger[128] of God that I cast out the demons, then the kingdom of God has come[129] to you."

Here, too, Jesus dramatically connects his exorcisms with the arrival of the kingdom, not just in some "sign-ifying" sense but in a real way: the liberation of people from demonic influences is not just a sign pointing to the kingdom's arrival but is itself a visible and dramatic manifestation of the kingdom's power in God's present restoration of Israel.[130] If, Jesus tells his opponents, I exorcise by the power of God, then God's final victory is being established and will tragically overtake you in your sins.[131]

Thus, we have in the exorcisms of Jesus evidence that he saw God's kingdom in operation. For those enslaved to the forces that bound them to sin and social exclusion, the experience of liberation is a tangible experience of the kingdom itself. These experiences do not point the liberated people to some ideal or theological construct that would lead them to see what "really" happened. Rather, when the kingdom comes there is liberation from Satan's clutches. In their deliverance, these people become sudden participants in the end-time act of God reigning over Israel in strength.[132]

The presence of the kingdom involves power: one experiences the kingdom tangibly in the invisible, but irresistible, growth of the king-

---

127. On the historicity of this logion, see esp. J. D. G. Dunn, "Matthew 12:28/ Luke 11:20 — A Word of Jesus?" in W. Hulitt Gloer, ed., *Eschatology and the New Testament: Essays in Honor of George Raymond Beasley-Murray* (Peabody, Mass.: Hendrickson, 1988) 29-49.

128. On "finger," see Meier, *A Marginal Jew*, 2.411, who shows that use of this term places Jesus (self-consciously) on the level of Moses and Aaron, at the very least. See also Manson, *Teaching*, 82-83.

129. On the meaning of *ephthasen*, "has come to/upon," see the helpful study of Kümmel, *Promise*, 106-8.

130. Twelftree, "Demon, Devil, Satan," 168.

131. See Meier, *A Marginal Jew*, 2.453.

132. See Otto, "Kingdom of God," in Chilton, ed., *Kingdom*, 32.

dom from a small, ragtag band of followers into a large, universal people of God. The same power is expressed in strength when Jesus heals people and restores them to their social location, granting them resocialization, the forgiveness of sins, and acceptance into the covenant with Israel. Finally, the kingdom is seen in the dramatic acts of powerful victory over Satan and his minions. Jesus comes to Israel at the turning of the ages, calling Israel to repent and to turn to covenant faithfulness as he announces the arrival of the kingdom. This call is buttressed by powerful acts of God's redeeming strength. It is no wonder, then, that when Jesus healed and exorcised "they praised the God of Israel" (Matt. 15:31).

The Kingdom's Call for Covenant Faithfulness

Every covenantal arrangement in Israel required a human response of trust and obedience (see, e.g., Genesis 12, 17; Exodus 20–24; Deuteronomy 24, 28; 2 Samuel 7). For those who, because of unfaithfulness and sinfulness, forfeited their enjoyment of covenant blessings and so found themselves exiled, the only way to revive their covenant participation was through repentance. The covenant itself generated and shaped a community that lived according to its ethical standards (cf. Luke 12:32). Accordingly, Jesus' kingdom message for Israel would necessarily have envisioned a kingdom community living by a kingdom ethic.

Covenant faithfulness does not form the complete context for Jesus' ethic, though; more fundamentally, eschatology informs everything about Jesus' ethical directives and gives those directives their singular focus and shape.[133]

Jesus addressed Israel and called the nation to repentance, faith, and righteous obedience as preconditions for participating in God's renewing of the covenant. If Israel responds properly, it will be sheltered from the coming wrath of God. It is in this context, the announcement to Israel of its coming disaster, that Jesus' ethics are to be understood. To encounter the kingdom Israel must repent, believe, and follow Jesus' restated Torah. The evidence will be sketched only in part at this point, since Chapters 5 and 6 will treat the topic more fully.

---

133. See Schweitzer, *Mystery*, 94, 115, 122.

Jesus' ethics are kingdom ethics, not abstract moral reflections. Neither are they simply casuistic pronouncements or legal inferences, such as those found in the Mishnah or Tosepta, but behavioral prescriptions that emerge from his message about God and the kingdom.[134] There is a correlation between kingdom and ethics: to the degree that the kingdom has been realized, its ethic can be realized. This point cannot be emphasized enough; when interpreters remove Jesus' ethics from their kingdom context, or fail to get a proper grasp of what he meant by kingdom, those ethics quickly devolve into either a sentimental utopianism or a repressive legalism. Both of these errors can be avoided if Jesus' ethic is given its proper place in his mission to Israel.

At this point it will suffice merely to examine the "entrance sayings" of Jesus, since it is these logia that expressly connect kingdom and ethics, and they perfectly express the context of Jesus: prophetic hope for righteousness, impending judgment, call to repentance, and obedience to God's will.[135] In their concrete variety, these sayings about entering the kingdom lead us to the heart of Jesus' ethics: an unconditional commitment to God's will in the concreteness of everyday living. An extensive analysis of the traditions that may have given rise to this type of saying by Jesus is not possible here, but one obvious traditional theme that influenced Jesus in various ways deserves mention: the demands placed on Israel as it prepared to enter the land of Canaan (cf., e.g., Deut. 4:1; 6:18; 16:20).

First, we begin with Mark 9:43-48:

> "If your hand causes you to stumble, cut it off; it is better for you to enter life maimed than to have two hands and to go to hell, to the unquenchable fire. And if your foot causes you to stumble, cut it off; it is better for you to enter life lame than to have two feet and to be thrown into hell. And if your eye causes you to stumble, tear it out; it is better for you to enter the kingdom of God with one eye than to have two eyes and to be thrown into hell, where their worm never dies, and the fire is never quenched."

134. See the excellent contextualizing by Becker, *Jesus von Nazaret*, 276-88.

135. See H. Windisch, "Die Sprüche vom Eingehen in das Reich Gottes," *ZNW* 27 (1928) 163-92; Dalman, *Words*, 116-18; Fuller, *Mission*, 29-31; Kümmel, *Promise*, 52-53, 125-26; R. Schnackenburg, *Die sittliche Botschaft des Neuen Testaments* (2 vols.; HTKNTS 1-2; Freiburg: Herder, 1986-88) 1.36-37. For a recent exegetical analysis, see Beasley-Murray, *Jesus and the Kingdom*, 174-87, though he fails to offer much of a synthesis.

"Stumbling" naturally describes sins and actions that defeat the activity of God. Just as John the Baptist informed Israel that anything excessive needed to be eliminated (Luke 3:7-14), so Jesus taught that whatever gets in the way must be hurdled; whatever slows one down must be discarded; whatever injures one's commitment to the will of God must be avoided — even to the point of self-mutilation. Many argue that, since mutilation was abominable in Judaism (Deut. 14:1; pagan mutilation can be seen in 1 Kgs. 18:28; Zech. 13:6), these logia are most likely to be taken metaphorically. However, in light of Matt. 19:10-12, it is indeed possible that Jesus exhorted his hearers to jettison anything that interfered with their entry into the kingdom, even if that meant self-inflicted bodily harm.[136] Such a view would be consistent with Jesus' demand to follow him even at the risk of suffering persecution (cf. Matt. 10:24-25) and at the cost of forsaking obligations of piety and family (Luke 9:57-62).

Critical in our passage (Mark 9:43-48) is the alignment of "life" and "kingdom of God" against their opposite, "hell," which is twice defined with a horrific image, the "unquenchable fire." Since "hell" describes the eternal state where God punishes, the future kingdom in all its fullness must be in view here. To enter into that kingdom, one must eliminate all obstacles. The arrival of the present kingdom calls for an unconditional commitment, because losing the future kingdom is to lose everything.

Second, we need to look at the case of the rich young ruler for another example of an entrance requirement (cf. Mark 10:17-27 pars.; italics added):

> As he was setting out on a journey, a man ran up and knelt before him, and asked him, "Good Teacher, what must I do to inherit eternal life?" Jesus said to him, "Why do you call me good? No one is good but God alone. You know the commandments: 'You shall not murder; You shall not commit adultery; You shall not steal; You shall not bear false witness; You shall not defraud; Honor your father and mother.'" He said to him, "Teacher, I have kept all these since my youth." Jesus, looking at him, loved him and said, "You lack one thing; go, sell what you own, and give the money to the poor, and you will have treasure in heaven; then come, follow me." When he heard

---

136. See the comments of R. Gundry, *Mark: A Commentary on His Apology for the Cross* (Grand Rapids: Eerdmans, 1993) 514.

this, he was shocked and went away grieving, for he had many possessions.

Then Jesus looked around and said to his disciples, *"How hard it will be for those who have wealth to enter the kingdom of God!"* And the disciples were perplexed at these words. But Jesus said to them again, *"Children, how hard it is to enter the kingdom of God! It is easier for a camel to go through the eye of a needle than for someone who is rich to enter the kingdom of God."* They were greatly astounded and said to one another, "Then who can be saved?" Jesus looked at them and said, "For mortals it is impossible, but not for God; for God all things are possible."

The critical words for our purpose are "How hard it will be for those who have wealth to enter the kingdom of God!" The rich find it impossible to extricate themselves from entanglements of wealth. Again, Jesus does not offer here some abstract, reflective principle about the kind of response God requires: rather, through this incident we learn that he called people to abandon their wealth in order to follow him, for in so doing they would enter the kingdom of God in the present.

A third passage worth looking at is Mark 10:15:

"Truly I tell you, whoever does not receive the kingdom of God as a little child will never enter it."

Jesus is speaking here of a childlike characteristic required by God for those who would enter into the kingdom: humility. To be sure, inasmuch as Jesus accepted the poor and the needy, the tax collectors and the sinners,[137] he accepted another marginalized group of ancient Jewish society: children. However, Jesus used this inherent attribute of children to probe the motives of his disciples, and he called them to have this characteristic. This much is clear also in a triple tradition: in their desire to be something special, the disciples were given to pride and to comparing themselves (Mark 9:33-37 pars.). According to Jesus, children are not like this; they are humble. To enter the kingdom now, one must be humble before God, accepting his judgment on Israel, admitting one's sinfulness,

137. See the important essay of J. D. G. Dunn, "Pharisees, Sinners, and Jesus," in J. Neusner, et al., eds., *The Social World of Formative Christianity and Judaism: Essays in Tribute to Howard Clark Kee* (Philadelphia: Fortress, 1988) 264-89.

just as Jesus himself participated in a corporate confession of Israel's sinfulness (Mark 1:1-11 pars.), and striking out in trust and obedience in light of the renewal that the kingdom brings to Israel.[138]

Fourth, there are two special entrance sayings in Matthew. Though consistent with the radical, concrete images found in the above two, they sound distinctive moral tones characteristic of Matthew. The language may be Matthean, but the ideas at least cohere with his teachings and practice.

> "For I tell you, unless your righteousness exceeds that of the scribes and Pharisees, you will never enter the kingdom of heaven." (Matt. 5:20)

> "Not everyone who says to me, 'Lord, Lord,' will enter the kingdom of heaven, but only the one who does the will of my Father in heaven." (Matt. 7:21)

Jesus' call for entrance into the kingdom requires a moral commitment to do the will of God as taught by Jesus.[139] In contrast to the Pharisees and scribes, Jesus' followers are to obey the will of God as Jesus teaches it; in so doing, they will fulfill the entire plan of God for Israel. If they do not, they will be called least and will be excluded from the kingdom in its final form. Confession is not adequate; those who wish to live in the land in perfection must live a life of obedience.

The final passage to mention here is Matt. 21:28-32:

> "What do you think? A man had two sons; he went to the first and said, 'Son, go and work in the vineyard today.' He answered, 'I will not'; but later he changed his mind and went. The father went to the second and said the same; and he answered, 'I go, sir'; but he did not go. Which of the two did the will of his father?" They said, "The first." Jesus said to them, "Truly I tell you, the tax collectors and the prostitutes are going into the kingdom of God ahead of you. For John came to you in the way of righteousness and you did not believe him,

---

138. See further Chilton, *Pure Kingdom*, 83-85.

139. See B. Przybylski, *Righteousness in Matthew and His World of Thought* (SNTSMS 41; Cambridge: Cambridge University Press, 1980); S. McKnight, "Justice, Righteousness," *DJG*, 411-16.

but the tax collectors and the prostitutes believed him; and even after you saw it, you did not change your minds and believe him."

Like the others, this entrance saying is concrete and speaks of the sorts of people who will enter the kingdom: "the tax collectors and the prostitutes." It was these kind of people who responded to John's call to national repentance and who, in so repenting, joined in the way of righteousness. They willingly abandoned their previous course of disobedience to the covenant to align themselves with the will of this prophet of God. Jesus appealed to this kind of incident as paradigmatic for those who would reconstitute Israel; it is not those of rank and social reputation who are necessarily Israel but those who do the will of God as made known by Jesus (and before him John).

In looking over these entrance sayings of Jesus, one immediately notices how incomplete they are.[140] They do not propound a simple formula for entering the kingdom but tailor the demand of Jesus to a person's particular need. The essence is this: the kingdom calls individuals out of their particular Israel and summons them to kingdom ethics, but that summons takes on all the shapes and contours of Jewish society. Jesus taught what John preached: to enter the kingdom one must abandon one's unfaithfulness to the covenant and strike out in a new direction in light of the advent of the kingdom (e.g., Matt. 22:1-10; Luke 14:16-24; *Gospel of Thomas* 64; Mark 10:23-25; Matt. 13:44-46). Those who respond, who repent and walk in obedience to Jesus, are promised entrance into the kingdom of God. These followers of Jesus form the end-time remnant; they become the true people of God.[141]

The Kingdom Actualized in Suffering and Death[142]

How Jesus envisioned the relationship of the kingdom to his death is often ignored. In standard monographs on the kingdom of God, one

---

140. See Chilton, *Pure Kingdom*, 79-80.

141. See Meyer, *Aims of Jesus*, 210-19.

142. Important studies of this theme include: Schürmann, *Gottes Reich*; Fuller, *Mission*, 50-78; Wright, *Jesus and the Victory of God*, 540-611; Chilton, *Temple of Jesus*, 91-159; idem, *Pure Kingdom*, 115-26; M. Hengel, *The Atonement: The Origins of the Doctrine in the New Testament* (trans. J. Bowden; Philadelphia: Fortress, 1981); Tan, *Zion Traditions*.

rarely finds a section on the death of Jesus as something that he saw as central to his kingdom vision.

Like John the Baptist, Jesus anticipated opposition and rejection. He even foresaw that he would, like John, end up dead for carrying out his mission. And he expected to die in Jerusalem (cf. Luke 13:31-33).[143] A key passage, of course, is Matt. 11:11-12. Also important are passages that record Jesus' perception of the treatment of prophets before him (e.g., Luke 11:49-51; Matt. 23:37-39; cf. Q: Matt. 5:11-12//Luke 6:22-23), even if some of these sayings were preserved more cryptically in parabolic form (Mark 12:1-12). Jesus anticipated his death at the hands of his nation as a result of his mission to offer to Israel the kingdom of God (Luke 12:49-50; 13:32-33; 17:25).

Furthermore, Jesus himself connected his own rejection and death with the eschatological woes. It is hard to imagine that a prophet as convinced as Jesus was of his role in ushering in the kingdom would not also know about the woes associated with that kingdom. From there it is but a small step to maintain that he connected his rejection with those woes. He saw his death; he saw the coming ordeal for Israel (cf., e.g., Dan 12:1); he need only have related his death to that ordeal as part of God's judgment on the nation.[144] Jesus' lament over Jerusalem reflects this theme poignantly:

> "Jerusalem, Jerusalem, the city that kills the prophets and stones those who are sent to it! How often have I desired to gather your children together as a hen gathers her brood under her wings, and you were not willing! See, your house is left to you, desolate. For I tell you, you will not see me again until you say, 'Blessed is the one who comes in the name of the Lord.'" (Matt. 23:37-39)

And Jesus thought he was acting to bring about that ordeal:

> Do not think that I have come to bring peace to the earth; I have not come to bring peace, but a sword. For I have come to set a man against his father, and a daughter against her mother, and a daugh-

---

143. See esp. Tan, *Zion Traditions*, 57-80.

144. See Meyer, *Aims of Jesus*, 206-8; D. C. Allison, *The End of the Ages Has Come: An Early Interpretation of the Passion and Resurrection of Jesus* (Philadelphia: Fortress, 1985) 5-25.

ter-in-law against her mother-in-law; and one's foes will be members of one's own household. Whoever loves father or mother more than me is not worthy of me; and whoever loves son or daughter more than me is not worthy of me; and whoever does not take up the cross and follow me is not worthy of me. Those who find their life will lose it, and those who lose their life for my sake will find it." (Matt. 10:34-39)

By simply connecting his rejection with the final ordeal, however, Jesus would not necessarily have invested his death with saving significance. To do that, Jesus described his mission in terms of Isaiah's Suffering Servant, who suffers *on behalf of the nation, the one for the many.* The classic text, though its authenticity is hotly disputed, is Mark 10:45:

"For the Son of Man came not to be served but to serve, and to give his life a ransom for many."

Along with this logion one needs to place the so-called passion predictions (Mark 8:31-32 pars.; 9:31 pars.; 10:33-34 pars.). Although subject to Christianization in the course of their transmission, these predictions clearly evince in their earliest stages Jesus' anticipation of rejection, death, and subsequent vindication — all as part of his mission on earth. As Bruce D. Chilton has recently argued so persuasively, Jesus' own temple action (Mark 11:1-19) and his alternative meal (the Lord's Supper; Mark 14:12-25) are most likely to be understood as Jesus' particular contribution to Judaism. Jesus saw the current temple as impure, and he offered his meal, and himself, as a revolutionary alternative to the current sacrificial system.[145] In other words, he offered himself as a sacrificial victim to God so that God would forgive the sins of Israel and restore the nation. Those who ate with him during that last meal began, as it were, a new order of sacrifice with a new covenantal arrangement: Jesus' meal, his own body and blood.

This means that Jesus saw his mission in terms of sacrifice, and he must have connected this sacrifice with the kingdom. It begs logic to think that Jesus did not connect the two. Jesus believed that he was sacrificing himself for the sake of ushering in the kingdom of God. He

---

145. See Chilton, *Temple of Jesus*, 138, 152-53. See also the lengthy analysis of Wright, *Jesus and the Victory of God*, 477-611.

took on the role of the Suffering Servant who offers himself for the many (Israel).

Summary

What set Jesus apart from all Jewish prophets is that he believed that the kingdom was a present and operative reality. Scholarship agrees at this point. However, the more important issue is in what sense this kingdom is present and how that presence is to be defined.

The kingdom is present in the sense that God's long-awaited and promised plans for the deliverance and restoration of Israel are now being fulfilled. Jesus preached the kingdom's presence, he acted in ways to show that it was effectively operating, and he did things that showed its power. In each of these acts, the promises made to Israel were being realized in the present: God was coming to restore the nation and end the exile. Whether we glimpse this realization primarily in Jesus' table fellowship with sinners, in his offer of forgiveness, in his mysterious parables, or in his miracles, the realization of the kingdom was nonetheless present.

The kingdom is seen in and through Jesus. Jesus was bold enough to announce that it was he, and not others, who was ushering in the kingdom. Whether one wants to call this ego-centeredness or incipient christology is beside the point; Jesus firmly believed that he was the prophet of the last day whom God had appointed to usher in the kingdom. He thought of this kingdom as continuous with the ancient covenants that God had made with Israel, but he also conceived of his activity as something new and restorative.

The kingdom is inauspiciously present in a myriad of ways. Drawing upon a tradition concerned with humility and God's surprising ways, Jesus likened the present kingdom of God to a mustard seed, to leaven, and to table fellowship with sinners. He called unlikely types of people to follow him: tax collectors, prostitutes, fishermen, and peasant artisans. Directly in the face of much of Jewish expectation, Jesus taught that the (future) kingdom would peacefully coexist with those outside it. In so teaching, Jesus eschewed the option of a violent revolution and depicted the kingdom as a gentle society for those who want peace. Peaceful means bring about God's kingdom of peace among his chosen nation Israel.

Although the kingdom is inauspicious in its essential nature, it is occasionally powerful in its display. Jesus' acts of power, especially his exorcisms and healings, are to be understood in this context. To show the exceptional power of God at work among Israelites, he performed miracles, not as tokens of the kingdom, but as revelations of the kingdom itself. He did not perform miracles to get attention or to coerce others to follow him, but to reveal a kingdom that would eventually embrace the world in a universal display of God's salvation.

A central theme of Jesus' teaching concerns behavior and relationship to God. This ethic of Jesus reveals what it takes to enter into this presently operative kingdom. The nation can enter into the blessings of the end of days simply by repenting, by turning to Jesus in light of the advent of the kingdom, and by striking out in a new way of obedience to Jesus. The end-time ethical hope of righteousness, Jesus announced, must be heard and heeded. Those who do so will find the hope for Israel's consolation.

All this constitutes only part of Jesus' message of the kingdom, for Jesus also taught about the kingdom that was yet to come. This theme, so dominant in the works of scholars like Weiß and Schweitzer, deserves a separate treatment.

CHAPTER 4

The Kingdom Yet to Come

Jewish social and political circumstances permitted the religious hope of Israel to have its own delightful and despairing history. At the same time, this hope shaped the social and political identity of the nation and exercised a profound influence on the teachings of Jesus. His teachings on the present operation of the kingdom were shaped fundamentally by his vision of the future kingdom. His calls to discipleship and his miracles are to be understood as present manifestations of the future kingdom, and both the present and future manifestations of the kingdom are to be seen as the fulfillment of the Jewish hope of the end of exile, the establishment of a true purity, the elimination of enemies from the land, and the sole rulership of the nation by God. Summarizing his thorough investigation of Jesus' view of the future kingdom of God, John P. Meier states, "Jesus did understand the central symbol of the kingdom of God in terms of the definitive coming of God in the near future to bring the present state of things to an end and to establish his full and unimpeded rule over the world in general and Israel in particular."[1]

We must now ask in what senses Jesus saw the kingdom as future. I shall address this topic under the following five headings: (1) key texts, (2) the continuity of the future kingdom with the present, (3) the time of the kingdom as uncertain, yet discernible and consummated within one generation, (4) the final judgment at the outset of the future

---

1. J. P. Meier, *A Marginal Jew: Rethinking the Historical Jesus* (ABRL; 3 vols.; New York: Doubleday, 1991-) 2.349.

kingdom, and (5) fellowship with God the Father as the essential feature of the final kingdom.

Many have attempted to offer global summaries of Jesus' vision of the future. I begin with the conclusion of E. P. Sanders:

> Thus the kingdom expected by Jesus is not quite that expected by Paul — in the air, and not of flesh and blood — , but not that of an actual insurrectionist either. It is like the present world — it has a king, leaders, a temple, and twelve tribes — but it is not just a rearrangement of the present world. God must step in and provide a new temple, the restored people of Israel, and presumably a renewed social order, one in which "sinners" will have a place.[2]

Ben F. Meyer summarizes Jesus' vision of the kingdom as follows:

> Jesus' scheme of the future was single and simple: crisis events (his own death, the persecution of his followers and martyrdom for some of them, the suffering of Israel, the attack on Jerusalem, the ruin of the temple) followed by resolution events (the day of the Son of man, the resurrection of the dead, the pilgrimage of the nations, the enthronement of the disciples, etc.).[3]

In what follows, I shall attempt to sketch the vision Jesus had for the future. To do this, we must look first at a few significant texts.[4]

2. E. P. Sanders, *Jesus and Judaism* (Philadelphia: Fortress, 1985) 232.

3. B. F. Meyer, *The Aims of Jesus* (London: SCM, 1979) 204-5; cf. his *Christus Faber: The Master-Builder and the House of God* (Allison Park, Penn.: Pickwick, 1992) 41-58. See also J. Jeremias, *New Testament Theology: The Proclamation of Jesus* (trans. J. Bowden; New York: Charles Scribner's Sons, 1971) 100.

4. An independent line has been pursued by B. Witherington, *Jesus, Paul, and the End of the World: A Comparative Study in New Testament Eschatology* (Downers Grove, Ill.: InterVarsity Press, 1992).

Key Texts

In Judaism, one spoke most often of the "age to come," which was a "comprehensive term for the blessings of salvation."[5] Even if not his favorite expression, "the age to come" does feature in the teaching of Jesus. For instance, in Mark 10:29-30 Jesus says:

> "Truly I tell you, there is no one who has left house or brothers or sisters or mother or father or children or fields, for my sake and for the sake of the good news, who will not receive a hundredfold now *in this age* — houses, brothers and sisters, mothers and children, and fields with persecutions — and *in the age to come* eternal life."

And, from a Q tradition concerning forgivable and unforgivable sins:

> Whoever speaks a word against the Son of Man will be forgiven, but whoever speaks against the Holy Spirit will not be forgiven, either *in this age* or *in the age to come.* (Matt. 12:32)

Thus, it appears that Jesus maintained the same division of time common among his contemporaries. The present age was merely preparatory for the age to come, in which age the fullness of God's salvation and blessing would be realized for Israel.

The Gospels portray a clear line running from the preaching of John the Baptist through Jesus to his followers in the essential content of their message:

> "Repent, for the kingdom of heaven has come near." (Matt. 3:2, of John)

> "Repent, for the kingdom of heaven has come near." (Matt. 4:17, of Jesus)

> "'The kingdom of heaven has come near.'" (Matt. 10:7, of the Twelve)

> "'The kingdom of God has come near to you.'" (Luke 10:9, of the Seventy)

5. G. Dalman, *The Words of Jesus Considered in the Light of Post-Biblical Jewish Writings and the Aramaic Language* (trans. D. M. Kay; Edinburgh: T & T Clark, 1902) 135.

"... the kingdom of God has come near." (Luke 10:11, of the Seventy)

Dispute has naturally arisen over whether these sayings are authentic and over whether the presentation of John's preaching has influenced that of Jesus' or vice versa. Establishing the authenticity of these logia is beyond the scope of this book, but few scholars question that these words at least give a fair summary of the essential message of John, Jesus, and some of Jesus' followers. The crucial matter in determining Jesus' perception of time is the meaning of the word *engizō*.[6] The term can mean either "has already arrived" or "has drawn near."[7] It is best taken to mean "has drawn very near but is not yet here."[8] The decisive evidence comes from a few key passages in Matthew: in Matt. 21:1, the travelers have drawn near to Jerusalem but are still in Bethphage (thus, "have drawn very near"); in Matt. 21:34, the time for the harvest has drawn near but has not yet arrived; and in Matt. 26:45, the hour of Jesus' death has drawn so near that its impact is now being felt, but it remains still in the future. Further evidence comes from Luke 21:31, "So also, when you see these things taking place, you know that the kingdom of God is near." The same usage of *engizō* features in texts outside the Gospels, like 1 Peter 4:7 and James 5:8. We may reasonably conclude, then, that these early Christian writers (in Greek)[9] used the word *engizō* to speak of the imminent arrival of a kingdom not yet fully present.[10] Thus, they considered the kingdom to lie in the future — even though it was making its presence felt already in the present.

The future kingdom, then, stood at the center of the preaching of John, Jesus, and their immediate successors. They were concerned not so much with the *present realization* of the kingdom as with its *fuller, final manifestation*. The kingdom, though now operative in some re-

---

6. The Greek term in each case is a perfect: ἤγγικεν.

7. For a fuller discussion, see G. R. Beasley-Murray, *Jesus and the Kingdom of God* (Grand Rapids: Eerdmans, 1986) 71-75.

8. See J. Y. Campbell, "The Kingdom of God Has Come," *ExpTim* 48 (1936-1937) 91-94; R. H. Fuller, *The Mission and Achievement of Jesus: An Examination of the Presuppositions of New Testament Theology* (SBT 12; London: SCM, 1954) 21-25; W. G. Kümmel, *Promise and Fulfillment: The Eschatological Message of Jesus* (trans. D. M. Barton; London: SCM, 1957) 19-25.

9. See R. F. Berkey, "ΕΓΓΙΖΕΙΝ, ΦΘΑΝΕΙΝ and Realized Eschatology," *JBL* 82 (1963) 177-87; Fuller, *Mission*, 24-25.

10. See also Luke 21:8, 20; 22:1; Acts 7:17; Rom. 13:12; Heb. 10:25.

spects, is primarily a future state of affairs in which Israel would do and be all that YHWH designed.

Various characters in the Gospels voice their expectation of the future kingdom. In Mark 11:10, the crowds greet Jesus on his way into Jerusalem:

> "Hosanna! Blessed is the one who comes in the name of the Lord!
> Blessed is the coming kingdom of our ancestor David!
> Hosanna in the highest heaven!"

The crowds express in thoroughly Jewish fashion that the kingdom of God is on the verge of realization with Jesus' entry into Jerusalem, but the kingdom is not yet here.

Mark tells us that Joseph of Arimathea, "who was also himself waiting expectantly for the kingdom of God" (Mark 15:42), had the same expectation: the kingdom was coming soon but was still in the future. A Lukan aside to one of Jesus' parables says:

> As they were listening to this, he went on to tell a parable, because he was near Jerusalem, and because they supposed that the kingdom of God was to appear immediately. (Luke 19:11)

The same future expectation surfaces in the words of the thief on the cross:

> "Jesus, remember me when you come into your kingdom." (Luke 23:42)

Acts 1:6 preserves an ancient sentiment of the earliest followers of Jesus:

> "Lord, is this the time when you will restore the kingdom to Israel?"

This early, Jewish, largely unencumbered-by-Christian-tradition hope conflicts with later depictions of the authority of the apostles and confirms that in the earliest traditions about Jesus the kingdom of God was yet future — in an imminent sense.

This is precisely what Jesus taught his disciples to pray: "Your kingdom come" (Matt. 6:10; Luke 11:2).[11] Consistent with the Jewish

---

11. See J. Weiß, *Die Predigt Jesu vom Reiche Gottes* (3d ed.; ed. F. Hahn; Göttingen:

Qaddish, which reads "May he let his kingdom rule in your lifetime and in your days and the lifetime of the whole house of Israel, speedily and soon. And to this, say: amen,"[12] Jesus shaped his prayer around the kingdom motif[13] and expressed his essential view of the kingdom: though presently operative, its fullness is yet future.[14] This bedrock tradition about Jesus clearly reflects his central idea of the kingdom. The disciples are to pray for its coming and set their hope on the future realization of its fullness.[15] According to John P. Meier,

> in the only prayer that Jesus ever taught his disciples (as far as we know), the first concern voiced in the petitions is not a need or problem of this present world but rather a strictly eschatological desire that God reveal himself in all his power and glory ("hallowed be your name") by coming to Israel to reign fully and definitively as king ("your kingdom come").[16]

Finally, in a saying taken by nearly all to be authentic (since it concerns an imminent expectation), or at least earlier than its parousia-oriented parallel in Mark 13:29, Jesus says:

> "So also, when you see these things taking place, you know that the kingdom of God is near." (Luke 21:31)

Jesus saw in the unfolding events associated with the coming destruction of Jerusalem a harbinger of the imminent kingdom of God. We can therefore conclude that Jesus viewed the kingdom of God as a future reality. This leaves us with no small problem: how can we combine these clear indications of a future kingdom with Jesus' teachings about the kingdom as a present, operative reality?

Vandenhoeck & Ruprecht, 1964) 69-73; Meier, *A Marginal Jew,* 2.291-302; B. D. Chilton, *Pure Kingdom: Jesus' Vision of God* (Grand Rapids: Eerdmans, 1996) 57-60; J. Gnilka, *Jesus von Nazaret: Botschaft und Geschichte* (rev. ed.; Freiburg: Herder, 1993) 142-44.

12. See J. Jeremias, *Prayers of Jesus* (trans. J. Bowden, C. Burchard, and J. Reumann; London: SCM, 1967) 98.

13. See H. Schürmann, *Gottes Reich — Jesu Geschick: Jesu ureigener Tod im Licht seiner Basileia-Verkündigung* (Freiburg: Herder, 1983) 11-12.

14. Weiß, *Predigt,* 72.

15. On "day," cf. Kümmel, *Promise,* 36-43.

16. Meier, *A Marginal Jew,* 2.302.

Continuity of the Future with the Present[17]

According to Jesus, those who would enter into the kingdom and enjoy its magnificence were none other than those who followed him and responded positively to his message and ministry. Since it was the essence of Jesus' preaching to declare that the kingdom was then operative (cf. Luke 4:43; 8:1; 9:11; Matt. 4:23; 9:35 with 24:14), those who were responding to him appropriately were in some sense being taken up into the kingdom itself. Thus, we read in Luke 14:15-24:

> One of the dinner guests, on hearing this, said to him, "Blessed is anyone who will eat bread in the kingdom of God!" Then Jesus said to him, "Someone gave a great dinner and invited many. At the time for the dinner he sent his slave to say to those who had been invited, 'Come; for everything is ready now.' But they all alike began to make excuses. The first said to him, 'I have bought a piece of land, and I must go out and see it; please accept my regrets.' Another said, 'I have bought five yoke of oxen, and I am going to try them out; please accept my regrets.' Another said, 'I have just been married, and therefore I cannot come.' So the slave returned and reported this to his master. Then the owner of the house became angry and said to his slave, 'Go out at once into the streets and lanes of the town and bring in the poor, the crippled, the blind, and the lame.' And the slave said, 'Sir, what you ordered has been done, and there is still room.' Then the master said to the slave, 'Go out into the roads and lanes, and compel people to come in, so that my house may be filled. For I tell you, none of those who were invited will taste my dinner.'"

This is the career mission of Jesus: to usher others into the kingdom through the proclamation of its arrival, through participation in meals, and through his mighty deeds. Consequently, to his special followers, Jesus says:

> "You are those who have stood by me in my trials; and I confer on you, just as my Father has conferred on me, a kingdom, so that you

---

17. This theme has been emphasized by Beasley-Murray, *Jesus and the Kingdom*, and J. Becker, *Jesus von Nazaret* (New York: de Gruyter, 1996) 124-30.

may eat and drink at my table in my kingdom, and you will sit on thrones judging the twelve tribes of Israel." (Luke 22:28-30)

That is, those who respond to Jesus now are those who will share the benefits of the kingdom that Jesus is presently inaugurating for Israel.

Jesus instructed and enabled the Twelve, and especially Peter, to extend his work for the kingdom:

"I will give you the keys of the kingdom of heaven, and whatever you bind on earth will be bound in heaven, and whatever you loose on earth will be loosed in heaven." (Matt. 16:19)

Though intense debate has been generated by this logion, it is nonetheless clear that Peter is granted the privilege to do what Jesus has already done: proclaim forgiveness and judgment in light of the dawning kingdom. Others, too, are granted this ministry of extending the kingdom; thus, in Luke 9:60, a would-be disciple is exhorted to "go and proclaim the kingdom of God," and this is broadened into the larger mission of the Twelve and the Seventy (cf. Luke 10:9, 11). Each of these extensions is connected with the ministry of preaching and actualizing the kingdom of God. Jesus charges the Seventy to proclaim these words:

"Whenever you enter a town and its people welcome you, eat what is set before you; cure the sick who are there, and say to them, 'The kingdom of God has come near to you.' But whenever you enter a town and they do not welcome you, go out into its streets and say, 'Even the dust of your town that clings to our feet, we wipe off in protest against you. Yet know this: the kingdom of God has come near.'" (Luke 10:8-11)

The result of this special opportunity is further extended to enable that same group of leaders to rule the twelve tribes in the kingdom (Matt. 19:28). The import of this text is clear: Jesus believed that he was inaugurating the kingdom, and he enabled the closest of his followers to be incorporated into this actualization of the promises of God by sending them out to extend the kingdom. In addition, he clearly taught that those who responded would later populate the kingdom that God would grant to Israel at the end of days.

The future kingdom is the incomparable effect of the present actualization of the kingdom by Jesus. In the parable of the seed growing secretly (Mark 4:26-29), the harvest emerges from the invisibly growing seed, but the seed is being planted *now*. The parable of the mustard seed makes a similar point: the small, insignificant seed that has been already planted and is presently growing (i.e., the ragtag group around Jesus) is the same seed that will grow into a plant large enough to shade Gentiles when God manifests the fullness of his rule — "when Israel becomes what her god intends her to become"[18] (Mark 4:30-32).

An Uncertain, but Imminent Time

The most debated topic about Jesus since the days of Reimarus, but especially since Weiß and Schweitzer, concerns time: when did Jesus think the kingdom would come in its fullness? Imminently, within a generation, as some texts seem to imply (Matt. 10:23; Mark 9:1; 13:30)? If so, was Jesus not mistaken?[19] If he was, how can he be worshipped as Son of God or confessed as savior? Or did Jesus think the kingdom would come in some distant future, as so many orthodox Christians have maintained for two millennia? How do we account for the evidence suggesting that Jesus anticipated an imminent end? In what follows, I will support the view that Jesus expected the imminent arrival of the kingdom. Scholars have too easily moved from this observation to accuse Jesus of human error or to offer a complete reinterpretation. But as Bruce D. Chilton has said, "What is inconvenient for modern purposes should not be wished away from ancient sources."[20]

---

18. N. T. Wright, *Jesus and the Victory of God* (Christian Origins and the Question of God, vol. 2; Minneapolis: Fortress, 1996) 241. Wright uses "god" in lower case. See his *The New Testament and the People of God* (Christian Origins and the Question of God, vol. 1; Minneapolis: Fortress, 1992) xiv-xv.

19. A good sketch of the issues can be found in Meyer, *Aims of Jesus*, 242-49. Meyer correctly notes that Jesus was a Jewish prophet and that prophetic knowledge is inherently ambiguous and metaphorical, rather than determinate.

20. Chilton, *Pure Kingdom*, 9.

Three Critical Texts

In the mission of the Twelve, as recorded by Matthew, we read:

> "When they persecute you in one town, flee to the next; for truly I tell you, you will not have gone through all the towns of Israel before the Son of Man comes." (Matt. 10:23)

Just before Mark records the transfiguration, he writes:

> "Truly I tell you, there are some standing here who will not taste death until they see that the kingdom of God has come with power." (Mark 9:1)

And, in his final discourse, Jesus says of the destruction of Jerusalem:

> "Truly I tell you, this generation will not pass away until all these things have taken place." (Mark 13:30 pars.)

What are we to make of these texts, which on nearly any reading suggest that Jesus thought something catastrophic, if not final and conclusive, would happen shortly, within a generation? No amount of exegetical gymnastics can evade their obvious import.[21] Jesus thought (and surely no one made such sayings up and put them onto the lips of Jesus) that God would bring final deliverance to Israel; he would forgive her sins and end her exile; he would restore the temple in all its purity and wipe her enemies from the land. All this, Jesus thought, would happen within one generation, that is, within about 30 to 40 years. In the following sections, I will argue that Jesus had an imminent expectation and that this view is consistent with the prophetic movement in Israel. His perception was not erroneous. In its limitation, ignorance, and ambiguity, prophetic knowledge is not erroneous knowledge, but it is different from everyday, empirical knowledge. Jesus' vision for the fu-

---

21. Some scholars argue that these logia are products of a later Christian eschatology that attributed belief in an imminent end to Jesus, a view more representative of German than either British or American scholarship. See, e.g., Meier, *A Marginal Jew*, 2.336-48; H. Merklein, *Jesu Botschaft von der Gottesherrshaft* (SBS 111; Stuttgart: Katholisches Bibelwerk, 1983) 51-58; Gnilka, *Jesus*, 154-55; Schürmann, *Gottes Reich*, 39-41.

ture kingdom was connected to his vision of the destruction of Jerusalem as God's judgment on Israel for her persistent refusal to turn back to the covenant. These were his prophetic particulars — his burden, if you will. He did not see beyond the destruction of Jerusalem but connected both the final judgment and the final deliverance with that event. In other words, like Jewish prophets of old,[22] Jesus saw the next event — in his case, the destruction in A.D. 70 — as the end event of history.

General Observations

First, it is unquestionable that Jesus excited apocalyptic, or at least enthusiastic, expectations about an imminent fulfillment of God's promises to Israel. Thus, we read in Luke 19:11:

> As they were listening to this, he went on to tell a parable, because he was near Jerusalem, and because they supposed that the kingdom of God was to appear immediately.

Later, in a comment by the author of Acts, we read:

> So when they had come together, they asked him, "Lord, is this the time when you will restore the kingdom to Israel?" (Acts 1:6)

So, besides the three critical texts cited above, we have here two further evidences of Jesus exciting his audiences about the future kingdom as an imminent reality to be actualized on earth.[23] Even if Jesus had to calm his audience down, and even if he had to do this regularly, it still remains that his audience thought he was teaching an imminent realization of the kingdom. And, to the degree that we think Jesus was a good teacher and capable of communicating his thoughts intelligibly and coherently (and few would deny this), we must also argue that, if his audiences thought like this, he must have believed in such and taught such about the future. In other words, since Jesus was such a

22. See Becker, *Jesus von Nazaret*, 267-75; Wright, *Jesus and the Victory of God*, 147-97.
23. See also Matt. 23:37-39; Luke 12:54-56; John 6:15.

good teacher, we have every right to think that the impulsive hopes of his audience were on target. This is not to say that they, at times, drew incorrect inferences or came to inaccurate conclusions about time or about content, but it is to admit that Jesus believed in an imminent realization of the kingdom to restore Israel and that he taught this with utter clarity.

Second, Jesus considered the time for the full realization of the kingdom to be incalculable. This is made clear in Luke 17:20-21:

> Once Jesus was asked by the Pharisees when the kingdom of God was coming, and he answered, "The kingdom of God is not coming with things that can be observed; nor will they say, 'Look, here it is!' or 'There it is!' For, in fact, the kingdom of God is among you."

Much debate has been given to the meaning of the words "not with things that can be observed." [24] This expression describes observation of various items, for example, physical symptoms, heavenly bodies, and even rules and commandments. One view contends that "not with things that can be observed" and "among you" are virtually synonymous expressions, the point being that the kingdom cannot be observed because it is an inward experience. Others have seen two different ideas being presented: a denial of an apocalyptic timetable and an affirmation of the presence of the kingdom in an inauspicious manner. Though some have seen in this expression a denial on the part of Jesus that the kingdom would come on Passover night,[25] it is better to see here a general denial by Jesus of the value of reckoning the date of the arrival of God's kingdom on the basis of previous revelations and correlating them to world events so that one might know where one is in the plan of the ages. The time for the arrival of the kingdom is unknown to humans.[26]

Third, the precise time of the arrival of God's final judgment and deliverance of Israel was unknown even to Jesus.[27]

---

24. On this logion, cf. Beasley-Murray, *Jesus and the Kingdom,* 97-103, upon whom I rely for the following discussion.

25. The view was maintained by A. Strobel, "Die Passa-Erwartung als urchristliches Problem in Lc 17.20f," *ZNW* 49 (1958) 157-96.

26. See Beasley-Murray, *Jesus and the Kingdom,* 99-100.

27. See Kümmel, *Promise,* 40-43; C. L. Holman, *Till Jesus Comes: Origins of Christian Apocalyptic Expectation* (Peabody, Mass.: Hendrickson, 1996) 134-37.

"But about that day or hour no one knows, neither the angels in heaven, nor the Son, but only the Father." (Mark 13:32)

No one can reasonably contest the authenticity of this verse, for no one in the early church would have attributed any kind of limitations of knowledge to Jesus. Although Jesus knew that the fullness of the kingdom was imminent (cf. Luke 21:31), and that "all these things" (Mark 13:30) would take place within one generation,[28] there were limitations to what he did know about that future: he did not know "that day or hour." He knew *in general* that "all these things" would take place within one generation, but he did not know *in particular* the precise time. Thus, imminence and ignorance (or limited knowledge) are compatible features of Jesus' vision of the future for Israel.

Fourth, Jesus' expectation of an imminent end had an ethical corollary: get ready! The imminent appearing of God for judgment, effected through the use of Rome in destroying Jerusalem and its temple, was supposed to compel Jesus' audience into preparedness:

"Beware, keep alert; for you do not know when the time will come. It is like a man going on a journey, when he leaves home and puts his slaves in charge, each with his work, and commands the doorkeeper to be on the watch. Therefore, keep awake — for you do not know when the master of the house will come, in the evening, or at midnight, or at cockcrow, or at dawn, or else he may find you asleep when he comes suddenly. And what I say to you I say to all: Keep awake." (Mark 13:33-37)

"Be dressed for action and have your lamps lit; be like those who are waiting for their master to return from the wedding banquet, so that they may open the door for him as soon as he comes and knocks. Blessed are those slaves whom the master finds alert when he comes; truly I tell you, he will fasten his belt and have them sit down to eat, and he will come and serve them. If he comes during the middle of the night, or near dawn, and finds them so, blessed are those slaves." (Luke 12:35-38, from L tradition)

28. I am unconvinced by the arguments of some that Mark 13:32//Matt. 24:36 refers not to the destruction of Jerusalem but to the final day. It is far simpler to explain the whole text (Mark 13 pars.) as referring to the destruction of Jerusalem.

"Keep awake therefore, for you do not know on what day your Lord is coming. But understand this: if the owner of the house had known in what part of the night the thief was coming, he would have stayed awake and would not have let his house be broken into. Therefore you also must be ready, for the Son of Man is coming at an unexpected hour."[29] (Matt. 24:42-44, from Q)

What this evidence implies is that Jesus' vision of the future was not simply an apocalyptic insight into what God was about to bring about for Israel. Rather, his knowledge of the future was granted to him in order to ready Israel for the coming day.

Jesus' limited knowledge generated a strand of ethical exhortation that was also typical of Judaism. Because Israelites did not know when all of history would be wrapped up, they were to be faithful to the covenant stipulations God had provided. So also with Jesus: because he did not know precisely when the kingdom would come, and because the time of tribulation would be "cut short for the sake of the elect" (Mark 13:20), his followers were to be faithful so that they would be saved (Mark 13:13; cf. Luke 17:26-27, 34-35 par.; 12:42-46 par.; Matt. 25:1-46). Neither Jesus nor the disciples knew exactly when the kingdom would come. But it was imminent.

Exegetical Observations

We need now to examine more carefully the three critical texts cited above (Matt. 10:23; Mark 9:1; 13:30).[30] Matthew 10:23, a logion with no parallel in either Mark or Luke, but with significant connections to the larger parallels in Mark 13,[31] states that the Twelve will not have returned from their mission to, or flight through, Israel (cf. Matt. 10:5-6) "before the Son of Man comes." It simply will not do to

---

29. I would also place Luke 18:1-6; Matt. 24:45-51; 25:1-13 in this category of data. On all this, cf. Kümmel, *Promise*, 54-64.

30. See M. Künzi, *Das Naherwartungslogion Matthäus 10,23: Geschichte seiner Auslegung* (BGBE 9; Tübingen: Mohr Siebeck, 1970); idem, *Das Naherwartungslogion Markus 9,1 par: Geschichte seiner Auslegung, mit einem Nachwort zur Auslegungs- geschichte von Markus 13,30* (BGBE 21; Tübingen: Mohr Siebeck, 1977).

31. See S. McKnight, "Jesus and the End-Time: Matthew 10:23," *SBLASP* (1986) 501-20; see also Kümmel, *Promise*, 61-64.

suggest that Jesus envisioned an indeterminate time, stretching perhaps for millennia, for the mission to the Jews. This attributes non-
sense to Jesus; why suggest to fleeing missionaries that they may, after all, never be delivered from their flight if the Son of Man waits for
millennia? The logion only makes sense if the limited mission of the
Twelve is in view, if their persecution and need to flee are up-front,
and if temporal imminence is suggested by the phrase "before the
Son of Man comes." Clearly then, something is in view that will give
them insufficient time to flee from persecuting Israelites.[32] Such a
time span would permit anything from a few weeks to a few decades,
depending on how long it took for them to raise enough hackles to
have to flee like mad to escape.

But what does the phrase "before the Son of Man comes" mean?
Several options are available.[33] First, it could refer to the Son of Man
descending from heaven to earth to reestablish his reign. While the
weight of much of Christian tradition is behind this view, this event
simply did not happen during the life of Jesus' disciples, and it would
be strange for a Christian writer to record this saying if Jesus was
wrong. Second, it could refer metaphorically to the Son of Man coming
in judgment and be understood as an image for the destruction of Jerusalem. Inasmuch as "kingdom of God" can refer to multiple events and
experiences, so might the "coming" of the Son of Man have a certain
plasticity in fulfillment. Third, it could refer, again metaphorically, to
the Son of Man's ascending before the Ancient of Days, with his people,
in vindication. In this case, we would need, if the referent corresponds
to an empirical event, to look for something in which Jesus himself was
vindicated before God in such a way that the disciples were able to find
consolation in the midst of their persecution. Since the first option
should be ruled out for the reasons given above, we need to decide between the second and third options.

Since the Son of Man is connected with judgment in other early
evidence (cf. Matt. 13:36-43; 24:37-41), there is support for the second
view. And, if one is to take history itself into view, the destruction of Je-

---

32. On the meaning of "finish" in the sense of "finish fleeing" rather than "finish
evangelizing," see McKnight, "Jesus and the End-Time," 517-20. Kümmel, *Promise*, 64,
extends the time limit: "before the *complete* discharge of their missionary commis-
sion."

33. An excellent discussion may be found in D. A. Hagner, *Matthew 1–13* (WBC
33A; Dallas: Word, 1993) 278-80.

rusalem corresponds in almost any prophetic view of history to what Jesus predicted. On the other hand, if we take Mark 13:24-27 (par. Matt. 24:29-31; Luke 21:25-28) as poetic, apocalyptic imagery for the vindication of the Son of Man before the Ancient of Days (i.e., God), then Matt. 10:23 could be made to conform to such a view quite easily and naturally. That is, the Twelve would not have time to finish evangelizing before the Son of Man (Jesus) would somehow be vindicated. While this might refer to such things as the resurrection, the gift of the Spirit at Pentecost, or the success of the Gentile mission, the clear association of the vindication in Mark 13:24-27 with the destruction of Jerusalem as God's seal of approval on Jesus would suggest that it refers most probably to that event. While it is difficult to decide between the second and third options, the preponderance of evidence favors the third view more than the second. The disciples will escape persecution because God will act to vindicate Jesus, as Son of Man, by permitting Rome to wreak God's vengeance on a disobedient people.[34] Accordingly, Jesus implies in this logion that the time is short for Israel to respond. If Israel does not turn back to covenant faithfulness, rejecting her present course, and turn to the forgiveness Jesus offers to those who wish to end the exile, she will be crushed. But Israel must shape up soon, because the time left is insufficient for the Twelve to go through the cities of Israel.

We turn now to Mark 9:1: "And he said to them, 'Truly I tell you, there are some standing here who will not taste death until they see that the kingdom of God has come with power.'"[35] Following Peter's confession of Jesus as Messiah, and Jesus' affirmation of the necessity of suffering, Jesus informs his followers that the kingdom of God certainly will appear in strength before some of them die.[36] All three synoptic Gospels place this logion in the context of the transfiguration. The expression "who will not taste death," in conjunction with "there are some standing

34. See Wright, *Jesus and the Victory of God*, 510-19.

35. A good recent study is D. A. Hagner, *Matthew 14–28* (WBC 33B; Dallas: Word, 1995) 485-87; also Chilton, *Pure Kingdom*, 62-66. For further analysis, cf. T. W. Manson, *The Teaching of Jesus: Studies of Its Form and Content* (Cambridge: Cambridge University Press, 1939) 279-84; Kümmel, *Promise*, 25-29; L. Goppelt, *Theology of the New Testament* (2 vols.; trans. J. E. Alsup; ed. J. Roloff; Grand Rapids: Eerdmans, 1981-82) 1.57.

36. For a careful discussion of these issues, see B. D. Chilton, *God in Strength: Jesus' Announcement of the Kingdom* (SNTSU B:1; Freistadt: Plöchl, 1979) 64-65, 251-74.

here," is a Jewish way of saying "before some of you die."[37] The logion therefore has in view the normal life span of those who heard Jesus speak, which perhaps extended another 30 to 40 years. But when this logion is followed in Mark 9:2 by "Six days later," we become suspicious that Mark is responsible for positioning the logion right before his account of the transfiguration. Thus, as G. R. Beasley-Murray summarizes the situation: "More important, it hardly seems realistic to suppose that Jesus would state that some of those standing there with him would not *taste death* before they would see the arrival of the kingdom of God if he were referring to an event [the transfiguration] that was to take place *six days later*."[38] Thus, we can reasonably conclude that Jesus stated that his disciples would not die before they saw something highly significant having to do with the kingdom of God.

What might that be? The church has given many answers, and one of the most popular is that Mark had it right: it refers to the transfiguration.[39] Others have variously suggested the resurrection, the parousia, and the destruction of Jerusalem. Because the natural rendering of the introductory clause favors an event toward the end of what might have been reasonably expected of the life span of the disciples, I would argue against the transfiguration or resurrection as the primary referent of this logion. This leaves us the option of the parousia or the destruction of Jerusalem. Matthew 10:23, however, seems to give us ground to see these two options as nearly identical in that the "the Son of Man coming in his kingdom" (which is how Matthew 16:28 renders what we have in our logion in Mark 9:1) may well be a metaphorical description of the vindication of the Son of Man. That is, before Jesus' disciples died they would see Jesus vindicated as the true prophet of God to the nation. It is reasonable, then, to argue that this vindication took place when Jerusalem was sacked by Rome as God's punishment for covenant unfaithfulness.

Jesus therefore predicted a vindication of himself and his followers before the death of the disciples. This view fits admirably with the previous context (Mark 8:34-38) and gives adequate ground for Mark's insertion of the logion before his account of the transfiguration. In the previous context, Jesus promises the disciples that, though they would

37. For an alternate view, see Chilton, *Pure Kingdom*, 65.
38. *Jesus and the Kingdom*, 188.
39. E.g., W. L. Lane, *The Gospel according to Mark* (NICNT; Grand Rapids: Eerdmans, 1974) 312-14.

suffer like him, they would be vindicated by God. And just as Jesus was to suffer the ignominy of a humiliating death at the hands of the leaders in Jerusalem, so he would be vindicated. The disciples need to be assured of Jesus' vindication, and this is precisely how the transfiguration ought to be understood — as proleptic vindication. Hence Mark's redaction.

Finally, we need to consider Mark 13:30, "Truly I tell you, this generation will not pass away until all these things have taken place." This little logion has been more resisted than understood. Jesus affirms here that "all these things" (an expression that probably refers to everything described in Mark 13:1-29, including the parousia pericope and the "it is near" statement of 13:29) will take place within one "generation" (cf. Mark 8:12, 38; 9:19; Matt. 11:16; 12:41-42, 45; 23:36).[40] "Generation" on the lips of Jesus is not a positive evaluation: the "generation" he sees in front of him is sinful, faithless, bent on violence, and destined for destruction (cf. Gen. 7:1; Deut. 1:35; 32:5; Ps. 95:10).[41] That generation, as history has informed us, suffered horribly at the hands of the Romans.

To summarize: Jesus clearly taught that a grand display of the kingdom of God and the coming of the Son of Man would take place within one generation. His followers would be persecuted and chased (Matt. 10:23) but delivered; those who followed him would not die before they saw this climactic event; and everything predicted about Jerusalem's destruction and God wrapping up his plan for Israel would take place before the current generation died out. Jesus believed in an imminent display of the kingdom of God, and he used the metaphor of the coming of the Son of Man to refer to this kingdom event. Furthermore, the evidence suggests that this event is especially, though not entirely, connected with Jesus' prophetic vision of the destruction of Jerusalem as God's unleashing of his punishment on Israel for its choice to follow a path leading to violence and covenant unfaithfulness. Exactly when that great event would occur was not clear to Jesus, but he knew that it would take place within one generation. He also encouraged his followers to pray with a yearning desire for the immediate fulfillment of the coming kingdom.

---

40. See Kümmel, *Promise*, 59-61.

41. See E. Lövestam, *Jesus and 'This Generation'* (CBNT 25; Stockholm: Almqvist & Wiksell, 1995); M. Reiser, *Jesus and Judgment: The Eschatological Proclamation in Its Jewish Context* (trans. L. M. Maloney; Minneapolis: Fortress, 1997) 215-17.

Was Jesus Mistaken?

At this point we need to consider briefly the question of whether or not Jesus was mistaken in his expectation of an imminent realization of the kingdom of God.[42] The evidence above clearly reveals a vision for the future with a limited horizon: Jesus prophesied that God would wrap things up within one generation. However, instead of saying that Jesus was mistaken, that he was either a false prophet or a misguided fanatic, we ought to admit that his knowledge of the future was limited in the same way that the Hebrew prophets' visions were limited to the events of their respective generations.[43] Further, Jesus' knowledge of the future was expressed in metaphorical and poetic images of collapse, judgment, and deliverance. Within this limitation, Jesus prophesied the destruction of Jerusalem as the climactic event in Israel's history that would end the privilege of Israel in God's plan. He also attached to this the final resolution of Israel through the images connected with remnant and redemption.[44] The historical particulars remain, because Jesus was himself limited in his knowledge of the future. But he was not wrong: Jerusalem *was* sacked (as he said it would be) as an act of God's judgment on Israel for its unfaithfulness to the covenant. Jesus' followers outlived that destruction. These people did not straggle along, limping for some hope to sustain them; instead, confidently and unflaggingly they carried what they thought was the good news about Jesus to the whole Roman empire and, at the same time, continued to believe in the hope they learned from both Judaism and Jesus: that some day God would act to bring all of ordinary history to a closure that would feature Israel as God's people and Jesus as his Messiah. I agree, then, with Ben F. Meyer: "The disparity [between prediction and history] is not well described as error. None of the prophets were mistaken, least of all the greatest of them."[45]

It remains for us now to explain how Jesus' fuller vision of the fu-

---

42. See Meyer, *Aims of Jesus*, 242-49; for an alternate view, see A. E. Harvey, *Jesus and the Constraints of History* (Philadelphia: Westminster, 1982) 66-97.

43. See esp. Meyer, *Aims of Jesus*, 246-47.

44. Translating this historical particularity into existential crisis, so typical of post-Bultmann German scholarship, is simply a convenient way of evading a historical issue and making Jesus congenial to modern sensibilities.

45. Meyer, *Christus Faber*, 56.

ture related to his prediction of the destruction of Jerusalem. Did he see a delay of millennia after the destruction, or did he tie the two items together?[46] Where did he place the final judgment? Did he envision a heaven "up above" into which true Israelites would enter? What about the age to come and rewards? Were these separate issues for Jesus, or were they all tied into his vision of A.D. 70? I will argue in what follows that Jesus saw no further than A.D. 70 and that he thought everything would be wrapped up in conjunction with that catastrophic event for Israel. In seeing the future in this way, Jesus was not mistaken; rather, he envisioned the future very much like Jewish prophets of the Israelite tradition did and not all that different from the way of contemporary Jewish prophets.[47]

The Judgment of God

Dominating the future for Jesus was God's final scrutiny of individual Israelites, who would have to give an account of their behavior if they wanted to enter the kingdom.[48] No Jewish prophet before or after Jesus ever gave more attention to eternal consequences than he did. What Christians have believed about hell has been constructed almost entirely out of the materials this supposedly soft and kind Galilean carpenter provided.[49] For Jesus this future judgment would be realized historically in the destruction of Jerusalem and would usher in the kingdom. In what follows I shall examine the following points about the judgment: (1) it will be Jesus' own decision, (2) it will be effected through the angels of the Son of Man and his twelve apostles, (3) it will

46. That delay was an integral part of Jewish eschatology has been shown by Holman, *Till Jesus Comes.* See also Kümmel, *Promise,* 64-87. The critical evidence includes Mark 2:19; 8:34; 10:35-45; 12:1-12; 14:25, 29; Matt. 10:28, 39; 23:38-39; Luke 6:22; 11:41; 17:22; 18:7-8.

47. See esp. W. Heard, "Revolutionary Movements," *DJG,* 689-98; P. W. Barnett, "The Jewish Sign Prophets — A.D. 40-70 — Their Intentions and Origins," *NTS* 27 (1981) 679-97; Wright, *Jesus and the Victory of God,* 145-474; R. Gray, *Prophetic Figures in Late Second Temple Jewish Palestine: The Evidence from Josephus* (New York: Oxford, 1993).

48. Reiser, *Jesus and Judgment.*

49. For a survey of the material, see A. E. Bernstein, *The Formation of Hell: Death and Retribution in the Ancient and Early Christian Worlds* (Ithaca, N.Y.: Cornell University Press, 1993); J. Lunde, "Heaven and Hell," *DJG,* 307-12; S. Travis, "Judgment," *DJG,* 408-11.

separate true Israelites from false Israelites eternally, and (4) it will involve all nations.[50]

We need to begin by sketching the evidence that Jesus predicted the destruction of Jerusalem. Some of Jesus' sayings are rather cryptic, but they remain clear if one recognizes that they envision a future event involving an earthly catastrophe. The data include the following logia:

> "Put your sword back into its place; for all who take the sword will perish by the sword." (Matt. 26:52)

> "What then will the owner of the vineyard do? He will come and destroy the tenants and give the vineyard to others." (Mark 12:9)

> "Jerusalem, Jerusalem, the city that kills the prophets and stones those who are sent to it! How often have I desired to gather your children together as a hen gathers her brood under her wings, and you were not willing! See, your house is left to you. And I tell you, you will not see me until the time comes when you say, 'Blessed is the one who comes in the name of the Lord.'" (Luke 13:34-35)

> As he came near and saw the city, he wept over it, saying, "If you, even you, had only recognized on this day the things that make for peace! But now they are hidden from your eyes. Indeed, the days will come upon you, when your enemies will set up ramparts around you and surround you, and hem you in on every side. They will crush you to the ground, you and your children within you, and they will not leave within you one stone upon another; because you did not recognize the time of your visitation from God." (Luke 19:41-44)

Besides these remarks of Jesus, and prior to the accusations leveled against him (cf. Mark 14:58; 15:29-30), stands Mark 13:1-32.[51] Af-

---

50. Notably absent from Jesus' vision of the final judgment are two typical Jewish features: (1) a final battle with Satan and the forces of evil; and (2) a battle with pagan nations. The first might be explained as something that has taken place in Jesus (cf. Luke 10:17-20); perhaps the second is missing because Jesus had an inclusive vision of who constituted Israel.

51. See also Wright, *Jesus and the Victory of God*, 339-68; Beasley-Murray, *Jesus and the Kingdom*, 322-37; Kümmel, *Promise*, 95-104; D. Wenham, *The Rediscovery of Jesus' Eschatological Discourse* (GP 4; Sheffield: JSOT, 1984).

ter predicting the toppling of the stones of the temple (13:2), Jesus is asked by his closest followers, "When will this be, and what will be the sign that all these things are about to be accomplished?" (13:4). In typically metaphorical and colorful language, Jesus draws from the language of the Hebrew prophets in speaking of the signs (13:5-8), the beginnings of troubles (13:9-13), the abomination of desolation (13:14-20), the rise of false messiahs (13:21-23), and then of the "coming of the Son of Man" (13:24-27). These are finished off with a parable (13:28-29) and a comment about his ignorance of the precise timing of these events (i.e., the destruction of the temple and its forewarnings; 13:30-32).

Most of what Jesus predicted came true; nearly all of it can be read in historical form in Josephus's *The Jewish War*.[52] What Jesus said would take place did take place in the events surrounding the Roman destruction of Jerusalem. Because many Christians have sought to find in Mark 13 a description of events that are still to come, as a prelude to the second coming of Christ, they often fail to observe that Jesus was primarily concerned with the destruction of Jerusalem in A.D. 70 and

---

52. The following enumerated items are themes of Jesus' prophecies about the future that have parallels in Josephus and that suggest predictive prophecy: (1) *false prophetic/messianic claims:* War 2.252-65; 2.585-94 (John of Gischala); 4.529-44 (Simon ben Gioras); (2) *hideous persecution:* 2.297-308, esp. 306-8 (Florus); 2.457-80; 2.494-98 (50,000 Alexandrian Jews slaughtered in A.D. 66); 3.59-63 (Galilee a "scene of fire and blood"); 3.336-39, esp. 3.336 (surrender of Jotapata); 3.414-27, esp. 426-27 (Joppa exodus leads to sea of blood); 3.485-91 (Tarichaeae valley full of corpses); 3.522-31 (massacre on Sea of Galilee: blood, corpses, stench); 4.305-44 (bloody insurrection in Temple courts led by Zealots and Idumaeans; high priest Ananus killed); 5.446-59 (500 crucifixions per day); 5.512-26 (death everywhere); 6.351-55 (city burns); 6.369 ("Not a spot in the city was left bare: every corner had its corpse, the victim of famine or sedition"); (3) *defiling of Temple:* 4.377-88 (by Zealots); 5.11-38, esp. 16-18 (lakes of blood in the Temple); 5.527-33 (high priestly murders); 6.1-8 (war ruined it all); 6.249-66 (Temple burned); (4) *horrors of famine:* 5.429-38; 6.193-213 (mother devours her own child); (5) *the ultimate in pain:* 5.442-45; (6) *flights ending in horrific murders:* 5.548-52 (2,000 Jewish refugees ripped open by Syrians and Arabs when it was discovered that one Jew had golden coins in his excrement); 6.366-73 (flights to caves and among rocks); (7) *constant observation that all this was the judgment of God* (6.93-110); (8) *corresponding events connected with the last days of Jerusalem before its total destruction:* 6.288-309 (star and comet [birth of Jesus?]; midnight light around the altar [birth of Jesus?]; cow gives birth to lamb; gates open of their own accord [death of Jesus?]; chariots in the sky, with battalions; invisible voice saying, "We are departing hence"; a prophet named Jesus [not Jesus of Nazareth] announces judgment).

that the details of his predictions were fulfilled in that very event. To ignore this evidence is to misinterpret the words of Jesus, to rip him from his historical context, and to deprive him of the prophetic status he deserves. To find just where Jesus predicts the destruction of Jerusalem, we must look to Mark 13:24-27:

> "But in those days, after that suffering
>> the sun will be darkened,
>>> and the moon will not give its light,
>> and the stars will be falling from heaven,
>>> and the powers in heaven will be shaken.
> Then they will see 'the Son of Man coming in clouds'
>> with great power and glory.
> Then he will send out the angels,
>> and gather his elect from the four winds,
> from the ends of the earth to the ends of heaven."

Here Jesus describes the sack of Jerusalem in apocalyptic, metaphorical language of the sort used by Jewish prophets for political crises.[53] These verses picture a political crisis and judgment (including, but not limited to, the destruction of Jerusalem in A.D. 70) in terms of the apocalyptic vindication of the Son of Man (cf. Isa. 13:9-10; 34:4; Ezek. 32:7; Amos 8:9; Joel 2:10; 3:15; Zech. 2:6-12; Mark 14:62). As others have recently argued, this pericope does not describe the descent of Jesus in some distant future to reclaim his church but what in fact did take place in the year 70: Jesus, the Messiah, was vindicated when his words about the nation came true.

Jesus announced the coming kingdom and its judgment, he called Israel to repent of its unfaithfulness, and he began to form a remnant of people who would be ready for that judgment when it came. He predicted that this would take place if Israel did not respond; when it did take place through Roman agency, the destruction itself functioned as a massive, earthly demonstration that Jesus, the last prophet to Israel, was

---

53. See G. B. Caird, *Saint Luke* (WPC; Philadelphia: Westminster, 1977) 231-32; R. T. France, *Jesus and the Old Testament: His Application of Old Testament Passages to Himself and His Mission* (London: Tyndale, 1971) 227-39, esp. 233-34; see also his *The Gospel according to Matthew* (TNTC; Grand Rapids: Eerdmans, 1985) 333-36, 343-46; Wright, *Jesus and the Victory of God*, 360-65. On the nature of apocalyptic, metaphorical imagery, see G. B. Caird, *The Language and Imagery of the Bible* (Philadelphia: Westminster, 1980) 110-17, 201-71.

right after all. Through the Romans Jesus was vindicated as the true herald of God. This is the limit of what Jesus predicted. He prophesied the coming judgment of God on Israel and saw the rest of history through this vision of the sacking of Jerusalem. As C. H. Dodd said, "Just as the Old Testament prophets saw in the Assyrian or the Babylonian peril the form in which divine judgment on Israel was approaching, so Jesus saw in the growing menace of a clash with Rome a token of coming disaster, in which the sins of the Jewish people would meet their retribution."[54]

We may now look at four features of the judgment itself. First, unlike Jewish prophets before him, but consistent with what he believed about himself (cf. Q: Luke 12:8-9//Matt. 10:32-33), Jesus stated that he would be involved in making the decisions in the final judgment:[55]

> Then the mother of the sons of Zebedee came to him with her sons, and kneeling before him, she asked a favor of him. And he said to her, "What do you want?" She said to him, "Declare that these two sons of mine will sit, one at your right hand and one at your left, in your kingdom." But Jesus answered, "You do not know what you are asking. Are you able to drink the cup that I am about to drink?" They said to him, "We are able." He said to them, "You will indeed drink my cup, but to sit at my right hand and at my left, this is not mine to grant, but it is for those for whom it has been prepared by my Father." (Matt. 20:20-23//Mark 10:35-40)

The mother here thinks of Jesus on the throne, as he surely intimated more than once that he would be, and of his having the say in who sits next to him. This is the foundation of Jesus' view of the future kingdom: he will be enthroned by and next to the Father, the Ancient of Days, to execute judgment.

Another relevant text is the parable of the ten virgins:

> "Then the kingdom of heaven will be like this. Ten bridesmaids took their lamps and went to meet the bridegroom. Five of them were

54. C. H. Dodd, *The Parables of the Kingdom* (London: Nisbet, 1936) 66. See also R. A. Horsley, *Jesus and the Spiral of Violence: Popular Jewish Resistance in Roman Palestine* (San Francisco: Harper & Row, 1987) 285-317, though he has a socio-political critique that I see as too restrictive for all the evidence.

55. See T. W. Manson, *Teaching*, 269; Kümmel, *Promise*, 39, 45, 88-95.

foolish, and five were wise. When the foolish took their lamps, they took no oil with them; but the wise took flasks of oil with their lamps. As the bridegroom was delayed, all of them became drowsy and slept. But at midnight there was a shout, 'Look! Here is the bridegroom! Come out to meet him.' Then all those bridesmaids got up and trimmed their lamps. The foolish said to the wise, 'Give us some of your oil, for our lamps are going out.' But the wise replied, 'No! there will not be enough for you and for us; you had better go to the dealers and buy some for yourselves.' And while they went to buy it, the bridegroom came, and those who were ready went with him into the wedding banquet; and the door was shut. Later the other bridesmaids came also, saying, 'Lord, lord, open to us.' But he replied, 'Truly I tell you, I do not know you.' Keep awake therefore, for you know neither the day nor the hour." (Matt. 25:1-13)

Consistent with an earlier allusive reference to himself as bridegroom (Mark 2:20), Jesus surely intended in this parable to speak of himself and of his future acting as judge. Watchfulness is required if one wants to be ready for the final day. In context, this parable is juxtaposed immediately alongside Jesus' predictions of the destruction of Jerusalem when God wreaks vengeance through Rome on unfaithful Israel. The "coming of the bridegroom" refers to a "coming" in judgment (cf. above on Matt. 10:23). Along lines similar to the parabolic words about Noah's generation (Q: Luke 17:26-27, 34-35//Matt. 24:37-41), here unfaithful Israelites will be taken in judgment, while faithful Israelites will survive to enjoy life in the kingdom. Thus, Jesus is the bridegroom who returns to claim his bride and the one who makes the decisions about who enters the party.

The parable of the talents uses a different scenario to make the same point (Matt. 25:14-30). Jesus likens himself to an owner of land who departs while his workers have time to gain a profit. When their time is done, the owner returns to settle accounts and give a final reckoning. Jesus' final comment is: "For to all those who have, more will be given, and they will have an abundance; but from those who have nothing, even what they have will be taken away" (25:29).

In the parable of the sheep and goats (Matt. 25:31-46), we read:

"When the Son of Man comes in his glory, and all the angels with him, then he will sit on the throne of his glory." (25:31)

Again, Jesus sees himself in the category of the judging Son of Man (cf. Dan. 7:1-28), who judges the nations on the basis of how people respond to Jesus in their treatment of his "little ones" (cf. Luke 12:8-9).

These teachings provoke the question whether we should distinguish between the destruction of Jerusalem (the specific focus of the teachings) and the final judgment, or whether we should see them as one. Since Jesus seems to have made no such distinction, and since the evangelists do not seem to entertain any great lapse of time between the two events, we are left with the conclusion that Jesus saw the destruction of Jerusalem unfolding into the final judgment. Indeed, we may reasonably infer that Jesus saw the destruction as the inauguration of the final judgment itself. Those who survived the Roman attack on Jerusalem would be those who would populate the kingdom.

To round off this picture of Jesus as the final judge, we ought to recall the words of the bandit next to Jesus at the crucifixion:

> "Jesus, remember me when you come into your kingdom." (Luke 23:42)

This man evidently believed that Jesus had a say in the final judgment, since he believed petitioning Jesus could do some good. While some may object to anyone thinking so highly of himself, Jesus apparently did believe that he would be the one making the decision about who would enter the kingdom and who would be excluded from it.

Second, Jesus claimed on a couple of occasions that others would be involved in this final determination. In a Q logion, Jesus promises the Twelve:[56]

> "You are those who have stood by me in my trials; and I confer on you, just as my Father has conferred on me, a kingdom, so that you may eat and drink at my table in my kingdom, and you will sit on thrones judging the twelve tribes of Israel." (Luke 22:28-30)

The Matthean rendering of this saying, though different, makes the same point:

56. See Kümmel, *Promise*, 47-48.

"Truly I tell you, at the renewal of all things, when the Son of Man is seated on the throne of his glory, you who have followed me will also sit on twelve thrones, judging the twelve tribes of Israel." (Matt. 19:28-29)

Matthew's rendering has "Son of Man" and makes the scene more eschatologically final, but his version still matches Luke's in two important ways: (1) the final judgment is effected by the Son of Man, Jesus (Luke has "my table" and "my kingdom"), and (2) the Twelve will judge the twelve tribes of Israel. This vision of Jesus reveals his focus on the nation of Israel as the center of the age to come and his promise to his followers that they would be the ones who would rule in that day.[57]

Jesus also asserted that angels would participate in the final judgment:

"The Son of Man will send his angels, and they will collect out of his kingdom all causes of sin and all evildoers, and they will throw them into the furnace of fire, where there will be weeping and gnashing of teeth. . . . So it will be at the end of the age. The angels will come out and separate the evil from the righteous and throw them into the furnace of fire, where there will be weeping and gnashing of teeth." (Matt. 13:41-42, 49)

It is difficult to tell whether Jesus had in mind different judgments being administered by different agents (here angels, there the Twelve). At any rate, these passages employ poetic imagery and should not be treated as clear snapshots of the future. Jesus evidently used different images under different circumstances to enhance the vision he was seeking to impress upon what he considered to be a disobedient people. Angelic involvement in the final judgment, however, is typically Jewish.[58] What is credited to the activity of angels in Matt. 13:49 is attributed in the parable of the sheep and goats to the Son of Man (Matt. 25:34, 41). However one tries to put all this together, Jesus evidently saw the final judgment as a process that he would enact, sometimes

57. The word "judge" here could describe executing a sentence or ruling. A polemical context would prefer the former meaning, whereas a more stable context (with Jesus as king and the Twelve as the judges) would prefer the latter. For discussion, see Beasley-Murray, *Jesus and the Kingdom*, 273-77; Reiser, *Jesus and Judgment*, 260-61.

58. Cf. Matt. 16:27; 25:31; see also *1 Enoch* 54:6; 63:1.

through his Twelve apostles, sometimes through angels, and sometimes by himself.

Thirdly, however, the impact of the judgment is not ambiguous: Jesus saw a final judgment by which true Israelites would be effectively separated from false Israelites eternally:

> "The Son of Man will send his angels, and they will collect out of his kingdom all causes of sin and all evildoers, and they will throw them into the furnace of fire, where there will be weeping and gnashing of teeth. Then the righteous will shine like the sun in the kingdom of their Father." (Matt. 13:41-43)[59]

Here we have a vision of a future condition in which the angels of the Son of Man will administer his judging will by collecting the sinners out of the kingdom[60] and throwing them into a burning furnace in order to destroy them (Q: Matt. 3:11-12//Luke 3:16-17).[61] The righteous, however, will survive and will remain in that kingdom to enjoy the blessing of God.[62]

Similarly, in the parable of the dragnet (Matt. 13:47-50), the fisher sits on shore with his catch and separates good fish from bad fish. Jesus adds:

> "So it will be at the end of the age. The angels will come out and separate the evil from the righteous[63] and throw them into the furnace of fire, where there will be weeping and gnashing of teeth." (Matt. 13:49-50)

Yet another piece of evidence along this line is Matt. 25:46:

> "And these will go away into eternal punishment, but the righteous into eternal life."

59. See also Matt. 7:24-29; 8:11-12.

60. A description of the nation of Israel, and possibly the land of Israel; cf. Matt. 8:11-12//Luke 13:28-30.

61. See Reiser, *Jesus and Judgment*, 167-93.

62. As with Matt. 24:37-41//Luke 17:26-27, 34-35, salvation is seen here as surviving judgment (the destruction of Jerusalem) and enjoying blessing in the land of Israel.

63. The Greek literally reads "the angels will come and separate the evil ones *out from the midst* of the righteous ones" (Matt. 13:49).

Here again we have the Son of Man effecting a separation of sinners from the righteous, and this in an eternal sense. A final judgment condemns those who defile the law of God and who are unfaithful to God's covenant, and those who survive the scrutiny of God are those who followed John and Jesus when they declared the imminent judgment of God and the need for Israel to repent.

Finally, we need to observe that at least one time Jesus envisioned this final judgment as a judgment on all nations. Thus, we read in the introductory words of the parable of the sheep and goats:

> "When the Son of Man comes in his glory, and all the angels with him, then he will sit on the throne of his glory. All the nations will be gathered before him, and he will separate people one from another as a shepherd separates the sheep from the goats, and he will put the sheep at his right hand and the goats at the left." (Matt. 25:31-33)

In this scene, at least, Jesus thinks of a universal judgment through which he also envisions a judgment of every human being alive.[64] This judgment is assessed according to how individuals have treated the "least of these my brothers" (Jesus' followers)[65] and results in an eternal condition.[66]

This parable is grossly misunderstood if it is torn from the overall context of Jesus' message and read apart from the apocalyptic material about the destruction of Jerusalem (Matthew 23–25 pars.). This parable, too, ought to be connected with Jesus' prediction of the imminent doom of Jerusalem and understood as one more piece of his overall picture of the last day: that day is imminent, and it will begin with a judgment by God on Israel for her disobedience to the covenant. That judgment is actualized, in Jesus' view, in the destruction of Jerusalem. This destruction will be the inauguration of the final judgment, which will separate true Israelites from false Israelites. The false ones will be banned from the kingdom, and the true ones will populate it. There

---

64. See Reiser, *Jesus and Judgment,* 263-301.

65. Cf. Matt. 10:5-16, 40-42. Identifying the "least of these my brothers" with those who have followed Jesus in no way relaxes Jesus' call for mercy and compassion upon all. See Hagner, *Matthew 14–28,* 744-45; Kümmel, *Promise,* 92-95.

66. See S. McKnight, "Eternal Consequences or Eternal Consciousness?" in W. V. Crockett and J. G. Sigountos, eds., *Through No Fault of Their Own? The Fate of Those Who Have Never Heard* (Grand Rapids: Baker, 1991) 147-57.

will be no second chances, though; either people respond to John and Jesus positively, by repenting and following Jesus, or they will be banned from that kingdom forever. Therefore, when Jesus speaks of a judgment on all nations, he has in mind a judgment on Israel (in A.D. 70) that, because of the presence of the worldwide Roman empire, becomes in effect a judgment on all the world. This judgment is based on how people have responded to Jesus and to those who have followed him.

This understanding of the parable of the sheep and goats coheres with what we have already determined: Jesus followed John in announcing an imminent judgment on Israel for disobedience; they both called all Israel to repentance and to righteousness; they threatened that if Israel did not turn from its course of destruction, it would experience an awful disaster; and they both envisioned that those who did respond would survive God's judgment to populate the kingdom forever.

Fellowship with the Father

The kingdom Jesus proclaimed presumes Jewish discourse about the final kingdom or age to come. In Judaism the kingdom typically included the conditions of peace, justice, love, obedience to the law of Moses, God's splendor evident in the temple in Jerusalem, and the preeminence of Israel. Jesus would have assumed all, or at least most, of these conditions. In what follows, however, I will focus on those features of the future kingdom that are either distinctive to Jesus or emphatic in his vision. In Jewish thinking and with Jesus, the kingdom usually assumes an earthly realization. If our goal is to understand Jesus aright, we must learn to rethink Jesus' vision. Popular notions of a timeless, golden spiritual existence in heaven need to give way to the dusty roads, but plush green grass, blue skies, and plentiful harvests associated with the revolution that was to take place in the land of Israel.

A distinctive trait of Jesus' vision is that the kingdom would reflect the Father's character, love, and glory. The subjects of the kingdom, God's purified people, would enjoy fellowship with the Father and would experience his fatherly approbation. The image of God as a loving and authoritative Father now assumes its full importance: the kingdom will be like a family sitting around a table basking in its father's love. Jesus' practice of table fellowship with his followers set the agenda for his vision of the future kingdom (e.g., Mark 2:13-17 pars.; Matt. 11:19//Luke 7:34; Luke 15:1-2):[67] the age to come will be a time of endless table fellowship with God the Father.

To examine this theme we need to revisit Jesus' regular and provocative practice of sharing table. It was an activity characterized by what John Dominic Crossan calls "open commensality," or inclusive fellowship. Jesus invited Israelites of all kinds, including tax collectors, prostitutes, and those otherwise known simply as "sinners," to sit with him and his followers for a meal.[68] These meals were marked by a mutual sharing of life, by Jesus' teaching and telling parables, and by general displays of loving concern for one another. If we are correct that meals provided the occasion for much of Jesus' teaching, then we can infer that Jesus was able to take over these meals by becoming their *de facto* host, setting the agenda and guiding the discussion. Undoubtedly, the most notable feature of Jesus' practice was his inclusion of sinners. Why? Because he dispensed forgiveness for Israel through his teachings and through his actions. By acting out fellowship, Jesus intended to dispense the forgiveness of sins and to create the new community of the restored Israel that would inherit the kingdom.

Jesus saw in his acting out of the restored Israel an anticipation of the future kingdom.[69] His table fellowship and the future kingdom are connected by the following logic: (1) his whole career was devoted to inaugurating and announcing the arrival of the kingdom as the fulfillment of Israel's hope; (2) the most characteristic activity in his ministry was table fellowship with his followers as the establishment of the true community; (3) inasmuch as he regarded the kingdom as both present and future, (4) it follows that his table fellowship with others was itself a social vision for Israel and a preliminary taste of the final kingdom.

This is made clear in one logion of Jesus:[70]

---

67. See Dalman, *Words,* 110-13; J. Priest, "A Note on the Messianic Banquet," in J. H. Charlesworth, ed., *The Messiah: Developments in Earliest Christianity* (Minneapolis: Fortress, 1992) 222-38.

68. See esp. J. D. Crossan, *The Historical Jesus: The Life of a Mediterranean Jewish Peasant* (San Francisco: HarperSanFrancisco, 1991) 303-51.

69. See Chilton, *Pure Kingdom,* 86, 89-90.

70. See Meier, *A Marginal Jew,* 2.309-17; Reiser, *Jesus and Judgment,* 230-41.

"I tell you, many will come from east and west and will eat with Abraham and Isaac and Jacob in the kingdom of heaven, while the heirs of the kingdom will be thrown into the outer darkness, where there will be weeping and gnashing of teeth." (Matt. 8:11-12//Luke 13:28-29)

In the context of his inclusion of Gentiles (Matthew), or at least his condemnation of unfaithful Israelites (Luke), Jesus pronounced that the kingdom of God would be a time of table fellowship for all of God's children, regardless of ethnic identity. This vision of the future kingdom influenced Jesus' practice, which was intended to be a present realization and application of his vision of the future kingdom.

Even more, Jesus promised his disciples, in his closing hour, that in the age to come he would reinstate his table fellowship with them: [71]

"Truly I tell you, I will never again drink of the fruit of the vine until that day when I drink it new in the kingdom of God." (Mark 14:25; par. Matt. 26:29)

Luke has a logion that presents the same motif:[72]

". . . and I confer on you, just as my Father has conferred on me, a kingdom, so that you may eat and drink at my table in my kingdom, and you will sit on thrones judging the twelve tribes of Israel." (Luke 22:29-30)

In both of these logia it is not hard to recognize the logic of Jesus: current practice is determined by a certain future.[73] The future kingdom will be characterized by table fellowship with Jesus and the Fa-

---

71. Matthew adds two touches: (1) after "when I drink" he has "with you," and (2) instead of "kingdom *of God*," he has "in my Father's kingdom." See Meier, *A Marginal Jew*, 2.302-9. J. Jeremias, *The Eucharistic Words of Jesus* (Philadelphia: Fortress, 1964) 207-18, interpreted Mark 14:25 as a vow of abstinence until the resumption of fellowship.

72. See now the interesting parallels from Qumran adduced by C. A. Evans, *Jesus and His Contemporaries: Comparative Studies* (AGJU 25; Leiden: Brill, 1995) 150-52.

73. Chilton has shown that "I will never drink . . . until" means "though I may not drink now (since I will die), nevertheless I certainly will drink with you in the kingdom" (*Pure Kingdom*, 88-89).

ther, so it becomes important to actualize that fellowship in present life.[74]

The request of the sons of Zebedee (through their mother[75]) may be of the same cloth:

> "Declare that these two sons of mine will sit, one at your right hand and one at your left, in your kingdom." (Matt. 20:21)

Is this a request to sit next to Jesus on his *throne* or *at table* in the final kingdom? The latter is more consistent with the vision of Jesus than the former (despite Matt. 19:28//Luke 22:28-29).

In short, when Jesus described the future it was often in terms of table fellowship. The parable of the marriage feast describes the age to come as table fellowship in a festive setting:

> Once more Jesus spoke to them in parables, saying: "The kingdom of heaven may be compared to a king who gave a wedding banquet for his son. He sent his slaves to call those who had been invited to the wedding banquet, but they would not come. Again he sent other slaves, saying, 'Tell those who have been invited: Look, I have prepared my dinner, my oxen and my fat calves have been slaughtered, and everything is ready; come to the wedding banquet.' But they made light of it and went away, one to his farm, another to his business, while the rest seized his slaves, mistreated them, and killed them. The king was enraged. He sent his troops, destroyed those murderers, and burned their city. Then he said to his slaves, 'The wedding is ready, but those invited were not worthy. Go therefore into the main streets, and invite everyone you find to the wedding banquet.' Those slaves went out into the streets and gathered all whom they found, both good and bad; so the wedding hall was filled with guests. But when the king came in to see the guests, he noticed a man there who was not wearing a wedding robe, and he said to him, 'Friend, how did you get in here without a wedding robe?' And he was speechless. Then the king said to the attendants, 'Bind him hand and foot, and throw him into the outer darkness, where there will be

74. Chilton, *Pure Kingdom*, 86, 89-90.
75. The Markan parallel (10:37) has the sons themselves make the request.

weeping and gnashing of teeth.' For many are called, but few are chosen." (Matt. 22:1-14)

The surprising turn of the man with the improper garment is not as important as the overall image: the final kingdom is a banquet for "both good and bad," and the banquet hall is filled with guests. The wine is flowing, the joy is abundant, and the fellowship is intimate as the guests enjoy the bounty of the patron. The man improperly dressed probably symbolizes the "sons of the kingdom" of Matt. 8:11-12, that is, those among Israel who have not repented, who have not seen in Jesus the kingdom being realized, and who have not aligned themselves with the new community of the restored Israel that Jesus has created around the Twelve. Tragically, they will be expelled from the kingdom (destroyed along with Jerusalem) and will not survive the judgment to enter into the kingdom of joy and feasting.[76] However this man be interpreted, the symbol of the party remains: the kingdom of God will be like a massive banquet in which God's true people experience the joys of feasting and fellowship.

Two more features of this final kingdom need to be observed. First, it is a time when the Father blesses the true people of God. While Christian usage has made the term "blessed" descriptive of far too many mundane items, the use of "blessed" in the Beatitudes describes not so much a present condition as a future promise: in the age to come, these people will have the approval of the Father, they will inherit the land,[77] they will enjoy total protection and complete satisfaction, and they will experience a fundamental reversal of their present condition (Matt. 5:3-12//Luke 6:20-26). To be sure, the term "blessed" conveys the same inaugurated eschatology as the word "kingdom": in Matt. 13:16 (par. Luke 10:23-24) the disciples are "blessed" because they understand Jesus' parables and witness his stupendous marvels (cf. Matt. 11:6//Luke 7:23; Matt. 16:17). Nonetheless, this blessing awaits a final fullness (Luke 12:35-48). The blessing about which Jesus

---

76. See Wright, *Jesus and the Victory of God,* 326-29.

77. On Jesus' use of land imagery, see W. D. Davies, *The Gospel and the Land: Early Christianity and Jewish Territorial Doctrine* (Berkeley: University of California Press, 1974); D. Mendels, *The Rise and Fall of Jewish Nationalism* (ABRL; New York: Doubleday, 1992; reprint, Grand Rapids: Eerdmans, 1997) 81-105, 243-75; W. Janzen, "Land," *ABD,* 4.143-54; R. L. Wilken, *The Land Called Holy: Palestine in Christian History and Thought* (New Haven: Yale University Press, 1992) 46-52.

speaks, especially in the Beatitudes, is therefore the realization of the fullness for which Israel has been longing: the return from exile, the coming of God to Zion, the inheritance of the whole land, the expulsion of God's enemies from the land, the creation of a new heart for obedience to God's Torah, the reversal of injustices, and the glorious fellowship of the unified family of God.

Second, this kingdom is one in which the Father expresses his sovereign love and authority. Although the use of "Father" with "kingdom" evidently belongs to later redaction, the substance is hardly worth debating; the final kingdom is God's kingdom, and God is the Father:

> "Do not be afraid, little flock, for it is your Father's good pleasure to give you the kingdom." (Luke 12:32)

> "Then the righteous will shine like the sun in the kingdom of their Father." (Matt. 13:43)

> Then the king will say to those at his right hand, "Come, you that are blessed by my Father, inherit the kingdom prepared for you from the foundation of the world." (Matt. 25:34)

> "I tell you, I will never again drink of this fruit of the vine until that day when I drink it new with you in my Father's kingdom." (Matt. 26:29)

Jesus chose the term "Father" to describe God because it resonated with his two primary notions about God: God is both personally loving and inflexibly holy in his authority. The final kingdom is the Father's kingdom because, following the destruction of Jerusalem and the judgment of God on unfaithful Israel, God will establish his perfect, holy will and loving relationship with all those who populate that kingdom. Then, Jesus contends, God will establish on earth what he promised so long ago. Those who attach themselves to him are to pray for its realization (Matt. 6:10).

Conclusions

When Jesus looked down the road to the final kingdom, what did he see? First, he believed that those who were following him, participating in his table fellowship, and witnessing his miraculous cures and teachings, would be the ones to populate the final kingdom. Second, though he believed that the kingdom would arrive within a generation, and though he prayed and taught others to pray for its arrival, he was uncertain of precisely when the kingdom would appear in all its fullness. Third, he believed that the future would begin with God's judgment on Israel's sinfulness in the form of the destruction of Jerusalem. Fourth, he believed that, following the judgment, the kingdom of God would be made up of Israelites who had survived the ordeal and who would become the restored Israel, constituted around the new tribal leaders, the Twelve. Fifth, he believed that the final kingdom would be a time of endless fellowship with the Father, who would shower peace, love, and justice on the land. For Jesus, the final kingdom would be the consummation of history, the goal toward which God had been directing his energies since the days of Abraham. It would be the complete end of exile and the restoration of God's people.

CHAPTER 5

The Ethic of Jesus: Conversion and Cost

W hat Jesus said about ethics, about how people are to live before God and with others, remains the most misunderstood dimension of his teachings.[1] The fundamental problem is that the ethic of Jesus has been ripped away from its moorings in what he affirmed about God and the kingdom. Reversing this process becomes all the more important: until God and kingdom are understood, there is no place for the ethic of Jesus.[2] What Jesus said about ethics constitutes a particular application of his understanding of God and kingdom. There is no

---

1. Recent studies of the ethics of Jesus include R. Schnackenburg, *Die sittliche Botschaft des Neuen Testaments* (2 vols.; HTKNTS 1-2; Freiburg: Herder, 1986-88), a revision of *The Moral Teaching of the New Testament* (trans. J. Holland-Smith and W. J. O'Hara; New York: Seabury, 1965); E. Lohse, *Theological Ethics of the New Testament* (trans. M. E. Boring; Minneapolis: Fortress, 1991); W. Schrage, *The Ethics of the New Testament* (trans. D. E. Green; Philadelphia: Fortress, 1988); see also A. N. Wilder, *Eschatology and Ethics in the Teaching of Jesus* (rev. ed.; New York: Harper and Bros., 1950). Valuable studies of New Testament ethics in general, but which lack separate sections on the ethics of Jesus, include R. B. Hays, *The Moral Vision of the New Testament: Community, Cross, New Creation: A Contemporary Introduction to New Testament Ethics* (New York: HarperSanFrancisco, 1996); R. N. Longenecker, ed., *Patterns of Discipleship in the New Testament* (MNTS; Grand Rapids: Eerdmans, 1996); F. J. Matera, *New Testament Ethics: The Legacies of Jesus and Paul* (Louisville: Westminster John Knox, 1996). See also W. A. Meeks, *The Origins of Christian Morality: The First Two Centuries* (New Haven: Yale University Press, 1993); A. E. Harvey, *Strenuous Commands: The Ethic of Jesus* (Philadelphia: Trinity Press International, 1990).

2. See H. Conzelmann, *Jesus* (trans. J. R. Lord; intro. J. Reumann; Philadelphia: Fortress, 1973) 60-61; Schnackenburg, *Die sittliche Botschaft*, 1.76-77; N. Perrin, *Rediscovering the Teaching of Jesus* (New York: Harper & Row, 1967) 109.

room here for pious sentimentalities. So, for example, Jesus urged his followers to "turn the other [cheek] also" (Matt. 5:39), and many have turned this saying into a general principle of conduct. This logion, however, represents neither a political program for passivism nor a bland prescription for ethical conduct, but a pronouncement about how Israel is to interact with Rome in light of Israel's current political trouble and in light of Jesus' call for the nation to repent in view of the coming judgment. Jesus' ethics are to be understood in light of how Israel is to live in light of the coming judgment.[3]

The trajectory of Jesus' ethic was established by the Deuteronomic ethical tradition (especially as it came to expression in the major prophets) and by its extension in the Wisdom tradition.[4] Jesus' ethic both reactualized those traditions and set itself over against them; thus, his ethic differed from Jewish tradition only as it responded to that tradition.[5] Christian scholarship, however, has tended to avoid the Jewish heritage of Jesus or even to set Jesus' ethic over against that heritage. Far too often scholars have tried to legitimate Jesus by showing how he differed with Judaism.[6] No difference between them explains the rise of the Jesus movement or grasps the reason for the eventual parting of ways between Judaism and emerging Christianity. Too often Christians have singled out the worst examples of Jewish ethics and practice, imputed them to Judaism as a whole, compared them with the ideal of Jesus, and then found Judaism wanting. What this approach gains is ru-

3. See B. Wiebe, *Messianic Ethics: Jesus' Proclamation of the Kingdom of God and the Church in Response* (Scottdale, Penn.: Herald, 1992).

4. Good studies can be found in S. Schechter, *Aspects of Rabbinic Theology* (intro. N. Gilman; Woodstock, Vt.: Jewish Lights Publishing, 1993); E. P. Sanders, *Judaism: Practice and Belief 63 BCE–66 CE* (Philadelphia: Trinity Press International, 1992) 190-240, with 241-78; T. W. Manson, *The Teaching of Jesus: Studies of Its Form and Content* (Cambridge: Cambridge University Press, 1939) 288-95; idem, *Ethics and the Gospel* (London: SCM, 1960). Two studies that focus attention on the wisdom background to Jesus' ethics are Harvey, *Strenuous Commands*, 39-67; and B. Witherington, *Jesus the Sage: The Pilgrimage of Wisdom* (Minneapolis: Fortress, 1994).

5. See J. Klausner, *Jesus of Nazareth: His Life, Times, and Teaching* (trans. H. Danby; New York: Macmillan, 1926) 381, 384-89.

6. See J. Jeremias, *The Sermon on the Mount* (trans. N. Perrin; FBBS 2; Philadelphia: Fortress, 1963) 4-6. Scholars have tended to see an improvement by Jesus in one of three areas: (1) his method of declaring ethics, (2) his concentration on the internal over against the externality of Judaism, or (3) his reduction of the will of God to love of God and others.

ined by what it loses: Jesus becomes a thoroughly unhistorical figure. We need to bear in mind the dictum of E. P. Sanders: "Religions, however, must be assessed on the basis of their highest ideals, not the failures of individuals."[7]

How, then, has the ethic of Jesus been understood?[8] Much of what has been written on the subject has stemmed from pastoral theology rather than historical research,[9] while studies of dogmatic and systematic theology have typically given the topic little emphasis.

The classical division of the ethics of Jesus into "ethics of perfection" (for the clerics and priests) and "ethics of the norm" (for the laity) has its origins in older Roman Catholic presentations. This dichotomy makes Jesus' ethics an ethics for the elite.[10] In particular, when Jesus' call seems extreme, as when he enjoins poverty (Mark 10:21), separation from family (Luke 14:26), or chastity (Matt. 19:11-12), it is treated as a special ethic for those who have committed themselves to the *vita religiosa*. While these so-called counsels of perfection may reflect an extreme element in Jesus' teachings, such a radical division of his ethic as a permanent feature finds no basis in what he actually said.[11] In all fairness, though, a survey of scholarship reveals that contemporary Roman Catholic scholars, many of whom have taken the vows connected with the "evangelical counsels," interpret the sayings of Jesus in a manner similar to their Protestant colleagues with much less credence given to the elitist dimension of Jesus' ethic. The sayings of Jesus, they seem to be arguing, are for all.[12]

---

7. Sanders, *Judaism: Practice and Belief*, 234.

8. For surveys, see especially the following: R. H. Hiers, *Jesus and Ethics: Four Interpretations* (Philadelphia: Westminster, 1968); Wiebe, *Messianic Ethics*, 15-54. See also the shorter treatments of J. T. Sanders, *Ethics in the New Testament: Change and Development* (rev. ed.; London: SCM, 1986) 1-29; L. D. Hurst, "Ethics of Jesus," *DJG*, 210-11; L. Goppelt, *Theology of the New Testament* (2 vols.; trans. J. E. Alsup; ed. J. Roloff; Grand Rapids: Eerdmans, 1981-82) 1.115-19.

9. A classic example is Dietrich Bonhoeffer's profound analysis of the ethic of Jesus written in resistance to the Third Reich; cf. his *The Cost of Discipleship* (rev. ed.; trans. R. H. Fuller and I. Booth; New York: Macmillan, 1963). This work now has a definitive critical edition: see *Nachfolge* (DBW 4; ed. M. Kuske and I. Tödt; Munich: Kaiser, 1989).

10. See E. Cothenet, et al., *Imitating Christ* (RES 5; St. Meinrad, Ind.: Abbey, 1974), a translation of "Imitation du Christ (Livre)," from *Dictionnaire de Spiritualité*, vol. 7.2, cols. 1536-1601, 2355-68.

11. See Bonhoeffer, *Cost*, 50-51.

12. See the introductory comments of J. L. Boyle, S.J., in Cothenet, *Imitating Christ*, vi.

The theological controversies that fermented during and helped precipitate the Reformation focused on grace and works. Too often Jesus was seen as a sophisticated theologian. Two facets of this debate deserve mention: the Lutheran use of the ethic of Jesus as merely a heightening and intensification of the law, which brings people to trust in grace; and the Calvinist focus on the theology of faith and grace in Paul, which virtually eclipsed the need for the ethic of Jesus, except to flesh out what Paul meant by the life of faith.

Lutheran theology, with its dichotomizing of law and faith, found in the Sermon on the Mount a Mosaic-like demand for righteousness. This led to severe tension with the Lutheran emphasis upon salvation by faith alone (understood as trust in God's gracious provision of salvation in Christ) and ultimately to a reinterpretation of the Sermon on the Mount in a manner totally out of harmony with its own conclusion (Matt. 7:13-27). Consequently, Jesus' ethic was perceived to be a concentration of Moses' law for the purpose of driving his listeners to see their absolute need for trust in God's grace rather than in their human capacity to obey. A full critique of this approach cannot be offered here;[13] suffice it to say that a theological dialectic has been permitted to do violence to the clear words of Jesus.[14]

The Calvinist emphasis upon God's elective grace and the absolute need for grace to awaken a person to faith and obedience led some theologians to a near total neglect of the ethic of Jesus.[15] Human response became only a facet of the elective sovereignty of God, and the ethic of Jesus as a necessary obedience was eclipsed.[16]

These two treatments of the ethic of Jesus have dominated the Lutheran and Reformed traditions as well as Evangelical orientations.[17]

---

13. See Jeremias, *Sermon on the Mount*, 6-9.

14. See further Jeremias, *Sermon on the Mount*, 7, 9. See also Bonhoeffer, *Cost*, 50-60; Schrage, *Ethics*, 46.

15. See, e.g., H. Ridderbos, *The Coming of the Kingdom* (trans. H. de Jongste; ed. R. O. Zorn; St. Catharines, Ont.: Paideia, 1962); G. Bornkamm, *Jesus von Nazaret* (12th ed.; Stuttgart: Kohlhammer, 1980) 83-84; Jeremias, *Sermon on the Mount*, 24-35; J. Piper, *'Love Your Enemies': Jesus' Love Command in the Synoptic Gospels and in the Early Christian Paraenesis* (SNTSMS 38; Cambridge: Cambridge University Press, 1979) 76-85.

16. A good example of this is the standard Calvinist textbook, L. Berkhof, *Systematic Theology* (4th ed.; Grand Rapids: Eerdmans, 1941).

17. A notable exception is the pastorally oriented study of M. J. Wilkins, *Following the Master: Discipleship in the Steps of Jesus* (Grand Rapids: Zondervan, 1992) 98-144.

Many within these movements seem to think that Jesus was born on the wrong side of the cross![18]

In direct contrast to these approaches, the Anabaptists of the sixteenth century formulated an absolutist ethic of demand upon every person seeking to follow Christ.[19] In this approach, Jesus' Sermon on the Mount was deemed applicable to every person seeking baptism and life within the Christian community, and Jesus was transformed into a better Moses. The ethic of Jesus, and all of it, is for all.

Both European and American Protestantism, however, found another angle from which to understand and appropriate the ethic of Jesus. Protestant liberalism made Jesus into a cultural ethicist of the highest good. Here the focus fell on Jesus' perception of human capacities for both sin and goodness, and on his wonderful ability to state his ethical concerns in proverbial and hyperbolic forms. Consequently, though the ethic of Jesus became the backbone for ethics in Protestant liberalism,[20] its appropriation entailed a serious revision of its original meaning. No longer was that ethic a stiff demand in the context of Jesus' eschatological call to Israel but a polite, if at times bold, call for the Christian citizen to be at peace with others, to practice acts of charity, and to live with integrity before God — all set in the context of an intense religious individualism[21] intent on working toward a better world.[22]

Alongside the Protestant liberal ethic seemed to be a compulsive

---

18. See the remarks of Ridderbos, *Coming,* 257.

19. A good sourcebook is G. H. Williams and A. M. Mergal, *Spiritual and Anabaptist Writers: Documents Illustrative of the Radical Reformation* (LCC; Philadelphia: Westminster, 1967). See also the narrative history of W. R. Estep, *The Anabaptist Story: An Introduction to Sixteenth-Century Anabaptism* (3d ed.; Grand Rapids: Eerdmans, 1996). See also H. Windisch, *The Meaning of the Sermon on the Mount* (trans. S. M. Gilmour; Philadelphia: Westminster, 1961); for a critique, cf. Jeremias, *Sermon on the Mount,* 1-6.

20. E.g., A. Harnack, *What Is Christianity?* (trans. T. B. Saunders; New York: Harper & Row, 1957).

21. See S. Mathews, *Jesus on Social Institutions* (ed. K. Cauthen; Philadelphia: Fortress, 1971) 60-62, 88-104; Manson, *Teaching,* 297-302.

22. See P. T. Phillips, *A Kingdom on Earth: Anglo-American Social Christianity, 1880-1940* (University Park, Penn.: Pennsylvania State University Press, 1996); W. Sanday, "Jesus Christ," in *A Dictionary of the Bible* (ed. J. Hastings; New York: Charles Scribner's Sons, 1902) 2.603-53, reprinted with only slight revision in his *Outlines of the Life of Christ* (2d ed.; Edinburgh: T & T Clark, 1906). See also C. A. Briggs, *The Ethical Teaching of Jesus* (New York: Charles Scribner's Sons, 1904) x, 259-79.

need to offer unstinted praise of Jesus' ethic in comparison with Judaism or Western civilization as a whole.[23] Although it has been fashionable to criticize the Protestant liberal ethic, and especially its supposed Romanticism, it remains one of the few theological movements to base itself squarely on the teachings of Jesus and to allow the prominence that Jesus assigned to love to have full sway.

The most important representative of Protestant liberalism was Adolf von Harnack, who identified four main thoughts in Jesus' ethic: (1) "Jesus severed the connexion existing in his day between ethics and the external forms of religious worship and technical observance"; (2) "in all questions of morality he goes straight to the root, that is, to the disposition and intention"; (3) "what he freed from its connexion with self-seeking and ritual elements, and recognised as the moral principle, he reduces to *one* root and to *one* motive — love"; and (4) "Jesus freed the moral element from all alien connexions, even from its alliance with public religion."[24] He concluded:

> In thus expressing his message of the higher righteousness and the new commandment of love in these four leading thoughts, Jesus defined the sphere of the ethical in a way in which no one before him had ever defined it. But should we be threatened with doubts as to what he meant, we must steep ourselves again and again in the Beatitudes of the Sermon on the Mount. They contain his ethics and his religion, united at the root, and freed from all external and particularistic elements.[25]

Albert Schweitzer's daring reinterpretation of Jesus' mission issued in a devastating critique of the liberal Protestant approach to Jesus' ethic.[26] Schweitzer, as we have noted, argued that Jesus expected an

---

23. This is what J. Klausner, the great Jewish scholar, had to contest; see his *Jesus of Nazareth*, 381, 384, 414.

24. Harnack, *What Is Christianity?* 71-72.

25. Harnack, *What Is Christianity?* 73-74. For Harnack's own social ethic, cf. pp. 88-101.

26. A. Schweitzer garnered the credit for this approach, but it was Johannes Weiß who laid the foundation: cf. J. Weiß, *Die Predigt Jesu vom Reiche Gottes* (3d ed.; ed. F. Hahn; intro. R. Bultmann; Göttingen: Vandenhoeck & Ruprecht, 1964); idem, *Jesus' Proclamation of the Kingdom of God* (trans. and ed. R. H. Hiers and D. L. Holland; Chico, Calif.: Scholars Press, 1985) 131-36.

imminent kingdom to appear on earth and that Jesus was an apocalyptic ethical alarmist. The impact of viewing Jesus' ethic in light of eschatology was enormous: instead of finding in Jesus' teaching a long-term ethic applicable for generations to come, Schweitzer saw an interim ethic for the brief period prior to the arrival of the kingdom, which Jesus anticipated in a matter of weeks or months.[27] The ethic therefore derived its energies from the temporal urgency of its commitment: it was heroic (no marriage or sex), sacrificial (no possessions), and intense (no compromises). Its legacy for the church, however, became almost irrelevant; all that remained was a call to follow and, through that following, to discern God's will for today. Schweitzer distilled this reading in a now famous formulation:

> He comes to us as One unknown, without a name, as of old, by the lake-side, He came to those men who knew Him not. He speaks to us the same word: 'Follow thou me!' and sets us to the tasks which He has to fulfil for our time. He commands. And to those who obey Him, whether they be wise or simple, He will reveal Himself in the toils, the conflicts, the sufferings which they shall pass through in His fellowship, and, as an ineffable mystery, they shall learn in their own experience Who He is.[28]

Another modernizing of Jesus' ethic can be found in existentialism, where the Protestant liberal, the eschatological Jesus, and the ethical individualist merge into an attractive mixture.[29] Without minimizing the differences among representatives of this approach, nor the role eschatology played in their respective views of Jesus' ethic,[30] we can still identify what they shared: the view that Jesus' ethic was a call to escha-

27. See A. Schweitzer, *The Mystery of the Kingdom of God: The Secret of Jesus' Messiahship and Passion* (trans. W. Lowrie; New York: Schocken, 1964) 94-105.

28. A. Schweitzer, *The Quest for the Historical Jesus: A Critical Study of Its Progress from Reimarus to Wrede* (trans. W. Montgomery; intro. J. M. Robinson; New York: Macmillan, 1968) 403.

29. Particularly influential treatments can be found in R. Bultmann, *Jesus and the Word* (trans. L. P. Smith and E. H. Lantero; New York: Charles Scribner's Sons, 1958); W. Marxsen, *New Testament Foundations for Christian Ethics* (trans. O. C. Dean, Jr.; Minneapolis: Fortress, 1993); G. Bornkamm, *Jesus of Nazareth* (trans. I. and F. McLuskey, with J. M. Robinson; New York: Harper & Row, 1960) 82-95; Conzelmann, *Jesus*, 59-67; Perrin, *Rediscovering*, 108-53.

30. See Bultmann, *Jesus*, 27-45, 57-132.

tological or authentic existence. As it turns out, authentic existence has few objective markers but is discovered in the call and in the act that particularizes it. Rudolf Bultmann spoke for other representatives of this approach when he said:

> The will of God is then for Jesus as little a social or political program as it is either an ethical system which proceeds from an ideal of man and humanity or an ethic of value. He knows neither the conception of personality nor that of virtue. . . . As he has no doctrine of virtue, so also he has none of duty or of the good. It is sufficient for a man to know that God has placed him under the necessity of decision in every concrete situation in life, in the here and now. And this means that he himself must know what is required of him, and that no authority and no theory can take from him this responsibility.[31]

In more recent studies of Jesus' ethic, the existential dimension has been almost completely dropped. Eschatology, however, has held on. Even if Schweitzer erred in some respects, the role eschatology plays in this discussion remains fundamental, and it is back to Weiß and Schweitzer that we must go if we want to appreciate the sharp contours of Jesus' mission and message.[32] If the message of Jesus was shaped and conditioned by his call to Israel (not the world or the subsequent church) and was designed to offer to the nation a commitment that could redeem Israel from a coming judgment of God on the nation, then any articulation of that ethic which does not consider its place in this historical setting will diminish its force. Although one may not agree with all the details of Schweitzer's position, he was one of the first to offer a historically sensitive account of the role the ethic of Jesus played in the context of his mission as it related to Israel. What follows will build upon the crucial insight that Schweitzer brought to the fore, namely, the relationship of the eschatology of Jesus to his ethics.

---

31. Bultmann, *Jesus*, 108.

32. Recent treatments of the eschatological character of Jesus' ethics include Goppelt, *Theology* 1.107-10; Sanders, *Ethics*, 1-11; B. F. Meyer, *The Aims of Jesus* (London: SCM, 1979) 139, 151; Schrage, *Ethics*, 18-40; Harvey, *Strenuous Commands*, 140-68, 192; Wiebe, *Messianic Ethics*; J. Becker, *Jesus von Nazaret* (New York: de Gruyter, 1996) 276-88; Schnackenburg, *Die sittliche Botschaft*, 1.35-39, 79-81.

Conversion to Jesus

We are faced with two issues in seeking to present Jesus' teaching about conversion: how to organize the mass of data and how to present it in light of modern advances in the sociology of religion.[33] The following treatment will avoid a simplistic discussion of the meaning of the word "repent" *(metanoein),* and will not confine itself to the so-called entrance sayings (e.g., Matt. 5:20; 7:21; 18:3, 8-9; 19:23-24; 23:13). Rather, it seems more comprehensive to present a synthesis of the data that may be gleaned from the earliest traditions about Jesus.

Jesus spoke of two dimensions to conversion: a positive movement summarized in the word "faith" or "belief" and a negative movement best described as "repentance."[34] These two dimensions, however, are not abstract reflections on religious issues pertaining to a higher union with God, but specific calls by Jesus to contemporary Israelites who are facing a coming disaster and a forfeiture of God's covenantal providence if they do not turn from their current unfaithfulness to God and obey his will. The ethic of Jesus, his call to conversion in particular, was directed to a particular people (Israel), in a particular context (the land of Israel), at a particular time (prior to A.D. 70).[35]

Before we look at these two dimensions of conversion, a brief description of the term "conversion" deserves consideration. An especially vivid statement comes to expression in one of the entrance sayings:

> "Truly I tell you, whoever does not receive the kingdom of God as a little child will never enter it." (Mark 10:15)

Matthew's version of the saying reads:

> "Truly I tell you, unless you change and become like children, you will never enter the kingdom of heaven." (Matt. 18:3)[36]

---

33. On the latter, see L. R. Rambo, *Understanding Religious Conversion* (New Haven: Yale University Press, 1993).

34. Some recent studies have emphasized the positive side of repentance; e.g., Schnackenburg, *Die sittliche Botschaft,* 1.42-50. An older study that did the same is A. Schlatter, *The History of the Christ: The Foundation for New Testament Theology* (trans. A. J. Köstenberger; Grand Rapids: Baker, 1997) 137-55.

35. See Wiebe, *Messianic Ethics,* 122.

36. On the extent of Matthean redaction here, see W. D. Davies and D. C.

The critical words "unless you change" in Matthew's version express the ideal of Jewish conversion in true prophetic fashion. The concept, drawing as it does on the prophetic calls to Israel and Judah to turn from various states of sin and unfaithfulness to the Sinai covenant, defines a range of ideas, including faith, repentance, obedience, covenant fidelity, social justice, and the final restoration of God's eschatological salvation (cf., e.g., Deut. 4:30; Jer. 24:7; 31:18; Lam. 5:21; Hos. 3:5; Amos 4:6–5:2; Mal. 3:7-12; 4:5-6). The act of turning away from sin and toward God's will forms the basis of the entire call. The historical context drives the hearer to recognize here a call to the nation of Israel once again to return to YHWH, to the God who formed a special covenant community with Israel, and to his laws as expressed in the Mosaic legislation.[37] Nearly all discussions of the concept of conversion/repentance in the Hebrew Bible demonstrate the personal, or theological, dimension; scholars agree that the concept describes turning to God, not to some system of philosophical thought.

Jesus utilized a concept of conversion that was intensely national and eschatological. In the context of the ancient prophetic call to Israel and in light of the dire circumstances facing Israel in his day, he called upon his fellow Jews to accept his offer of the kingdom. Those who responded in conversion would be spared disaster and would enter the kingdom. Those who did not would experience condemnation. Disciples of Jesus are Israelites who have converted in light of this context.

Before committing themselves to following Jesus, those who heard him would have seen in him the one who would lead them out of exile. Although it would be impossible to argue that the earliest followers of Jesus saw in him the incarnation of God, it is entirely reasonable to think that they saw him functioning as savior of Israel, as the coming of God for them.[38] Thus, following Jesus meant acknowledging that he was the one who ended the exile, led the nation out of bondage to Rome, regained control of the land, regathered the twelve tribes, and restored the fortunes of Israel and Judah. Any summary of the ethic of

Allison, Jr., *A Critical and Exegetical Commentary on the Gospel According to St. Matthew* (3 vols.; Edinburgh: T & T Clark, 1988-97) 2.756-57; J. Jeremias, *New Testament Theology: The Proclamation of Jesus* (trans. J. Bowden; New York: Charles Scribner's Sons, 1971) 155.

37. See F. Laubach, "Conversion," *NIDNTT*, 1.355.

38. See N. T. Wright, *Jesus and the Victory of God* (Christian Origins and the Question of God, vol. 2; Minneapolis: Fortress, 1996) 612-53.

Jesus that neglects this national dimension of his teaching fails to give an adequate historical account of his ministry.

Positive Conversion: Faith

Many of those whom Jesus called and who followed him would not be classified as the "wicked" in Judaism, and so his call to conversion amounted to more than a call to turn from wickedness and concrete sins.[39] It was a progressive following of Jesus involving just as much positive appropriation as negative dissociation. Jesus did not call upon people to admit to a personal fallenness or to confess to being marked by original sin but to identify with the national condition, to accept God's word on that condition, and to live appropriately before God. The response he elicited was a dialectic of denial and affirmation, a constant interplay of the two.

Faith in God and faithfulness to God form a solid platform in the traditions of Israel upon which Jesus built (cf., e.g., Gen. 15:6; Exod. 14:31; Ps. 118:5-9; Isa. 7:9; 40:25-31; 57:13; Hab. 2:4). Isaiah 57:13 says, "whoever takes refuge in me shall possess the land and inherit my holy mountain." This tradition identifies faith as the response of Israel at the climax of history, when the exile ends and the kingdom arrives. One can infer from this sort of context that to believe in Jesus meant to set one's hope (for Israel's salvation) on God as he was speaking through Jesus. It is unhistorical to see faith merely as some private sense of trust in God for personal redemption. Faith for Jesus meant what it did for Israel's prophets: confidence in God's word to the nation, trust in his ushering in the fortunes of Israel, and hope that his promises would soon materialize.[40]

The exile-restoration tradition forms an indispensable context for understanding the concept of faith in the teaching of Jesus (cf. Isa. 28:16; Hab. 2:4; 1QpHab 7:17–8:3; T. Dan 5:13; 6:4; T. Ash. 7:6-7). The general concept of faith[41] for Jesus involved the following terms and

39. See E. P. Sanders, *Jesus and Judaism* (Philadelphia: Fortress, 1985) 176-88; J. D. G. Dunn, "Jesus, Table-Fellowship, and Qumran," in J. H. Charlesworth, ed., *Jesus and the Dead Sea Scrolls* (ABRL; New York: Doubleday, 1992) 254-72.

40. See Wright, *Jesus and the Victory of God*, 261.

41. See Schnackenburg, *Die sittliche Botschaft*, 1.50-58; Wright, *Jesus and the Victory of God*, 258-64.

images: faith (Mark 1:15), imitation (Mark 1:16-20; 2:14-15), public confession or identification with Jesus and his other followers (Matt. 10:32-33), loving Jesus more than one's kin (Luke 14:26-27//Matt. 10:37-39), becoming like children (Mark 10:15//Matt. 18:3), obeying the words of Jesus (Mark 4:15; Matt. 7:24-27//Luke 6:47-49), assuming Jesus' yoke (Matt. 11:28-30), and making a deliberate decision (Luke 12:33; 14:28-33). Conversation with these diverse images leads to four distinguishable aspects of the positive movement toward Jesus.

This positive movement begins with trusting Jesus as the one sent by God to deliver Israel:[42]

> Again they came to Jerusalem. As he was walking in the temple, the chief priests, the scribes, and the elders came to him and said, "By what authority are you doing these things? Who gave you this authority to do them?" Jesus said to them, "I will ask you one question; answer me, and I will tell you by what authority I do these things. Did the baptism of John come from heaven, or was it of human origin? Answer me." They argued with one another, "If we say, 'From heaven,' he will say, 'Why then did you not believe him?' But shall we say, 'Of human origin'?" — they were afraid of the crowd, for all regarded John as truly a prophet. So they answered Jesus, "We do not know." And Jesus said to them, "Neither will I tell you by what authority I am doing these things." (Mark 11:27-33)

Although this tradition originally was concerned with the relationship of Jesus and John, it reveals a constant concern of Jesus: the level of commitment necessary in order to see him for who he really was and for what he really offered. The leaders of Israel's establishment wanted answers but were not willing to commit themselves on the issue at hand, John's ultimate authority. Their unwillingness to declare their colors led Jesus to an equal unwillingness to divulge his ultimate authority. Jesus demanded public commitment; he tolerated no fence-sitting. This negative example shows that the positive movement in conversion involved a personal act of openness, an act of allegiance to Jesus as the one who could restore Israel.

Allegiance to Jesus finds frequent expression in the term *faith.*

---

42. On decision, or commitment, as the essential starting point of conversion, see Rambo, *Understanding Religious Conversion,* 124-41.

Most Christian interpreters have understood Jesus' conception of faith in Pauline terms, but Paul's idea of justification by faith had a different orientation. In the Gospels "faith" primarily means trust in Jesus to perform physical healing or deliverance (e.g., Matt. 8:13; 9:28; 21:22; Mark 5:36//Luke 8:50).[43] This perception of faith clearly differs from Paul's teaching on justification by faith — at least in emphasis. Although the predominant sense in the Gospels is that of trust in Jesus for healing, there are times when trust is focused on Jesus as the agent of salvation (e.g., Mark 1:15; 9:42; Matt. 27:42).[44] This type of faith is the recognition that God is eschatologically active in Jesus for the deliverance of Israel and that God is calling Israel to unreserved reliance upon Jesus' actions, teachings, and mission.[45]

Jesus' statement that those who wish to follow him must "receive the kingdom of God as a little child" (Mark 10:15) or, as Matthew presents it, "become like children," deserves consideration as part of this initial act of faith. Faith in Jesus surrenders faith in all other persons, gods, and systems; reaches out to Jesus in trust; and willingly risks Israel's future in this act of faith.[46] Another image conveys the same message: conversion to Jesus begins with "coming" to him (Matt. 11:28-30). The burdened and worried Israelite is invited to come to Jesus and to recognize in him the solution to the national problem of Israel.

The positive movement toward Jesus, however, is not an impulsive act but a deliberate deed:

"For which of you, intending to build a tower, does not first sit down and estimate the cost, to see whether he has enough to complete it? Otherwise, when he has laid a foundation and is not able to finish, all who see it will begin to ridicule him, saying, 'This fellow began to build and was not able to finish.' Or what king, going out to wage war against another king, will not sit down first and consider whether he is able with ten thousand to oppose the one who comes against him

---

43. See Schnackenburg, *Die sittliche Botschaft*, 1.54-56; Perrin, *Rediscovering*, 130-42; Jeremias, *Proclamation of Jesus*, 159-66; G. Vermes, *The Religion of Jesus the Jew* (Minneapolis: Fortress, 1993) 196-200.

44. Cf. also Matt. 21:25, 32. See the survey of evidence in R. T. France, "Faith," *DJG*, 223-26.

45. See further Wright, *Jesus and the Victory of God*, 263.

46. See Jeremias, *Proclamation of Jesus*, 155-56, who reads too much into this logion when he argues that it indirectly describes learning to say "Abba."

with twenty thousand? If he cannot, then, while the other is still far away, he sends a delegation and asks for the terms of peace." (Luke 14:28-32)[47]

Prior to building, the construction manager contemplates the cost to avoid shame in his society; prior to going to war, the king weighs the probabilities of success before he risks his own life and those of his soldiers. Thus, Jesus called upon his fellow Israelites to consider carefully what they were getting themselves into, what chances there were for endurance in such a vocation, and what kind of commitment they had to his mission.[48] Failure to live up to his conditions would lead to disaster.

In the parable of the soils (Mark 4:1-9, 13-20) only one response to Jesus is acceptable: fruit-producing growth. It is not stretching the parable to see here the same call that is found in the parables of the tower builder and the warrior king: to follow Jesus, Israelites must decide whether they can make a firm commitment.[49]

The positive movement toward Jesus also included a public identification with him. If we could transport ourselves to first-century Galilee, we would immediately encounter the public character of religious allegiance. Privatization and internalization of religious faith characterize modern society but not the first-century Jewish world. Jesus, an untrained, unauthorized, unorthodox prophet and teacher, attracted undistinguished persons through a consistent flaunting of Jewish purity customs and traditions of interpretation. He demanded that true Israelites join his ragtag movement and even went so far as to claim that those who did not join would not inherit the kingdom but experience the judgment of God. In essence, then, Jesus required of his followers a public commitment to his group and thereby a public identification with himself. How this public commitment worked out no doubt varied from person to person, but it began with eating with Jesus in a forum open enough for others to take note. Indeed, the primary form of public confession of Jesus was very likely expressed in table fellowship with him.

47. The interpretive logion applying this parable to possessions (14:33) is probably secondary.

48. See Becker, *Jesus von Nazaret,* 292-97.

49. This is true despite the highly condensed form of the call-to-discipleship narrative in Mark 1:16-20, which depicts a hasty conversion on the part of Jesus' disciples (cf. Mark 2:13-17; compare Luke 5:1-11 and John 1:35-51).

In a Q tradition, Jesus warns his listeners of the consequences of identifying with him or not joining his movement:

"And I tell you, everyone who acknowledges me before others, the Son of Man also will acknowledge before the angels of God; but whoever denies me before others will be denied before the angels of God." (Luke 12:8-9//Matt. 10:32-33)

Though one might be tempted to think here of a private hearing in some celestial location, this would dehistoricize and decontextualize Jesus' message. For Jesus, the kingdom was an earthly reality. Thus, he taught that those who heard him and acknowledged him, who publicly confessed him by identifying and eating with him, would be approved when the Son of Man was vindicated in his kingdom (compare Mark 8:38 with Matt. 16:27). Public identification with Jesus is therefore required to enter the kingdom.

For this reason, Jesus had to call his followers to "hate" their families:

"Whoever comes to me and does not hate father and mother, wife and children, brothers and sisters, yes, and even life itself, cannot be my disciple. Whoever does not carry the cross and follow me cannot be my disciple." (Luke 14:26-27)

"Whoever loves father or mother more than me is not worthy of me; and whoever loves son or daughter more than me is not worthy of me; and whoever does not take up the cross and follow me is not worthy of me." (Matt. 10:37-38)

In social terms, to "love" Jesus meant to identify with him publicly as the one through whom God was bringing salvation to Israel; to "hate" one's family meant to leave them because the dividing line had been drawn and the family had decided that Jesus was not the savior for Israel.[50] One had to choose Jesus if one wanted to enter the kingdom of God. This language of "hating" and "loving more" did not emerge from privatized religion, or from psychological tensions within one's imme-

50. Again, Luke's version of the Q tradition appears more primitive. See also the tradition in *Gospel of Thomas* 55, 101.

diate family, but from a steely determination of commitment to Jesus in fiery battle among alternative options of how Israel was to be redeemed.

The decision to commit oneself to Jesus as the savior of Israel, expressing itself in public identification with him, demanded obedience in following him. The notion of "following" had its basis in the Jewish scriptures. Negatively, the term was used for devoting oneself to foreign gods and participating in sinful practices like idolatry (cf. Deut. 4:3; Judg. 2:12; Jer. 2:5; 35:6-7).[51] Positively, the term described commitment to the Torah in faithful obedience to God's covenant with Israel; it also defined solidarity with a chosen leader (cf. Lev. 19:2; Deut. 13:4; Judg. 8:21-23; 1 Kings 14:8; 18:21; 2 Kings 23:3; Prov. 1:8; 2:1; 3:1; Isa. 54:13; 1 Macc. 2:51-64; see also 1 Kings 19:20; Isa. 8:16; Hebrews 11). By the time of the rabbis, the term had become a fixed expression describing the relationship of a student to his teacher (cf. *m. Abot* 1:1; 6:6).[52]

In the Gospels, the term "follow" is used both literally (e.g., Matt. 4:25; 8:1; 9:19) and metaphorically (e.g., Mark 1:16-20; Matt. 8:18-22), the latter connoting religious commitment and adherence to Jesus. In particular, his disciples are those who adhere to his example and his teachings because they see in him the one who will deliver Israel and restore the nation. The metaphorical sense has three components.[53] First, there is an invitation.[54] Thus, in Mark 1:16-18 Jesus calls the disciples to come after him, and they follow him; the Q tradition of would-be disciples shows the same (Luke 9:57-60//Matt. 8:18-22).[55] Second, there is a demand for commitment to him, his group, his teachings, and his vision for Israel:[56]

51. On "following," cf. Schnackenburg, *Die sittliche Botschaft*, 1.58-67; Cothenet, *Imitating Christ*, 1-13.

52. See M. Hengel, *The Charismatic Leader and His Followers* (trans. J. Greig; SNTW; Edinburgh: T & T Clark, 1981) 16-37.

53. See J. D. Kingsbury, "The Verb AKOLOUTHEIN ("To Follow") as an Index of Matthew's View of His Community," *JBL* 97 (1978) 56-73.

54. Schnackenburg, *Die sittliche Botschaft*, 1.59-62.

55. In addition, see the evidence at Mark 2:13 pars.; 8:34 pars.; 10:21 pars.; Matt. 10:38.

56. See B. Gerhardsson, *Memory and Manuscript: Oral Tradition and Written Transmission in Rabbinic Judaism and Early Christianity* (ASNU 22; Lund: Gleerup, 1961; reprint, Grand Rapids: Eerdmans, 1998) 181-89.

He called the crowd with his disciples, and said to them, "If any want to become my followers, let them deny themselves and take up their cross and follow me. For those who want to save their life will lose it, and those who lose their life for my sake, and for the sake of the gospel, will save it. For what will it profit them to gain the whole world and forfeit their life? Indeed, what can they give in return for their life? Those who are ashamed of me and of my words in this adulterous and sinful generation, of them the Son of Man will also be ashamed when he comes in the glory of his Father with the holy angels." (Mark 8:34-38)

Third, there is the cost of commitment: to follow Jesus means a life-changing, life-surrendering pilgrimage of wholehearted reliance upon him as the savior of Israel.

To sum up the discussion thus far: conversion to Jesus involved a positive movement toward him, beginning with a confrontation that led one to weigh the consequences of being associated with him and his call that Israel repent in order to avoid the coming disaster.[57] Accordingly, a positive decision to follow Jesus involved a public act of identification with him, best described by the image of "following" him. The whole process involved a call and a commitment, regardless of the cost.

Negative Conversion: Repentance

Alongside the positive movement to Jesus in faith and obedience was the negative side of conversion: those who acknowledged Jesus as the one who would lead Israel out of exile also had to repent from the whole nation's condition as part of their own sinfulness.[58] Jesus used a host of terms and metaphors to describe this negative side of conversion: "repentance" (Mark 1:15; 6:12), self-denial (Mark 8:34-35; Matt. 10:34-35; 18:4), taking up the "cross" (Mark 8:34; Matt. 10:38), "selling everything" (Mark 10:21; Luke 12:33), "leaving all" (Mark 1:16-20; 2:14; 10:28; Luke

---

57. See Hengel, *Charismatic Leader*, 34-35.

58. See Jeremias, *Proclamation of Jesus*, 151-58; Goppelt, *Theology*, 1.77-86; R. A. Horsley, *Jesus and the Spiral of Violence: Popular Jewish Resistance in Roman Palestine* (San Francisco: Harper & Row, 1987) 195-99; Wiebe, *Messianic Ethics*, 112-21. See also G. F. Moore, *Judaism in the First Centuries of the Christian Era: The Age of the Tannaim* (2 vols.; New York: Schocken, 1971) 1.507-34; Schnackenburg, *Die sittliche Botschaft*, 1.42-50.

14:33), and "hating all else" (Luke 14:26-27). The theme is therefore implicit in a variety of images, whether or not the term "repentance" was a characteristic term in his preaching.[59] As Leonhard Goppelt argued:

> "Repentance" is a collective term used by the evangelists primarily to summarize what Jesus wanted people to do. Jesus himself, however, spoke with differentiating concreteness about the life to which people were now being called, namely, to become poor as described in the Beatitudes and to invest themselves totally as described in the individual directives of the Sermon on the Mount.[60]

The various images for repentance may be synthesized into two categories: internal and external, or self-denial and world-denial. Under the category of internal repentance fall the expressions "repentance," "self-denial," and "taking up the cross"; under external repentance are the terms "selling all," "leaving all," and "hating all else." The former concern self-crucifixion and the latter, world-crucifixion. The two categories are integrally related, however; the first leads to the second, though the second does not necessitate the first. That is, internal repentance is not just a private affair but manifests itself in external ways. However, neither is external repentance a reliable indicator of internal repentance (cf. Isa. 66:2; Hos. 6:6; Amos 5:22; Micah 6:6-8).

Internal repentance concerned the disposition of individual Israelites in the context of the nation's bondage to Rome and of their personal relationship to the covenant God had made with Israel. This kind of repentance entailed "not just a change of mind about something but also a change of attitude, of intention, of will, if not a total transformation of one's conduct and orientation."[61] In the history of Israel, the call of God

59. See Wright, *Jesus and the Victory of God*, 246-58; Schrage, *Ethics*, 41; *contra* Sanders, *Jesus and Judaism*, 106-13. Sanders argues that evidence for Jesus preaching a national repentance is either scanty or unreliable, but several scholars have disagreed with him. See D. C. Allison, Jr., "Jesus and the Covenant: A Response to E. P. Sanders," *JSNT* 29 (1987) 57-78; B. D. Chilton, "Jesus and the Repentance of E. P. Sanders," *TynBul* 39 (1988) 1-18. See now M. Reiser, *Jesus and Judgment: The Eschatological Proclamation in Its Jewish Context* (trans. L. M. Maloney; Minneapolis: Fortress, 1997) 249-55. That some of the data on repentance derives from the evangelists, however, is beyond question. See Schnackenburg, *Die sittliche Botschaft*, 1.45-46.
60. Goppelt, *Theology*, 1.77.
61. Schrage, *Ethics*, 41-42.

through the prophets was a call for the nation to turn from its idolatries, its sinfulness, its injustices, and its unfaithful alliances with other nations for protection back to the God of the covenant who had brought them out of Egypt, protected them, recalled them to their ways by continual acts of discipline, and would forgive their sins and restore them to a twelve-tribe nation with his glory flooding the temple (e.g., Isa. 44:21-22; 45:22; 55:7).[62] This is the context of Jesus' call to his nation.

Beginning with John the Baptist and continuing through the ministry of Jesus, the call to repentance transcended a mere personal religious conversion. No first-century Israelites could think of themselves exclusively in individualistic terms.[63] They shaped their identity in the context of how the nation was faring. Thus, repentance meant undertaking an action for the good of the nation, for the sake of Israel's salvation, and for the sake of God's returned favor to the nation. This applies to Jesus' baptism and to his call: just as his baptism signified his agreement with John's call to the nation, so his call to repentance elicited a corporate response. Thus, Jesus issued his call to the whole nation rather than just to individual sinners in need of moral reform and personal conversion (cf. Matt. 11:21-24 par.; 12:38-42 par.; Luke 13:1-5).

Many texts could be brought forward to illustrate this point, but the parable of the prodigal son will serve the purpose well (Luke 15:11-32).[64] This parable describes the repentance of a sinful son in order to picture the restoration of the nation. In it, the individual act of repentance represents the prototypical act of the true Israelite. The younger son recognizes his sinfulness and candidly admits that he has sinned; he perceives that he has sinned against his father, thereby defiling his familial relationship and standing; he goes to his father and confesses his sinfulness; he hopes only for enough restoration and forgiveness to become a hired hand;[65] and he

---

62. A brief survey of the evidence in Judaism can be found in Sanders, *Jesus and Judaism*, 106-8; Wright, *Jesus and the Victory of God*, 246-52.

63. See B. J. Malina, *The New Testament World: Insights from Cultural Anthropology* (rev. ed.; Louisville, Ky.: Westminster John Knox, 1993) 63-89; M. McVann, "Family-Centeredness," in J. J. Pilch and B. J. Malina, eds., *Biblical Social Values and Their Meaning: A Handbook* (Peabody, Mass.: Hendrickson, 1993) 70-73; B. J. Malina and R. L. Rohrbaugh, *Social-Science Commentary on the Synoptic Gospels* (Minneapolis: Fortress, 1992) 99-101 (on surrogate family).

64. On the national as opposed to individualistic overtones of this parable, see Wright, *Jesus and the Victory of God*, 125-31.

65. See Jeremias, *Proclamation of Jesus*, 156-57.

ends up leaving his former lifestyle of sinfulness and arrogant distance from the land of Israel for a new obedience and faithfulness, even if that means living only on the border of the estate. In all this, the son's behavior is a paradigm for how the nation of Israel ought to respond to the Father's continual love: "Return to my land and house!" the Father calls out.

That repentance has a national component can also be seen in Q warnings that address the larger communities within Israel:

"Woe to you, Chorazin! Woe to you, Bethsaida! For if the deeds of power done in you had been done in Tyre and Sidon, they would have repented long ago, sitting in sackcloth and ashes. But at the judgment it will be more tolerable for Tyre and Sidon than for you. And you, Capernaum, will you be exalted to heaven? No, you will be brought down to Hades." (Luke 10:13-15//Matt. 11:21-22)

"The queen of the South will rise at the judgment with the people of this generation and condemn them, because she came from the ends of the earth to listen to the wisdom of Solomon, and see, something greater than Solomon is here! The people of Nineveh will rise up at the judgment with this generation and condemn it, because they repented at the proclamation of Jonah, and see, something greater than Jonah is here!" (Luke 11:31-32//Matt. 12:41-42)

And from an independent L tradition:

At that very time there were some present who told him about the Galileans whose blood Pilate had mingled with their sacrifices. He asked them, "Do you think that because these Galileans suffered in this way they were worse sinners than all other Galileans? No, I tell you; but unless you repent, you will all perish as they did. Or those eighteen who were killed when the tower of Siloam fell on them — do you think that they were worse offenders than all the others living in Jerusalem? No, I tell you; but unless you repent, you will all perish just as they did." (Luke 13:1-5)

To focus on national repentance is not to deny the need for personal repentance. Individual Israelites no doubt found in John's and Jesus' calls to righteousness a powerful conviction of their own sinfulness. Both the personal and the national dimensions were important, but the latter took precedence. The nation needed to change, but it could so only when individuals repented of their nation's past and walked in the faith that Jesus envisioned for the people of God.

We may now summarize what Jesus meant by conversion. There are two dimensions of conversion in Jesus' teachings: a positive movement toward Jesus and a negative movement away from sinfulness and unfaithfulness. The positive movement is best expressed in the concept of faith, while the negative movement finds its most lucid description in repentance. Faith involved a deliberate decision to commit oneself to Jesus and to his vision for the restoration of Israel as well as a whole-hearted commitment to his teachings and example. Repentance entailed internal self-denial as well as external signs. Conversion, then, was the decision to join the Jesus movement, to sit at table with Jesus in a public acknowledgment of his role in God's plan, to enlist oneself in his vision for the restoration of Israel, and to live the necessary lifestyle that such inclusion involved. Although conversion was a personal matter, it had national significance; it involved recognition of Jesus as the one who was calling the whole nation of Israel to restoration.

The Cost of Conversion to Jesus

Repenting and following Jesus came with a price. The following section will address the cost of conversion to Jesus under four headings: vocation, family, possessions, and self-denial.

Vocation

On various occasions, Jesus called people to abandon their vocations (the kind of vocation does not seem to have mattered[66]), to follow him, and to trust God to meet their needs (e.g., Q: Luke 12:22-31//Matt. 6:25-34). Examples are not hard to find. For instance, we find in Mark 1:16-20 a highly stylized report of the call of the first four disciples:

66. That Jesus called people who belonged to despised vocations to follow him, like the toll collector Levi/Matthew, is indeed remarkable (Mark 2:13-17; cf. Luke 7:34; 19:1-10).

> As Jesus passed along the Sea of Galilee, he saw Simon and his brother Andrew casting a net into the sea — for they were fishermen. And Jesus said to them, "Follow me and I will make you fish for people." And immediately they left their nets and followed him. As he went a little farther, he saw James son of Zebedee and his brother John, who were in their boat mending the nets. Immediately he called them; and they left their father Zebedee in the boat with the hired men, and followed him.

This tradition reflects massive compression (perhaps under the influence of 1 Kings 19:19-21), as we can see from the independent tradition about Peter in Luke 5:1-11, which gives a more detailed conversion/call story. However, the main outlines of the Gospel call stories remain historically credible.[67] For these Israelites, following Jesus meant abandoning their vocations, not because what they were doing (fishing and toll collecting) was unworthy of life in the kingdom, but because any vocation would have interfered with the call of Jesus.

Following Jesus involved not only abandoning one's livelihood but trusting Jesus and his Father to provide for one's daily needs. This is the point of several passages, especially a Q text in Luke 12:22-31// Matt. 6:25-34:

> He said to his disciples, "Therefore I tell you, do not worry about your life, what you will eat, or about your body, what you will wear. For life is more than food, and the body more than clothing. Consider the ravens: they neither sow nor reap, they have neither storehouse nor barn, and yet God feeds them. Of how much more value are you than the birds! And can any of you by worrying add a single hour to your span of life? If then you are not able to do so small a thing as that, why do you worry about the rest? Consider the lilies, how they grow: they neither toil nor spin; yet I tell you, even Solomon in all his glory was not clothed like one of these. But if God so clothes the grass of the field, which is alive today and tomorrow is thrown into the oven, how much more will he clothe you — you of little faith! And do not keep striving for what you are to eat and what you are to drink, and do not keep worrying. For it is the nations of the world

67. See also Mark 2:13-17 pars. for a similar condensed description. Condensations can relay historically reliable information.

that strive after all these things, and your Father knows that you need them. Instead, strive for his kingdom, and these things will be given to you as well."

Following Jesus in his new vision for Israel, the kingdom of God, means striving primarily for that kingdom instead of one's provisions. The Father who has anointed Jesus is the same Father who cares for those whom Jesus enlists in the kingdom. This text might appear simplistically optimistic about God's provision; the missionary instructions, however, make clear that God's provision is not a reenactment of the manna miracle but rather a situation in which new converts provide for those called to kingdom ministries (cf. Mark 6:8-11 par. and supplemented by Matt. 10:9-14; Luke 10:4-11).

The call to abandon one's vocation emerged from the call to announce the kingdom or, as the early tradition records it, to fish for more converts in Israel. Even if some of the disciples were drawn from the marginalized classes of Galilee, their decision to abandon their vocations was not simply an act of social protest against the ruling establishment but a commitment to announce the vision of Jesus to the nation and to bring the kingdom into their lives through acts of power (cf. Luke 10:3, 5-12). Leaving one's job means committing oneself to another task, kingdom proclamation:

"Follow me and I will make you fish for people." (Mark 1:17)

Christian interpretation has unfortunately sentimentalized this call, when it actually evokes a harsh reality: "fishing for people" recalls an image of both deliverance and judgment.[68] Several passages in the Old Testament utilize the image of fishing as a graphic image of God's judging sinful people (Jer. 16:16; Ezek. 29:4-5; Amos 4:2; Hab. 1:14-17). For instance, Jeremiah proclaimed in the name of the LORD:

I am now sending for many fishermen, says the LORD, and they shall catch them; and afterward I will send for many hunters, and they shall

68. The most complete analysis is W. H. Wuellner, *The Meaning of "Fishers of Men"* (Philadelphia: Westminster, 1967). See also C. W. F. Smith, "Fishers of Men: Footnotes on a Gospel Figure," *HTR* 52 (1959) 187-203; J. Mánek, "Fishers of Men," *NovT* 2 (1958) 138-41.

hunt them from every mountain and every hill, and out of the clefts of the rocks. For my eyes are on all their ways; they are not hidden from my presence, nor is their iniquity concealed from my sight. And I will doubly repay their iniquity and their sin, because they have polluted my land with the carcasses of their detestable idols, and have filled my inheritance with their abominations. (Jer 16:16-18)

On the other hand, Luke's wording, "from now on you will be catching people" (Luke 5:10), uses a Greek term that denotes capturing alive and that is decidedly more positive.[69] Another passage employing fishing imagery, the parable of the dragnet (Matt. 13:47-50), suggests that the metaphor is intended to describe both a restoring to life and a dragging into judgment, precisely the two results of the ministries of John, Jesus, and their followers (cf. Mark 6:10-11; Luke 10:5-12).[70]

Jesus' call for some to abandon their vocations, then, emerged from his vision for Israel as a nation on the edge of decision: if Israel decides for Jesus' vision, then the kingdom will come; if not, God will act in judgment. Into such a call Jesus, like Moses, Amos, and Jeremiah before him, initiated a few of his followers to accompany him. They, too, were to call the nation to either restoration or judgment.[71]

Family

Attached to the account of James and John leaving their vocation to follow Jesus is the note that "they left their father Zebedee in the boat with the hired men" (Mark 1:20//Matt. 4:21; cf. Luke 5:10). Thus another potential cost of following Jesus was departure from one's family. Only recently has the social significance of family in the ancient world become clear. The family provided for each individual social status and personal meaning, because identity for that person was fundamentally relational. To abandon the family in Jesus' world was an act of extreme hubris that required much deliberation and that brought with it serious social reprisals, if not persecution. Regular table fellowship with Jesus in the evenings thus engendered division.

69. Cf. BAGD, 340 (on ζωγρέω).
70. See Hengel, *Charismatic Leader,* 76-78.
71. See Hengel, *Charismatic Leader,* 73.

But there was a reason for this call to part from one's family: the coming judgment.[72] This is the context in which Jesus called his disciples to leave their families.[73]

The Gospel Evidence

Jesus' call to abandon family should not be allowed to obscure his fundamental affirmation of the family and its institutions.[74] In affirming the family, Jesus fell in line with Jewish tradition, and in spite of his harsh words about the family, he did affirm the obligation of children to parents (cf. Mark 7:9-13). Because this tradition conflicts with his call to abandon parents, we are on firm ground in assigning such a teaching to Jesus. Consistent with this tradition is his affirmation of the permanence of marriage (cf. Mark 10:1-12 par.; Luke 16:18; Matt. 5:31-32)[75] and the sinfulness of adultery (Matt. 5:27-30). One suspects that the tradition now found in John 19:26-27, where Jesus affirms his love for his mother in his dying breath, preserves an important historical record of Jesus' disposition toward his mother and to family in general. In line with both this strand of the Jesus tradition and the consistent Jewish tradition, it is not surprising that early Christian catechesis and ethics emerged in a family/household setting (Eph. 5:21–6:9; Col. 3:18–4:1; 1 Pet. 2:11–3:12; see also 1 Cor. 7:32-35; 11:2-16; 14:33-34; 2 Cor. 11:1-6).[76]

Jesus' radical call to leave family did not stem from an anti-authoritarian, bohemian desire to live on the fringe of society, nor did it reflect a countercultural, Cynic-type posture.[77] Rather, it had its ori-

72. See Weiß, *Jesus' Proclamation*, 109-12.

73. See further Schnackenburg, *Die sittliche Botschaft*, 1.144-55; Becker, *Jesus von Nazaret*, 388-98.

74. For Jesus' positive view of the family, see Schnackenburg, *Die sittliche Botschaft*, 1.144-55. On the family in Judaism, see Moore, *Judaism*, 2.119-40; S. Safrai, "Home and Family," in S. Safrai and M. Stern, eds., *The Jewish People in the First Century: Historical Geography, Political History, Social, Cultural, and Religious Life and Institutions*, (CRINT 1.2; Assen: Van Gorcum; Philadelphia: Fortress, 1976) 728-92.

75. See Goppelt, *Theology*, 1.110-12.

76. On family honor in Judaism, see G. Blidstein, *Honor Thy Father and Mother: Filial Responsibility in Jewish Law and Ethics* (New York: Ktav, 1975) esp. 75-121.

77. Two important studies that seek to portray Jesus as a Jewish Cynic are F. G. Downing, *Jesus and the Threat of Freedom* (London: SCM, 1987) and J. D. Crossan, *The Historical Jesus: The Life of a Mediterranean Jewish Peasant* (San Francisco: Harper-

gins in the biblical tradition, and it must be understood in light of the eschatological urgency of Jesus' message to the nation of Israel.

At least four separate traditions mention or focus on Jesus' call to abandon family honor in order to live honorably before God in the final hour. In addition to Mark 1:20 and Luke 5:9-11, mention must be made of the Q tradition behind Luke 9:59-60 (and 61-62).[78]

> To another he said, "Follow me." But he said, "Lord, first let me go and bury my father." But Jesus said to him, "Let the dead bury their own dead; but as for you, go and proclaim the kingdom of God."
>
> Another said, "I will follow you, Lord; but let me first say farewell to those at my home." Jesus said to him, "No one who puts a hand to the plow and looks back is fit for the kingdom of God."

The cutting edge is sharp; the call to follow Jesus has precedence over the obligation enshrined in the Torah to honor one's parents. Martin Hengel is therefore fully justified in saying that there "is hardly one logion of Jesus which more sharply runs counter to law, piety and custom than does Mt 8.22 = Lk 9.60a."[79] Luke 9:59-60 in particular frames Jesus' demand in a graphic and socially provocative manner: let those who do not subscribe to his vision for the restoration of Israel (the spiritually dead) take care of burying the physically dead. If it was binding in Judaism to bury one's father,[80] no matter what the cost and inconvenience (but cf. Lev. 21:11-12; Num. 6:6), then it was all the more binding to choose to follow Jesus as he inaugurated the kingdom for Israel. Jesus' demand called into question not only the biblical injunction to honor one's parents (Exod. 20:12) but also the pious practice of performing loving and merciful deeds (cf. Tobit 4:3-4; 6:15; 14:9, 11-12; *m. Abot* 1:2). Jesus' vision for Israel superseded Jewish custom, Jewish prayers, Jewish familial relations, and perhaps even the scriptures themselves. Those who followed him had to give up everything.

Another relevant passage, from Q, is found at Luke 12:51-53; 14:26//Matt. 10:34-39:

SanFrancisco, 1991). See also the brief critique of Wright, *Jesus and the Victory of God*, 66-74.

78. See esp. Hengel, *Charismatic Leader*.

79. Hengel, *Charismatic Leader*, 14; Sanders, *Jesus and Judaism*, 252-55.

80. The classic rabbinic text is *m. Ber.* 3:1.

"Do you think that I have come to bring peace to the earth? No, I tell you, but rather division! From now on five in one household will be divided, three against two and two against three; they will be divided:

> father against son
>   and son against father,
> mother against daughter
>   and daughter against mother,
> mother-in-law against her daughter-in-law
>   and daughter-in-law against mother-in-law."

"Whoever comes to me and does not hate father and mother, wife and children, brothers and sisters, yes, and even life itself, cannot be my disciple."

This text implies what a later tradition states: family breakups may occur, and celibacy may be required (Matt. 19:10-12). A similar theme emerges in Mark 13:12, in a logion relocated by Matthew to the missionary instructions (Matt. 10:21):

> "Brother will betray brother to death, and a father his child, and children will rise against parents and have them put to death."

These three traditions about the familial strife generated by the vision of Jesus have two different angles. The Markan tradition at 13:12 and the Q tradition at Luke 12:51-53 express in graphic fashion what takes place when family members disagree among themselves over the "Jesus question." The tradition of Q in Luke 14:26, however, approaches family tension from the angle of Jesus: no matter how stiff the opposition, one must follow him and abandon one's family. In a Jewish context of family honor and shame, two responses emerge: (1) those who do not think Jesus could possibly be the end-time prophet are dishonored and so lose social standing when a member of their family joins the Jesus movement; consequently, they fight for their honor with their own family members; and (2) those who do think Jesus is the one who can deliver and restore Israel are forced to make a decision; Jesus and such a family are incompatible. We can only try to imagine the turmoil such a dilemma generated within ancient Galilee.[81]

---

81. See R. A. Horsley, *Galilee: History, Politics, People* (Valley Forge, Penn.: Trin-

Sociological and Jewish Contexts

Recent use of social models for understanding earliest Christianity has an important contribution to make at this point. B. J. Malina and R. L. Rohrbaugh, for example, have argued persuasively that people in the first-century Mediterranean world were group oriented; their sense of self and conscience was bound up with their identity as members of a kin group, village group, and neighborhood. When, therefore, Jesus used terms like "love" and "hate" in his call to abandon family, he was really talking about "group attachment" and "disattachment."[82]

L. R. Rambo has analyzed the "crisis" involved in the process of conversion. Sociologists differ over whether the crisis comes prior to the encounter with the new religious option (and therefore generates a quest for conversion) or subsequent to the encounter (which then creates an introspection leading to a crisis). Two kinds of crises are analyzed: ones that call into question the fundamental orientation to life and ones that are somewhat mild but become the final event leading to a conversion. Crises come about as a result of various situations, including mystical experiences, illness and healing, a desire for transcendence, pathology, and apostasy. As Rambo has noted, "Some conversions require explicit and enacted rejection of past affiliations . . . . Apostasy inevitably elicits grief over lost relationships, ideas, beliefs, rituals, and connections with friends and family. The harshness with which some new converts denigrate their past can be understood when we realize that strong ties are being severed or realigned in a new religious orientation. . . . Denigration, then, is one tool for making the change more palatable or amenable."[83]

These insights on the nature of conversion shed light on Jesus' language about abandoning one's family. His harsh remarks ought to be seen as those of the "rhetorical Jesus," the way Jesus chose to express himself, rather than the "real Jesus," the Jesus who loved, cared, showed compassion, invited sinners to table, and who in general created peaceful relationships.[84] To show how important it was for his followers to

---

ity Press International, 1995) 195-201; idem, *Jesus and the Spiral of Violence: Popular Jewish Resistance in Roman Palestine* (San Francisco: Harper & Row, 1987) 209-45.

82. Malina and Rohrbaugh, *Social-Science Commentary,* 57-58.

83. Rambo, *Understanding Religious Conversion,* 53-54.

84. On the "rhetorical Jesus," see L. Gregory Bloomquist, "The Rhetoric of the Historical Jesus," in W. E. Arnal and M. Desjardins, eds., *Whose Historical Jesus?* (SCJ 7;

submit to his new vision, Jesus expressed himself in a rhetorical, but sociologically explicable, manner by urging his followers to abandon the family. Jesus spared no words to summon his disciples to total alignment with the kingdom.

Abandoning family was probably most visibly expressed in regular table fellowship with Jesus. The follower of Jesus would have left his family's table for Jesus' table and would thereby have offended his family. One can only imagine how Jesus' table fellowship affected the social reality of various families sharing a "backyard" court, where they mixed, shared meals, and observed various purity traditions.

Jesus' harsh remarks about family life and institutions, including marriage and procreation, were not unheard of in Judaism. Although his words were contrary to customary Jewish practice, they were not scandalously innovative. For instance, the prophetic life and celibacy are combined in Judaism (*b. Šabb.* 87a; Philo, *De Vit. Mos.* 2.68-69; *m. Soṭa* 9:15).[85] This evidence might suggest that Jesus' and John's advocacy of celibacy, for themselves and some of their followers, was a prophetic act and not simply radical behavior for its own sake. Thus, declining marriage and procreation was a potential cost of following Jesus but was understandable within Jewish tradition.

Furthermore, there was ample precedent in Jewish tradition for abandoning family in order to heed God's call. Abraham, for Jews the archetype of obedience to God, had to leave home and family so that God could lead him to the land of Canaan and establish a new people through him (Gen. 12:1-9). Jeremiah was instructed by God not to marry or to father children as a sign of the impending judgment on the kingdom of Judah (Jer. 16:1-4; cf. Ezek. 24:15-24). The story of Ruth depicts a convert leaving her family and native land. The Maccabee sons refused to let family commitments come between them and their zeal to restore the land (cf. 2 Macc. 15:17-19; 4 Macc. 8:1–14:10). Such zeal became typical in Judaism for those who believed they could save the nation from disaster. Thus, Jesus' calling some of his followers to abandon family is explicable within the Jewish prophetic tradition of obedience to God in order to restore the nation. Because Jesus was

Waterloo, Ont.: Wilfrid Laurier University Press, 1997) 98-117. Cf. G. B. Caird, *The Language and Imagery of the Bible* (reprint, Grand Rapids: Eerdmans, 1997) 111.

85. See G. Vermes, *Jesus the Jew: A Historian's Reading of the Gospels* (London: Fontana, 1976) 99-102.

prophet-like and his movement bore so many similarities to prophetic movements, and because his actions were so radical in orientation, we have no reason to doubt that he called some of his followers to break with family as so many other radical, prophetic-type leaders in Judaism had done.[86]

The Eschatological Context

Jesus' call to abandon family derived from his eschatological vision.[87] His stance toward the family was directly related to his vision of the eschatological community of Israel that would populate the kingdom.[88] Three texts deserve consideration for this point to be established:

> Then his mother and his brothers came; and standing outside, they sent to him and called him. A crowd was sitting around him; and they said to him, "Your mother and your brothers and sisters are outside, asking for you." And he replied, "Who are my mother and my brothers?" And looking at those who sat around him, he said, "Here are my mother and my brothers! Whoever does the will of God is my brother and sister and mother." (Mark 3:31-35 pars.)

> Jesus said, "Truly I tell you, there is no one who has left house or brothers or sisters or mother or father or children or fields, for my sake and for the sake of the good news, who will not receive a hundredfold now in this age — houses, brothers and sisters, mothers and children, and fields with persecutions — and in the age to come eternal life." (Mark 10:29-30 pars.)[89]

> Some Sadducees, who say there is no resurrection, came to him and asked him a question, saying, "Teacher, Moses wrote for us that 'if a man's brother dies, leaving a wife but no child, the man shall marry

86. On these prophet-like leaders, see P. W. Barnett, "The Jewish Sign Prophets — A.D. 40-70 — Their Intentions and Origin," *NTS* 27 (1981) 679-97; S. C. Barton, *Discipleship and Family Ties in Mark and Matthew* (SNTSMS 80; Cambridge: Cambridge University Press, 1994) 23-56, upon whom I have drawn in this section.
87. Hengel, *Charismatic Leader*, 15, 61-63.
88. See Goppelt, *Theology*, 1.110-12; Becker, *Jesus von Nazaret*, 388-98.
89. To this tradition, Matthew adds a Q tradition about the future for those who have left family; cf. Matt. 19:28; Luke 22:28-30. See Sanders, *Jesus and Judaism*, 98-102.

the widow and raise up children for his brother.' There were seven brothers; the first married and, when he died, left no children; and the second married her and died, leaving no children; and the third likewise; none of the seven left children. Last of all the woman herself died. In the resurrection whose wife will she be? For the seven had married her." Jesus said to them, "Is not this the reason you are wrong, that you know neither the scriptures nor the power of God? For when they rise from the dead, they neither marry nor are given in marriage, but are like angels in heaven. And as for the dead being raised, have you not read in the book of Moses, in the story about the bush, how God said to him, 'I am the God of Abraham, the God of Isaac, and the God of Jacob'? He is God not of the dead, but of the living; you are quite wrong." (Mark 12:18-27 pars.)

Here, in three separate traditions, we find a strand of Jesus' teachings about family abandonment that appears to be anchored in his vision of Israel in the kingdom: family ties there will no longer obtain.[90] His vision of the future community shaped his understanding of behavioral relations within the present family. The future community is not one of physical relations but of a totally new order (Mark 12:25). As R. A. Horsley observes, "Jesus had a highly positive sense of the family, but he transformed the criterion for membership from physical kinship and adherence to patriarchal authority to doing the will of God. . . ."[91] Resurrected Israelites who enter the kingdom of God would be sexless in their relations to one another; they would be related as spiritual beings, and procreation would no longer have any use. Levirate marriage laws would be suspended as each person serves God like the angels (cf. *b. Ber.* 17a). Thus, Jesus viewed marital ties and family relations as impermanent arrangements that would give way to a higher order of relations in God's kingdom.

In light of this future vision, Jesus' words about present relations take on a new meaning: because the final order, the kingdom of God, transcends the present order, present relations may very well need to be surrendered in order to live for and attain the kingdom. So, when Jesus

90. See Hengel, *Charismatic Leader*, 13; Horsley, *Jesus and the Spiral of Violence*, 231-45.

91. Horsley, *Jesus and the Spiral of Violence*, 237; cf. Wiebe, *Messianic Ethics*, 129-31.

186

identified his true family members as those who do the will of God, he was not denying his own family relations to Mary, or to his brothers and sisters, but contending that those who followed him would inherit the final kingdom and that it was to them that he had to give his attention and affection. Accordingly, when the dividing line was drawn (as can be seen in Mark 10:29-30), Jesus expected those he called to leave their families to join the restored nation. But he promised that on the other side of the divide stood a surrogate family: his other followers. For Jesus, this new community would be an earthly family, not a heavenly, spiritual one.[92]

We may conclude, then, that Jesus called some of his followers to leave their families but did so in light of his vision of the future kingdom, which would include family relations that transcend current physical relations. Those who leave their families now, however, are not left desolate; they immediately are ushered into a new family of those who have joined Jesus' movement for a restored Israel. Jesus may have thought of this new family as the remnant of the restored Israel. In all likelihood, only those followers whose families objected to Jesus' mission had to leave their families behind. One can easily imagine whole families seeing in Jesus God's final envoy to Israel. For such families there would be no discord (Q: Luke 12:51-53; 14:26-27), for they would now belong to the eschatological community around Jesus.

Possessions

The call of the first disciples contains yet one more element of the cost of following Jesus: they not only abandoned their vocations and families; they gave up their possessions.[93] Jesus' call to abandon possessions stemmed from his understanding of the incomparable claim of God on the lives of Israelites in light of the dawning kingdom.[94]

At the outset, we should acknowledge that Jesus personally benefited from the wealth and possessions of others. He stayed in other peo-

---

92. See Horsley, *Jesus and the Spiral of Violence*, 239.

93. See Schlatter, *History*, 166-74; Schnackenburg, *Die sittliche Botschaft*, 1.135-43; Jeremias, *Proclamation of Jesus*, 221-23; Goppelt, *Theology*, 1.79-84; Harvey, *Strenuous Commands*, 116-39.

94. See Weiß, *Jesus' Proclamation*, 107-8.

ple's homes (e.g., Mark 1:29), he consumed their food (Matt. 11:19; Luke 7:36; 14:1; John 12:1-3), he availed himself of their financial support (Luke 8:1-4; cf. also Mark 7:9-13), and he encouraged them to give out of their abundance (Luke 6:29-30, 34-35; 14:12-13; Matt. 6:1-4; 25:40). He evidently enjoyed the generosity of others. In none of these circumstances did he call the wealthy to abandon their homes or their possessions. Yet, although he did not in principle disapprove of owning property, "an unrestricted right to private property would never have entered Jesus' head."[95]

Jesus clearly taught the necessity of a personal reorientation around the kingdom before one could properly value possessions and wealth. He assigned top priority to seeking the kingdom; it had to control every movement and decision of his followers:

> "For what will it profit them to gain the whole world and forfeit their life?" (Mark 8:36 pars.)

> "Truly I tell you, there is no one who has left house or brothers or sisters or mother or father or children or fields, for my sake and for the sake of the good news, who will not receive a hundredfold now in this age — houses, brothers and sisters, mothers and children, and fields with persecutions — and in the age to come eternal life." (Mark 10:29-30 pars.)

> "But strive first for the kingdom of God and his righteousness, and all these things will be given to you as well." (Matt. 6:33//Luke 12:31)

> "The kingdom of heaven is like treasure hidden in a field, which someone found and hid; then in his joy he goes and sells all that he has and buys that field. Again, the kingdom of heaven is like a merchant in search of fine pearls; on finding one pearl of great value, he went and sold all that he had and bought it." (Matt. 13:44-46)

> Someone in the crowd said to him, "Teacher, tell my brother to divide the family inheritance with me." But he said to him, "Friend, who set me to be a judge or arbitrator over you?" And he said to them, "Take care! Be on your guard against all kinds of greed; for

95. Schrage, *Ethics*, 105.

one's life does not consist in the abundance of possessions." Then he told them a parable: "The land of a rich man produced abundantly. And he thought to himself, 'What should I do, for I have no place to store my crops?' Then he said, 'I will do this: I will pull down my barns and build larger ones, and there I will store all my grain and my goods. And I will say to my soul, 'Soul, you have ample goods laid up for many years; relax, eat, drink, be merry.' But God said to him, 'You fool! This very night your life is being demanded of you. And the things you have prepared, whose will they be?' So it is with those who store up treasures for themselves but are not rich toward God." (Luke 12:13-21)

The general thrust of this stream in the Jesus tradition is obvious: it is far more important to follow Jesus, to orient one's life around the kingdom, and to do God's will than to pursue wealth and amass possessions for one's social elevation or personal comfort. Following Jesus meant pursuing the kingdom, and pursuing the kingdom meant orienting one's whole life around Jesus' call to Israel to repent so as to restore the nation. Pursuing riches was the alternative, and that meant living one's life as if the current course of events was more than adequate for achieving what God had planned for Israel or as if one did not care about Israel's fortunes. Thus, Jesus' call to orient one's economic life around the kingdom was a social protest against the status quo in Israel. Among other things, his protest deemed Roman occupation of the land of Israel unacceptable and regarded compromising arrangements with the imperial economy as abominable. For Jesus' followers, joining in this social protest meant suffering physical deprivation — as Matt. 6:25-34//Luke 12:22-31 indicate.[96]

In Roman Galilee and Judea, one's possessions were indicators of one's social status (cf. Josephus, *Ant.* 11:254; Luke 15:22). When Israelites reoriented their lives around Jesus and the kingdom, they lost honor, assumed social shame, and dragged their family name along with them. Jesus' call of the first disciples (Mark 1:16-20 pars.; Luke 5:1-11) was no doubt opposed by their respective families, and social tensions were sure to have followed (cf. Luke 12:51-53 par.). Jesus' call to reorient one's attitude toward possessions around the kingdom

96. See G. Theissen, *Sociology of Early Palestinian Christianity* (trans. J. Bowden; Philadelphia: Fortress, 1978) 13.

was therefore a call to social shame, to self-denial, and to personal crucifixion.[97]

Jesus warned his disciples of the inherent dangers of wealth and accumulation. Possessions are impermanent (Matt. 6:19-21; cf. Luke 12:13-21; 16:9, 19-31). They are like metallic objects that rust and houses that get robbed. Enjoyment of them ends the moment one dies. Wealth can render a person insensitive toward God:

> "No one can serve two masters; for a slave will either hate the one and love the other, or be devoted to the one and despise the other. You cannot serve God and wealth." (Matt. 6:24//Luke 16:13)[98]

Jesus pictured the relation with God and wealth in terms of servitude, assuming that each requires and can command devotion, allegiance, and worship. When the so-called rich young ruler faces the alternative of following Jesus and abandoning his wealth or maintaining his current lifestyle, he chooses the latter because it is too hard for him to give up his opulent life (Mark 10:17-31 pars.). Luke, drawing upon one of his favorite traditions, tells several stories about the dangers of accumulation (Luke 12:13-21; 16:19-31) but only one story of a person who escaped its clutches (Zacchaeus: 19:1-10). Jesus did not explicate *why* wealth and possessions are dangerous; he stated only *that* they are dangerous. Preoccupation with possessions is inconsistent with the core value of restoring the nation.

Jesus' warnings against the dangers of wealth drew in part on themes in the Hebrew Bible.[99] Two traditions need to be noted here. According to one, the people of God can grow fat on their wealth, their "blessing," and can forsake God (cf. Deut. 32:10-18; Isa. 2:6-8; Jer. 5:7-9; Hag. 1:7-12). According to another, wealth can sometimes result not

---

97. See J. H. Neyrey, "Loss of Wealth, Loss of Family and Loss of Honour," in P. F. Esler, ed., *Modelling Early Christianity: Social-scientific Studies in the New Testament in Its Context* (London: Routledge, 1995) 139-58.

98. Cf. *Gospel of Thomas* 47a: "Jesus said, 'A person cannot mount two horses or bend two bows. And a servant cannot serve two lords; that servant will honor one and offend the other.'"

99. See M. Hengel, *Property and Riches in the Early Church: Aspects of a Social History of Early Christianity* (trans. J. Bowden; Philadelphia: Fortress, 1974); S. E. Wheeler, *Wealth as Peril and Obligation: The New Testament on Possessions* (Grand Rapids: Eerdmans, 1994).

from God's blessing but from injustice or fraud (Micah 6:9-12; Isa. 5:8-10; 10:1-11; Amos 5:10-12; 8:4-8). Jesus was evidently wary of a simplistic reading of the Deuteronomic tradition, which often seems to regard prosperity as an automatic sign of God's blessing. At any rate, he did not counter the Deuteronomic view simply with a call to help the poor or to engage in moral reform. Instead, he saw wealth as a direct challenge to loving God. For Jesus the law of God was at stake here: "you shall have no other gods before me" (Exod. 20:3).[100]

His most particular demand in this regard, accordingly, was that his followers develop a radical detachment from possessions, though this need not have entailed a total and permanent abandonment of all of them. Those who find in Jesus the pearl of great price are willing to leave all other pearls to obtain the great one (Matt. 13:45-46); they find an uncommon capacity to surrender their hold on their possessions. One is reminded of a story about the Maccabees: Mattathias, after his famous defiance of the officers of Antiochus Epiphanes, calls out for other like-minded Israelites to join him. To this Josephus adds the comment, "So saying, he set out with his sons into the wilderness, leaving behind all his property in the village. And many others did the same . . ." (*Ant.* 2.271-72).

Jesus enjoined detachment from possessions on two levels — a practical level and a radical level. One the one hand, he expected his followers to detach themselves from the idolatry of wealth and possessions, but on the other hand, he called some of them to abandon everything.

On the first level, Jesus advocated an attitude toward wealth that expresses itself in the course of everyday life. He told his followers to be carefree in their orientation toward their possessions and economic security:

> "Therefore I tell you, do not worry about your life, what you will eat, or about your body, what you will wear. . . . And do not keep striving for what you are to eat and what you are to drink, and do not keep worrying. For it is the nations of the world that strive after all these things, and your Father knows that you need them. Instead, strive for his kingdom, and these things will be given to you as well." (Matt. 6:25-34//Luke 12:22-31)

100. Goppelt, *Theology*, 1.83.

This tradition, which may well have emerged originally from missionary instructions, exhorts the followers of Jesus not to allow themselves to be distracted from their orientation toward the kingdom by the cares of this world (cf. Mark 4:19). Instead, they are to focus on the restored nation and let God provide for them. Anxiety and trust are incompatible.[101]

In this carefree attitude, the followers of Jesus are to trust in God for their ordinary provisions (Luke 12:30-31; Mark 6:8-10 pars.). Above all, this is the implication of the Lord's Prayer:

> "When you pray, say:
> Father, hallowed be your name.
> Your kingdom come.
> Give us each day our daily bread."[102] (Luke 11:2-3)

This prayer is rooted in the harsh reality of those who adopted an itinerant lifestyle in response to Jesus' call to restore the nation of Israel. Only a carefree attitude toward provisions permitted the followers of Jesus to embark on a path that brought no guarantees of food, clothing, and shelter. Trust in God became for Jesus the only antidote to the anxiety that naturally arises in the human heart to provide for itself. Trust in the Father also formed the basis for coping with loss of family, once the major system of provision for Jesus' followers.

At times, Jesus called his followers to abandon every form of financial security, including their vocations, their families, and their social networks. In the story of the rich young ruler (Mark 10:17-31 pars.), the critical moment in the dialogue is this:

> Jesus, looking at him, loved him and said, "You lack one thing; go, sell what you own, and give the money to the poor, and you will have treasure in heaven; then come, follow me."

To this man, because he has turned his possessions into gods and lords (cf. Isa. 3:16-24; Ezek. 7:19-20), comes the call to abandon possessions

101. See Harnack, *What Is Christianity?* 86.
102. On the meaning of "daily bread," see Davies and Allison, *Matthew,* 1.607-10. Jesus likely had in mind an earthly, physical provision rather than an eschatological one.

completely. Peter's reaction to this confrontation is to tell Jesus, "Look, we have left everything and followed you" (Mark 10:28). The call to the rich young ruler is an *exceptional* call, even though Luke records Jesus as having said:

> "So therefore, none of you can become my disciple if you do not give up all your possessions." (Luke 14:33)

This saying is hyperbolic in form and so cannot mean that all must give up all their possessions *since not all did*.[103] True repentance to follow Jesus in his call to Israel involves a total personal reorientation. Those who build towers and who go to war consider carefully the cost and whether they are capable of pulling it off; likewise, those who follow Jesus must carefully consider what they are doing and surrender themselves totally to Jesus, so that the nation can experience a reversal of fortunes. Those who surrender give up all their possessions to Jesus in their personal reorientation.

The call to abandon wealth is part of the larger picture we have been sketching throughout this study, namely, Jesus' status as the end-time agent of God, the incoming kingdom or restoration of the nation, and the threat of a coming disaster. Those who were swept up by Jesus into this vision for Israel were more than willing to abandon their servitude to mammon, because they found in Jesus the restoration of Israel and the consummation of God's promises to Israel.[104]

In all this Jesus was responding to the Deuteronomic view of wealth as a blessing from God and poverty as a curse from God (Deuteronomy 28). He turned that tradition on its head by calling his followers to a provocatively public action of not only giving up all but also including the poor in the new Israel of God. Jesus called his followers to another perspective on wealth in light of the coming kingdom, and so the Deuteronomic tradition, so honored by his contemporaries, had to give way to the new wine of God's kingdom.[105]

---

103. Lohse, *Theological Ethics*, 49.
104. Jeremias, *Proclamation of Jesus*, 223.
105. Hengel, *Property and Riches*, 30; see also Harnack, *What Is Christianity?* 82-83.

Self-Denial

We touched on the topic of the personal cost of following Jesus above in the section on internal repentance, but more needs to be said at this point in order to draw attention to the integral relation of self-denial and world-denial.

The followers of Jesus chose to enlist in his cause, to embrace his vision for the restoration for Israel, but to do this they had to go through a process of personal abnegation, an aspect of internal repentance best seen in the twin images of self-denial and taking up the cross.[106] The critical text for this discussion is Mark 8:34 pars.:[107]

> He called the crowd with his disciples, and said to them, "If any want to become my followers, let them deny themselves and take up their cross and follow me."

The logion is a simple chiasm: (A) follow — (B) deny — (B′) die — (A′) follow. Such a logion requires that the two central elements be understood similarly; self-denial and assumption of the cross both speak of the appropriate disposition of the follower of Jesus. But what did self-denial and taking up the cross mean for Jesus?

There are two elements to the act of self-denial: *personal condemnation* and *kingdom-through-Jesus affirmation*. Personal condemnation finds expression in the B units of the chiasm in Mark 8:34 par. ("deny" and "die"); the kingdom-through-Jesus affirmation, in the A units ("follow" and "follow"). To deny oneself without affirming Jesus and the kingdom is nothing but self-disciplined asceticism, a sort of picking oneself up by the bootstraps in an act of personal courage. To affirm the kingdom-through-Jesus without self-denial, on the other hand, trivializes the God of Israel by taking hold of his offer of restoring Israel without the necessary act of surrender that permits one to enter the covenant relationship.

The long popular notion that bearing one's cross pertains to personal problems that need to be endured in life (e.g., an insensitive

---

106. See Bonhoeffer, *Cost*, 95-104; Cothenet, *Imitating Christ*, 13-15; M. Borg, *Jesus: A New Vision: Spirit, Culture, and the Life of Discipleship* (San Francisco: Harper & Row, 1988) 112-15.

107. The redactional elements of Matthew are insignificant; Luke's addition of "daily" (Luke 9:23), however, is clearly an attempt to make the text an ever-present reality.

spouse, a demanding employer, a physical weakness, a personal struggle) both trivializes the logion of Jesus and sacrifices its historical sense on the altar of personal relevance. To be sure, what Jesus had in mind can include physical suffering, but only because of an attachment to Jesus, not the frailty of mortal existence.[108] Perhaps at no point in the mission of Jesus is the historical context more needed than when we interpret Jesus' summons to self-denial.

Crucifixion would have been a graphic image of self-denial at the time of Jesus.[109] This particular form of death was a sadistic penalty used by the Romans against especially violent or unruly criminals, and it was designed to be a public deterrent. Personally, it humiliated the Jewish victim because of nudity, but, even more, all the members of the family were publicly shamed by the incident. Those so put to death were refused a normal burial, which was an insult both to the one crucified and to the family. By using this image to describe the cost of discipleship, Jesus intended to express that following him would involve a self-humiliating act of total surrender in a shameful public context of intense physical suffering. Accordingly, discipleship meant identifying with Jesus, even to the point of joining him in enduring personal and social shame. It meant surrendering oneself even to the point of physical death. The memorable line of Dietrich Bonhoeffer says it all: "When Christ calls a man, he bids him come and die."[110]

We can unpack this point historically as follows: Jesus had a vision for Israel; those who chose to follow him needed to understand that their act would provoke opposition, because his vision was unacceptable to the majority in Israel. Those who felt the gravity of the opposition to Jesus' new vision for the nation now had in the cross, the Roman instrument of personal torture and public humiliation, another image that expressed the heart of Jesus: you must die if you want to follow me and to bring this vision to fruition, but God is on our side.

Once again, however, a social context needs to be kept before us. Self-denial, or taking up the cross to follow Jesus, meant social identification with Jesus as one who claimed to be the end-time prophet ushering in the kingdom of God. Following Jesus required accepting his vi-

---

108. See Bonhoeffer, *Cost*, 98.

109. See esp. M. Hengel, *Crucifixion* (trans. J. Bowden; Philadelphia: Fortress, 1977).

110. Bonhoeffer, *Cost*, 99.

sion for Israel and living by that vision. The language of self-denial, then, was a way of talking about refusing the current approach to maintaining Israel's covenant with God and putting in its place a countervision of how to keep that covenant. Thus, the call to self-denial entailed more than a personal, private act of faith; it demanded a public act of identification with Jesus. Self-denial was denial of the current vision of Israel and acceptance of another vision of Israel. Taking up the cross was therefore a programmatic image of realizing God's vision for the restoration of the nation.

It remains for us to ask, in the next chapter, what sort of ethical behavior Jesus envisioned for those who embraced such a vision for Israel and followed him. What is the moral character of the life to which Jesus called those who had converted and paid the necessary cost of following him?

CHAPTER 6

The Ethic of Jesus: Morality

Having examined the first two features of the ethic of Jesus, conversion and the cost of discipleship, we will now look at the moral teachings of Jesus. In our discussion of the kingdom of God, we saw that kingdom and morality are correlated in the ethic of Jesus. Since this correlation affects our understanding of Jesus' teaching of morality, a word of explanation is in order. The starting point here is the understanding that the kingdom of God is presently operative in Jesus and his offer to Israel. The ancient hope, so majestically articulated by the prophets, of a kingdom where peace, justice, and love obtained, where oppression would no longer exist, and where every Israelite would long to obey the law of God — this ancient hope is now fulfilled in history as Jesus brings those promises into operation.[1] Jesus thought that a new day had dawned and that the Israelites of his generation had the opportunity to live under conditions that were only a dream for the prophets. Part of that dream involved morality (Matt. 13:16-17). Although this realization of the ethical ideal of the prophets differs from what Paul meant by the indwelling of the Spirit, Jesus anticipated that theme in Pauline theology. The antitheses of the Sermon on the Mount ("you have heard it was said . . . but I say to you . . .") emerged from just this perception: a new day for Israel has dawned, a new day of salvation, of restoration, of the end of exile, and therefore of a new obedience. Accordingly, the ethic of Jesus was a kingdom ethic, though we must rec-

---

1. See esp. A. N. Wilder, *Eschatology and Ethics in the Teaching of Jesus* (rev. ed.; New York: Harper and Bros., 1950) 145-62.

197

ognize a necessary dialectic between present fulfillment and future consummation.[2]

Although the ethic of Jesus concerned life in the kingdom, he did not neatly distinguish between present moral capacities and future ones but spoke of what God wants for his people when the kingdom arrives. He intended his ethic to consummate God's will revealed through Moses and the prophets but also to extend the scriptural tradition. But Jesus did not say that "this can be done now" and "this, however, can't be done until later." Rather, he stated the will of God in all its ruggedness and boldness. The one who met his ethical demands could apply the will of God to every aspect of life, even allowing shortcomings and failings. Accordingly, Jesus refused to accommodate his ethic to the weaknesses of human nature, on the conviction that his ethic derived ultimately from the nature of God (cf. Matt. 5:48; Luke 6:36). God's nature and kingdom, therefore, form an intimate connection, because the nature of God will be on display in the final kingdom and will determine all that takes place.

The kingdom was not completely fulfilled but only inaugurated by Jesus. Because there is more of the kingdom yet to be realized, there is also more of the ethic of the kingdom to be realized. The fullness of the ethical dream of the prophets, and even of Jesus, is not achievable, because the fullness of the kingdom is not yet here. "Jesus, then, prescribes an ethics for the life of a community living in expectation of the eschatological future. Indeed, the ethics is the anticipation in the life of the community of that eschatological future in the present."[3] So Jesus did allow a kind of accommodation to current conditions; perfection cannot be achieved until a perfect kingdom has been realized, but it can be taught. The time of glory, magnificence, and purity remains a hope; so too the full realization of the ethic connected to those.

The corollary is obvious: to the degree that the kingdom has been realized, its ethic can also be realized by the nation Jesus is now restoring. Jesus looked upon his day as a time of inauguration, a time of partial but real fulfillment of the kingdom. Yet, the complete realization of God's will in the lives of individual Israelites who enjoy God's covenant faithfulness would come in the future. The ethic Jesus advocated in the

---

2. Wilder, *Eschatology and Ethics,* 160.

3. B. Wiebe, *Messianic Ethics: Jesus' Proclamation of the Kingdom of God and the Church in Response* (Scottdale, Penn.: Herald, 1992) 123.

present was only a partial realization of this future, consummated ethic.[4]

This means that correlation of kingdom and ethics dominated the expectation of Jesus for how his followers were to implement the will of God in Israel. The morality of a follower of Jesus is therefore a morality in anticipation, a morality that takes off in the direction of the kingdom but carries with it all the obvious features of real life in a real world that is not yet fully capable of achieving the will of God. It is an Israelite's actualization of the kingdom in anticipation of the kingdom. Thus, as Joachim Jeremias said:

> When we consider the individual demands made by Jesus, it is striking how *incomplete* they are. Jesus does not give instructions for all spheres of life; he does not offer a moral theology or a code of behaviour. Rather, his demands give symptoms, signs, examples of what happens when the reign of God breaks into a world that is still in the power of sin, death and the devil. The *basileia* [kingdom] lays claim to the whole of life. Jesus uses illustrations to demonstrate the appearance of the new life. His disciples are to apply them to every other aspect of their life. They themselves are to be signs of the reign of God, signs that something has happened.[5]

A convenient principle of organization for presenting the teachings of Jesus on morality is to categorize them in relational terms: how a follower relates to *God*, to *self*, and to *others*. The relationship governs the ethic, so that one's relationship to one's self differs from one's relationship to others and to God. To complicate the picture, the relation to God governs the relation to self and to others. There is, then, a dialectical relationship among God, self, and others with the self standing in the middle, a self transformed by God's grace through repentance and trust. The self that relates to others is a self that has already related to God and, in the process, is renewed to be a different self. From another angle, God is in the middle: both the self and others relate to God and can only relate to one another in light of their relation to God.

4. See W. Schrage, *The Ethics of the New Testament* (trans. D. E. Green; Philadelphia: Fortress, 1988) 29-30.

5. J. Jeremias, *New Testament Theology: The Proclamation of Jesus* (trans. J. Bowden; New York: Charles Scribner's Sons, 1971) 230. See also G. B. Caird, *New Testament Theology* (completed and edited by L. D. Hurst; Oxford: Clarendon, 1994) 390-91.

Fundamentally, the moral teaching of Jesus centered on relations to other persons, not to laws or institutions.[6] At the base of his teaching is not the question "Which law is the most significant?" but "How are we to relate to God, to self, and to others?" Particular institutions, even if held in high honor by Jesus, are ultimately shaped by the relation in question. Jesus' strong words about divorce (Mark 10:1-12 pars.; Matt. 5:31-32), for instance, are appeals not to the potential beauty or permanence of marriage, but to the fundamental relation of a man to a woman and a woman to a man in the order of creation. When the Pharisees appealed to Deut. 24:1-3 to legitimate divorce by appeal to the law of Moses, Jesus pointed to a deeper connection of marriage, also found in the law (Gen. 1:27 and 2:24), to the formation of "one flesh" by a God who did not intend separation. He went further and said that divorce puts a woman at risk and leads her into adultery (cf. Mark 10:1-12). Jesus, then, appealed to the relations in question rather than to the institution.

Relation to God

Two terms accurately grasp what Jesus said about a follower's relationship with God: *righteousness* and *love*. Undoubtedly, other terms deserve consideration; our concern here, though, is not to offer a comprehensive survey but to show how the national mission of Jesus shaped his moral teachings.

Righteousness[7]

Though we find the term *righteousness* chiefly in the Gospel of Matthew,[8] we have good reasons for thinking that Jesus not only used

---

6. See, for instance, L. Goppelt, *Theology of the New Testament* (2 vols.; trans. J. E. Alsup; ed. J. Roloff; Grand Rapids: Eerdmans, 1981-82) 1.109; G. Vermes, *The Religion of Jesus the Jew* (Minneapolis: Fortress, 1993) 44-45.

7. See S. McKnight, "Justice, Righteousness," *DJG*, 411-16.

8. I cannot agree, however, that Jesus avoided the term because it expressed the supposedly inferior concept of "works" in Judaism; this view goes back at least as far as G. Dalman, *Jesus-Jeshua: Studies in the Gospels* (trans. P. P. Levertoff; New

the term (and its cognates), but also intended for it to express a fundamentally critical relation of his followers to God. Unfortunately, scholars have often allowed the Pauline use of this term to intrude upon Jesus' usage of it, even though Jesus employed the term in a way that was decidedly un-Pauline. For Paul (at least as commonly understood by Protestants), *righteousness* denotes a relation to God that is granted to a believing person as a result of God's gracious forgiveness, a relation that cannot be earned, because humans sin and their sinfulness prevents them from being acceptable to God without his intervention. In Galatians and Romans, Paul adapts the term from his religious and especially legal world and uses it differently for the new relation to God.[9] Paul's usage stands in marked contrast with the emphasis of the term both in Judaism and in the teaching of Jesus.[10]

In Judaism the word primarily describes a person's relationship to God and his law in a moral, behavioral sense (cf. Job 22:6-9, 23; Ps. 1:4-6; Ezek. 45:9; *Ps. Sol.* 15:1-13). Deuteronomy 6:25 typifies the standard use of the term: "If we diligently observe this entire commandment before the LORD our God, as he has commanded us, we will be in the *right*." That the term is primarily describing a relationship of a person to a standard is ably demonstrated by Gen. 38:26 and 1 Sam. 24:17; in each case what might be described as less than ideal behavior becomes an act of righteousness. Paul, however, believed that no person, whether Israelite or not, could ever again be righteous in this sense; he therefore used the term to describe what takes place when God, in spite of the sinfulness of human beings, chooses to make them acceptable in his presence through the sacrifice of Jesus. But this is not the emphasis Jesus gave to the term. We should therefore bracket the Pauline understanding of *righteousness* and reacquaint ourselves with the context out of which Jesus was speaking, in which the term primarily described one's behavior with respect to the law.

The spheres of covenant obedience and discipleship form the con-

---

York: Macmillan, 1929) 69, and it continues to appear now and again in current scholarship.

9. A fine summary of the issues can now be found in J. D. G. Dunn, *The Theology of Paul the Apostle* (Grand Rapids: Eerdmans, 1997) 334-89.

10. The contrast between Judaism and Jesus, on the one hand, and Paul on the other is mitigated in the analysis of Dunn, *Theology*, 334-89.

text of Jesus' use of the term *righteousness*.[11] Righteousness for Jesus encompassed both covenant faithfulness, as advocated by the ancient prophets, and obedience to his understanding of the will of God. More importantly, in light of the dawn of God's kingdom, a kingdom characterized by righteousness (Psalms 97–99; Isa. 11:1-5; *1 Enoch* 62:1-16), Jesus' call to righteousness needs to be understood in eschatological terms: the righteousness to which he called his followers was the long-expected righteousness pertaining to the restoration of the nation. The moral vision of those who followed him in this eschatological vision was to be characterized by righteousness; they were to live their lives in obedience to God's final will and conform their behavior to God's final code of conduct.[12]

Jesus' call to righteousness stood in continuity with the ministry of John the Baptist, who had called on his fellow Israelites to lead moral lives conformed to God's will for the nation. Both John and Jesus called the nation to return to the covenant that God had made with Israel, and both of them envisioned an eschatological restoration of Israel for those who responded. The ingredient of righteousness, of obeying God's will as uncovered in their interpretation of the Torah, formed an integral aspect of the social and communal nature of this restoration of Israel (cf., e.g., Mark 2:13-17).

The call to restoration in terms of righteousness, made by John and continued by Jesus, can be seen in two separate traditions:

"For John came to you in the way of righteousness and you did not believe him, but the tax collectors and the prostitutes believed him; and even after you saw it, you did not change your minds and believe him." (Matt. 21:32)

John said to the crowds that came out to be baptized by him, "You brood of vipers! Who warned you to flee from the wrath to come?

11. On the relation of Jesus to the law of Moses, see esp. R. Banks, *Jesus and the Law in the Synoptic Tradition* (SNTSMS 28; Cambridge: Cambridge University Press, 1975); S. Westerholm, *Jesus and Scribal Authority* (CBNT 10; Lund: Gleerup, 1978).

12. The "surpassing righteousness" of Matt. 5:20 would therefore describe a moral, behavioral conformity to the will of God that has now been revealed even more completely in the wake of the arrival of the kingdom in Jesus as he proclaims God's will to Israel. See B. Przybylski, *Righteousness in Matthew and His World of Thought* (SNTSMS 41; Cambridge: Cambridge University Press, 1980) 80-87; Banks, *Jesus and the Law,* 224-26.

Bear fruits worthy of repentance. Do not begin to say to yourselves, 'We have Abraham as our ancestor'; for I tell you, God is able from these stones to raise up children to Abraham. Even now the ax is lying at the root of the trees; every tree therefore that does not bear good fruit is cut down and thrown into the fire." And the crowds asked him, "What then should we do?" In reply he said to them, "Whoever has two coats must share with anyone who has none; and whoever has food must do likewise." Even tax collectors came to be baptized, and they asked him, "Teacher, what should we do?" He said to them, "Collect no more than the amount prescribed for you." Soldiers also asked him, "And we, what should we do?" He said to them, "Do not extort money from anyone by threats or false accusation, and be satisfied with your wages." (Luke 3:7-14)

The details of John's call to those who sought his baptism are precisely the kinds of practices considered "acts of righteousness" or "deeds of mercy" in the historic traditions of Israel: sharing possessions freely, collecting taxes justly, and treating others kindly. When this is coupled with his call to repentance, and to his rejection of ancestry as an inadequate foundation for a covenant relationship to the God of Israel — not to mention his challenge of the Roman power (Mark 6:17-29) — it is not surprising that the M tradition sees in John the one who came in the way of righteousness (Matt. 21:32), a reference no doubt to how he himself lived and to how he called Israel to act in light of the coming judgment. John's call to social reformation provided for Jesus a foundation for his own call to repentance and righteousness.

Jesus *may* have described Israelites as righteous because they were morally obedient to God, because they did God's will and wanted God's will to be done throughout the nation. Two Q traditions point in this direction:

"Truly I tell you, many prophets and righteous people longed to see what you see, but did not see it, and to hear what you hear, but did not hear it." (Matt 13:17//Luke 10:24)

"Woe to you, scribes and Pharisees, hypocrites! For you build the tombs of the prophets and decorate the graves of the righteous. . . . so that upon you may come all the righteous blood shed on earth, from the blood of righteous Abel to the blood of Zechariah son of

203

Barachiah, whom you murdered between the sanctuary and the al-tar." (Matt 23:29, 35)

Many scholars regard all four uses of the term *righteous* in these two pas-sages as stemming from the hand of Matthew.[13] Where the Matthean wording has "righteous people," the Lukan parallel (apparently repre-senting the wording of Q more faithfully) has "kings" (Luke 10:24). With respect to the second tradition, however, some have argued that the term *righteous* describes not the followers of Jesus but ancient Israelite heroes and that the occurrence of the term therefore does not owe to Matthean redaction (since most of Matthew's editorial work concerns the followers of Jesus). However, its absence in the Lukan parallels in both logia (Luke 11:47, 50) speaks in favor of Matthean redaction. Arguing on the basis of this evidence, we can say only that the usage in Matt. 23:29, 35 coheres with the usage in Matt. 13:17. But, since Matt. 13:17 probably manifests redactional reworking, we must exclude these two traditions as firm evi-dence for how Jesus used the category *righteous*. It is possible, however, that these traditions are early; hence the cautious claim that Jesus *may* have used this term for Israelites.

Jesus also described as righteous those who obeyed his own teach-ings. Here is the firmest ground for understanding how Jesus expected his disciples to relate to God in the area of morality. In so doing, Jesus redefined the term in a manner parallel to what we find in the Dead Sea Scrolls, where the instruction of the Teacher of Righteousness sets a new standard for the sectarian community at Qumran (CD 4:7; 20:20-21; 1QpHab 2:2; 7:3-5). In separate traditions we find final judgment and resurrection scenes being populated by those who are "righteous" in the sense that they have embraced the vision of Jesus for Israel and have lived faithfully in accordance with his teachings.[14] In the parable of the net, the wicked are separated from the righteous (Matt. 13:49). In the Lukan account of Jesus having dinner at the home of a Pharisee (Luke 14:1-11), Jesus encourages his host to invite "the poor, the maimed, the lame, [and] the blind" to his banquets, promising him "you will be repaid at the resurrection of the righteous" (Luke 14:13-

13. See J. S. Kloppenborg, *Q Parallels: Synopsis, Critical Notes, and Concordance* (Foundation and Facets Reference Series; Sonoma, Calif.: Polebridge, 1988) 112.
14. We should probably exclude Matt. 13:43, since it stems from the interpreta-tion of the parable of the weeds, which shows many traces of special Matthean vocabu-lary.

14). In the parable of the sheep and goats, it is the righteous (those who do good deeds) who are approved (Matt. 25:46).

The force and authenticity of another relevant text, Matt. 6:1-2, relies upon a play on words: "Beware of practicing your piety before others in order to be seen by them; for then you have no reward from your Father in heaven. So whenever you give alms. . . ." The words translated *practicing your piety* and *alms* are nearly identical in Hebrew and Aramaic: "beware of doing your *righteous acts . . .* whenever you give *righteous acts. . . .*" This text can only be explained as a translation of a Semitic original going back to Jesus, and this would mean that Jesus deemed acts of righteousness to include almsgiving, prayer, and fasting.

Jesus probably also used the term *righteousness* to denote standing before God in humble recognition of one's sinfulness:

> He also told this parable to some who trusted in themselves that they were righteous and regarded others with contempt: "Two men went up to the temple to pray, one a Pharisee and the other a tax collector. The Pharisee, standing by himself, was praying thus, 'God, I thank you that I am not like other people: thieves, rogues, adulterers, or even like this tax collector. I fast twice a week; I give a tenth of all my income.' But the tax collector, standing far off, would not even look up to heaven, but was beating his breast and saying, 'God, be merciful to me, a sinner!' I tell you, this man went down to his home justified rather than the other; for all who exalt themselves will be humbled, but all who humble themselves will be exalted." (Luke 18:9-14)

Here *righteousness* clearly describes a person's standing before God: the tax collector (so frequently the paradigm of something good for Jesus) stands acceptable before God on account of his humble admission of his own sinfulness, whereas the Pharisee (the prototypical foil for Jesus; cf. Matt. 15:1-20; 23:1-39) thinks he is righteous because of his self-exalting "acts of righteousness."[15] Even if the teaching here differs from what Paul was later to develop,[16] it nevertheless laid the foundation for the doctrine that so informed Paul's mission.

15. Here "acts of righteousness" are, as in Paul, "boundary markers," behaviors that permit the group to define itself over against other groups, especially the Gentiles: tithes and Sabbath observance. On this, see Dunn, *Theology*, 354-59.
16. See J. A. Fitzmyer, *The Gospel according to Luke X–XXIV* (AB 28A; Garden City, N.Y.: Doubleday, 1985) 1184-85.

Several other passages in the Gospels use "righteousness" language, but in each case critical scholars doubt that the wording goes back to Jesus. Matthew 5:6 ("hunger and thirst for righteousness") probably stems from Matthean redaction (Luke 6:21 has "hunger now"). Most scholars also regard Matt. 5:20 as redactional, though wholesale composition is unlikely. Matthew 6:33 adds "and his righteousness," when the Lukan parallel reads only "strive for his kingdom." The logion in Matt. 10:41 has no parallel and is full of favorite Matthean vocabulary. The beatitude now at Matt. 5:10 may be authentic, even though it is unparalleled in Luke.

We may conclude, then, that Jesus taught his followers to be righteous as a result of a repentance that embraces Jesus' vision of the kingdom, a kingdom where God's will is done completely in a morally restored Israel. Those who joined Jesus' movement were to relate to God by a consistent obedience to his will concerning morality as Jesus taught it. In particular, they were to act mercifully toward the poor and imprisoned, practice piety, and rigorously commit themselves to the teachings of Jesus.

Love

Transcending even righteousness (a highly important aspect of piety in the Judaism Jesus both countered and established) is love.[17] Jesus so centralized love as to make it the fundamental moral category in the act of relating to God. In his teaching, righteousness is but a particular outworking of love. In Israelite tradition, love was something other than emotions. Three Deuteronomic texts form the basis of the understanding of love that informed Jesus' teaching:

> Hear, O Israel: The LORD is our God, the LORD alone. You shall love the LORD your God with all your heart, and with all your soul, and with all your might. (Deut. 6:4-5)

17. See J. Moffatt, *Love in the New Testament* (New York: Smith, 1930) 65-130, esp. 83-96; L. L. Morris, *Testaments of Love: A Study of Love in the Bible* (Grand Rapids: Eerdmans, 1981); G. Bornkamm, *Jesus of Nazareth* (trans. I. and F. McLuskey, with J. M. Robinson; New York: Harper & Row, 1960) 109-17; R. Schnackenburg, *Die sittliche Botschaft des Neuen Testaments* (2 vols.; HTKNTS 1-2; Freiburg: Herder, 1986-88); A. Schlatter, *The History of the Christ: The Foundation for New Testament Theology* (trans. A. J. Köstenberger; Grand Rapids: Baker, 1997) 166-74; see also 158-63.

So now, O Israel, what does the LORD your God require of you? Only to fear the LORD your God, to walk in all his ways, to love him, to serve the LORD your God with all your heart and with all your soul, and to keep the commandments of the LORD your God and his decrees that I am commanding you today, for your own well-being. Although heaven and the heaven of heavens belong to the LORD your God, the earth with all that is in it, yet the LORD set his heart in love on your ancestors alone and chose you, their descendants after them, out of all the peoples, as it is today. Circumcise, then, the foreskin of your heart, and do not be stubborn any longer. For the LORD your God is God of gods and Lord of lords, the great God, mighty and awesome, who is not partial and takes no bribe, who executes justice for the orphan and the widow, and who loves the strangers, providing them food and clothing. You shall also love the stranger, for you were strangers in the land of Egypt. You shall fear the LORD your God; him alone you shall worship; to him you shall hold fast, and by his name you shall swear. He is your praise; he is your God, who has done for you these great and awesome things that your own eyes have seen. Your ancestors went down to Egypt seventy persons; and now the LORD your God has made you as numerous as the stars in heaven. (Deut. 10:12-22)

Moreover, the LORD your God will circumcise your heart and the heart of your descendants, so that you will love the LORD your God with all your heart and with all your soul, in order that you may live. (Deut. 30:6)

Four features of this understanding of love need to be kept in mind: (1) Love is *elective.* God chose Israel from among all the nations of the world to receive his love. God called Abram out of Ur to journey to the promised land; he delivered Abraham's descendants from slavery in Egypt, gave them the law, and led them to the land; he continued to shower his faithful mercies upon Israel and the land even when the people disobeyed his law. In all of this, it is God who acts in love, who chooses to show his goodness to the nation, and who stubbornly refuses to give up on his chosen one (Hos. 11:1-12). (2) Love is *responsive.* It derives from having a circumcised heart and takes its cues from how YHWH has loved Israel. (3) Love is *expressed in covenant obedience.* Far too often love and obedience are depicted as implacable oppositions, two forms of religious devotion, but the biblical tradition regards them as two facets of one response to God (cf. Deut. 6:4-9; 10:12-13). (4) Love is *central* to the main confession of Israel, the *Shema:* "You shall love the LORD your God with all your heart, and with all your soul, and with all your might" (Deut. 6:5). It is wrong to regard Jesus as the first figure in religious history to teach love as the primary response to God.[18] Jesus certainly regarded love as primary, but in so doing he quoted the *Shema*. He affirmed what he had already learned from his father and mother, from his Jewish teachers, and from the sacred writings of Israelite religion: the love of God and neighbor.

Jesus, then, regarded love as the paramount response that God expected of Israelites who had found in Jesus the agent of the long-awaited restoration of the nation. If we were to confine ourselves to occurrences of the term *love* listed in a concordance, we would be misled: the word does not appear frequently in the Gospels, but one can never equate frequency of word with centrality of focus.[19] If one were to eliminate from consideration all passages that do not contain the term *love*, we would be forced to withdraw from consideration Jesus' parable of the prodigal son, his practice of table fellowship with sinners, his compassion, and his journey to Jerusalem to give himself for his nation in death. The reality of love in the mission of Jesus is in no way mitigated by the paucity of the term in the Gospels.

Jesus' reduced the will of God to loving God and loving others:

> One of the scribes came near and heard them disputing with one another, and seeing that he answered them well, he asked him, "Which commandment is the first of all?" Jesus answered, "The first is, 'Hear, O Israel: the Lord our God, the Lord is one; you shall love the Lord your God with all your heart, and with all your soul, and with all your mind, and with all your strength.' The second is this, 'You shall love your neighbor as yourself.' There is no other commandment greater than these." Then the scribe said to him, "You are right, Teacher; you have truly said that 'he is one, and besides him there is no other'; and 'to love him with all the heart, and with all the under-

18. See, e.g., R. Schnackenburg, *The Moral Teaching of the New Testament* (New York: Seabury, 1965) 90-91. This section has been completely revised in *Die sittliche Botschaft*, 1.88-89.

19. The Greek word *agapē* occurs approximately 36 times in the Synoptics (not eliminating parallel uses) and 44 times in the Gospel of John.

standing, and with all the strength,' and 'to love one's neighbor as oneself,' — this is much more important than all whole burnt offerings and sacrifices." When Jesus saw that he answered wisely, he said to him, "You are not far from the kingdom of God." After that no one dared to ask him any question. (Mark 12:28-34)[20]

Whether calling the command to love God and neighbor "the first" means that it is *greater* than all the other commandments or is the *climax* of the whole Torah and Prophets (Matt. 22:40) matters little here; the command expresses what God wants of his people.[21] And to say that Jesus reduced the law of Moses to love of God and neighbor is not to trivialize or eliminate the other commandments but only to insist that when one loves God and others one fulfills all that God required in his revelations to Israel.

Some scholars take this text to mean that humans love God when they love other persons. Love of others and love of God are related, but as cause to effect and not as identity. It is right to recognize an organic connection between loving God and loving others, but the connection is not described properly when the two are identified.

What then is love for God? First, love for God is a work of God in the heart of his people, who respond to what he has done for them. Jesus' command to love one's enemies (Matt. 5:43-47) shows that God's nature and God's actions set the tone for human action. The order of Mark 12:30-31 reflects the same: love God and then love others. Second, to love God is to give him what he deserves: to honor him by obeying him, worshipping him, and trusting him. To love God means to set one's central affections on him by allowing him to be God and Lord and by responding to his love and forgiveness in faith, love, and forgiveness (cf. Luke 7:36-50). In Jesus' vision, a restored Israel is to love God with all its heart, soul, mind, and strength, that is, to love God completely. It must be emphasized that love of God and obedience are not two separate religious responses, with the former superior and more enlightened. Love among Israelites includes obedience as the manner in which love is expressed. In the Gospel tradition, to love God

20. On the historical reliability of this tradition, cf. R. H. Fuller, "The Double Commandment of Love: A Test Case for the Criteria of Authenticity," in L. Schottroff, et al., eds., *Essays on the Love Commandment* (trans. R. H. and I. Fuller; Philadelphia: Fortress, 1978) 41-56.

21. On the historical background, see Fuller, "Double Commandment," 51-52.

involves embracing Jesus as the bearer of the good news of salvation for Israel, to take upon oneself the yoke of Jesus' commands, and to live in light of the coming restoration of Israel.

Relation to Self

Relating morally to God through righteousness and love requires a new self, a self that has been denied so as to affirm the vision of Jesus, a self that has been transformed to obey the will of God as Jesus teaches it. Inquiring into how Jesus thought a follower should relate to his or her own self may appear to be asking either an anachronistic or too philosophical question. However, we should not assume that Israelites did not think philosophically, even if their approach was not the classical philosophy of ancient Greece, nor that they did not reflect in some senses on the self (even if it be called "heart").[22] But more importantly, what Jesus said about relations to others implies a relation to the self. He self-consciously reflected, as did many prophets and rabbis, on the important distinction between heart (as the real self) and appearance. Such a reflection justifies delving into how Jesus thought his followers ought to view themselves.

Humility

What Jesus said about one's relations to either God and others implies an understanding of self.[23] Likewise, what Jesus said about humility before God implies a perception of one's self. At least two of the Beatitudes, though both from an apparently independent tradition, speak to this theme:

"Blessed are the meek, for they will inherit the earth." (Matt. 5:5)

"Blessed are the pure in heart, for they will see God." (Matt. 5:8)

22. A good study is H.-J. Fabry, "Leb, Lebab," TDOT, 7.399-437, esp. 412-34.
23. See D. Bonhoeffer, The Cost of Discipleship (rev. ed.; trans. R. H. Fuller and I. Booth; New York: Macmillan, 1963) 172-79.

In Matt. 5:3 we find another beatitude that speaks to the issue of self: "Blessed are the poor in spirit." Surely Matthew has added "in spirit" to the original Q wording "poor" (Luke 6:20), but in the original logion of Jesus "poor" would have described that class of pious Israelites who, though economically destitute, were nonetheless obedient and trustful of God.[24]

Thus, Matthew's formulation, though not reflecting the original wording of the logion, focuses the attention on one important facet of the meaning of "poor." Together, these two (perhaps three) beatitudes show that Jesus valued those who admitted their social status as low but nonetheless trusted in God and lived before him with an integrity and a purity that stemmed from humility. But Jesus also regarded humility as a character trait of the ideal disciple from beginning to end. Thus, when Jesus called the disciples to convert, he was calling the same group who had been following him for some time to live in constant humility before God (Mark 10:13-16) by checking the desire for greatness (Mark 9:33-37 pars.). This concern finds expression in a humorous parable at Luke 14:7-11 and an important addendum at 14:12-14:

> When he noticed how the guests chose the places of honor, he told them a parable. "When you are invited by someone to a wedding banquet, do not sit down at the place of honor, in case someone more distinguished than you has been invited by your host; and the host who invited both of you may come and say to you, 'Give this person your place,' and then in disgrace you would start to take the lowest place. But when you are invited, go and sit down at the lowest place, so that when your host comes, he may say to you, 'Friend, move up higher'; then you will be honored in the presence of all who sit at the table with you. For all who exalt themselves will be humbled, and those who humble themselves will be exalted."
>
> He said also to the one who had invited him, "When you give a luncheon or a dinner, do not invite your friends or your brothers or your relatives or rich neighbors, in case they may invite you in return, and you would be repaid. But when you give a banquet, invite the poor, the crippled, the lame, and the blind. And you will be

24. See R. A. Guelich, *The Sermon on the Mount: A Foundation for Understanding* (Waco, Tex.: Word, 1982) 69.

blessed, because they cannot repay you, for you will be repaid at the resurrection of the righteous."

The followers of Jesus probably knew where they belonged in public gatherings, as most first-century Jews would have known their social status.[25] But, to avoid shaming themselves, they were purposefully to seat themselves in the humbler seats at banquets so they might be exalted by God. This describes a conscious and willful act of humbling oneself. Disciples, like Jesus, are not to seek recognition (cf. Mark 1:35-39) but are to avoid publicity by humbling themselves. Jesus' concern is concentrated in a saying that is surely authentic:

> "All who exalt themselves will be humbled, and all who humble themselves will be exalted." (Matt. 23:12; cf. Matt. 6:1-6, 16-18)

Humility before God, then, implies a perception of the self that includes a confession of the need for guidance (revelation) and goodness (salvation) as an ongoing relation to the God of Israel and the self. It only follows that humility before God and self also entails a humility in one's relation to others. True humility does not look for recognition but does the deed of mercy as an act of loving obedience to God and as an act of love for the other. This kind of humility is a response to Israel's condition, not simply to one's personal standing before God. Israelites flocked to John the Baptist to confess the nation's sin and to seek deliverance and restoration, and Jesus called his followers to acknowledge Israel's current standing before God. He called them to humble themselves before God as he was about to restore Israel through Jesus.

Trust

If humility before God implies a view of the self, so also does trusting God, for those who trust God do not trust in themselves. Jesus expected his followers to forsake anxiety because it reflects both an absence of trust in God and a desire to secure one's life through one's own re-

---

25. See B. J. Malina and R. L. Rohrbaugh, *Social-Science Commentary on the Synoptic Gospels* (Minneapolis: Fortress, 1992) 367-68.

sources (Matt. 6:25-34//Luke 12:22-31). When a person learns to trust in God for provisions, that person must also forsake reliance upon self, and this implies a rearrangement of the personal system of trust. What the letter of James calls being "double-minded" (James 1:8; cf. Deut. 6:5; 13:3) is synonymous with what Jesus called being of "little faith" (cf. Luke 12:28//Matt. 6:30; 8:26; 14:31; 16:8; 17:20). The person of "little faith" is the person who wants to believe but who has anxiety as well. The follower of Jesus who has truly trusted in God puts away this anxiety and lack of faith in the knowledge that because God provides and restores, he can be trusted.

Transformation of the Self

Judaism in its various branches looked forward to the day when all Israel would obey God's law completely from the heart. The prophet Jeremiah expressed this hope in the context of the anticipated restoration of Israel following its return from exile in Babylon (Jer. 31:23-30, 38-40):

> The days are surely coming, says the LORD, when I will make a new covenant with the house of Israel and the house of Judah. It will not be like the covenant that I made with their ancestors when I took them by the hand to bring them out of the land of Egypt — a covenant that they broke, though I was their husband, says the LORD. But this is the covenant that I will make with the house of Israel after those days, says the LORD: I will put my law within them, and I will write it on their hearts; and I will be their God, and they shall be my people. No longer shall they teach one another, or say to each other, "Know the LORD," for they shall all know me, from the least of them to the greatest, says the LORD; for I will forgive their iniquity, and remember their sin no more. (Jer. 31:31-34)

Jesus called those who saw in him the fulfillment of what Jeremiah anticipated to be transformed from the inside out.[26] We find this call in a passage that rests at the very foundation of the Gospel tradition:

---

26. Perhaps this theme finds its most extreme form in W. Marxsen, *New Testament Foundations for Christian Ethics* (trans. O. C. Dean, Jr.; Minneapolis: Fortress,

When he had left the crowd and entered the house, his disciples asked him about the parable. He said to them, "Then do you also fail to understand? Do you not see that whatever goes into a person from outside cannot defile, since it enters, not the heart but the stomach, and goes out into the sewer?" (Thus he declared all foods clean.) And he said, "It is what comes out of a person that defiles. For it is from within, from the human heart, that evil intentions come: fornication, theft, murder, adultery, avarice, wickedness, deceit, licentiousness, envy, slander, pride, folly. All these evil things come from within, and they defile a person." (Mark 7:17-23)

Here Jesus counters external piety with internal piety and contends that what is inside is more important than what is outside. In this he reoriented Levitical purity and defilement concerns. For Jesus, what really mattered is what comes from the heart. Externalities like food purity can only be legitimate when they correspond substantively to one's heart. Yet, Jesus did not completely dismiss the need for the external act itself but instead saw the internal and the external as a unity.[27]

Two other sayings of Jesus deserve mention at this point:

"For where your treasure is, there your heart will be also." (Matt. 6:21//Luke 12:34)

"Blessed are the pure in heart, for they will see God." (Matt. 5:8)

We can be sure that the second logion (Matt. 5:8) pits itself against the concern for external purity, a purity of hands or body, and therefore expresses what is found in the Markan tradition about internal *versus* external cleanness (Mark 7:1-23). The logion about the treasure and the

1993) 23-141. See also the variety of viewpoints in T. W. Manson, *The Teaching of Jesus: Studies in Its Form and Content* (Cambridge: Cambridge University Press, 1939) 285-312; M. Borg, *Jesus: A New Vision: Spirit, Culture, and the Life of Discipleship* (San Francisco: Harper & Row, 1988) 108-10; N. T. Wright, *Jesus and the Victory of God* (Christian Origins and the Question of God, vol. 2; Minneapolis: Fortress, 1996) 282-87.

27. Wright, *Jesus and the Victory of God*, 283. A traditional example is Borg, *Jesus: A New Vision*, 110: "The conflict was between a way of being religious that depended upon observance of externals (the way of conventional wisdom) and a way of being religious that depended upon inner transformation."

heart (Matt. 6:21//Luke 12:34) only serves to emphasize that for Jesus the external world and the internal world were correlated, with the internal world having prominence.

Alongside these various logia, we must also observe that Jesus used other images which suggest that he believed in the importance of self-transformation when talking about morality to those who wanted to follow him. At least three traditions deserve to be noted: the image of treasures (Matt. 6:19-21//Luke 12:33-34), of the single eye (Matt. 6:22-23//Luke 11:34-36), and of the good tree and good fruits (Matt. 7:16-20; 12:33-37//Luke 6:43-45). Each of these images implies that Jesus viewed self-transformation as a process in which the external changes so as to correspond to the heart.[28]

Jesus' teaching on the subject of personal transformation also implies that God's grace is operative in the follower of Jesus to effect the transformation.[29] Yet, Jesus did not make divine enabling a central emphasis of his teaching; consequently, we misrepresent him when this theme is exaggerated and made the central platform upon which the whole edifice of his teaching is built. Such a building is Pauline, to be sure, and historically an important part of Christian theology, but it was not built by Jesus. If we are to be honest about Jesus, we must be honest about the texts that describe him.

Hypocrisy

Jesus was violently opposed to hypocrisy. In his view, hypocrisy was conscious pretense and purposeful deceit intended to lead others astray by one's behavior or teachings.[30] Hypocrisy willfully presents a false image of one's self. For Jesus, the real self had to be on public display and had to correspond to what one did and how one appeared to others.

It is no surprise, then, that Jesus connected hypocrisy with the heart. Although Mark uses the term "hypocrisy" in the context of a

28. See also Matt. 18:23-35; Luke 7:41-50 (with Matt. 25:14-30 and Luke 19:12-27) for other traditions that speak in some sense of an inner transformation. See further Caird, *New Testament Theology*, 391.

29. See T. W. Manson, *Ethics and the Gospel* (London: SCM, 1960) 68.

30. See D. E. Garland, *The Intention of Matthew 23* (NovTSup 52; Leiden: Brill, 1979) 91-123; R. H. Smith, "Hypocrite," *DJG*, 351-53; Goppelt, *Theology*, 1.84-86.

quotation from Isaiah (Mark 7:6: "Isaiah prophesied rightly about you hypocrites!") and Matthew has it aimed directly at Jesus' audience (Matt. 15:7: "You hypocrites!"), we can be sure that the term was used by Jesus for those whose hearts were at odds with their teachings. What Jesus found so disgusting about hypocrites was (1) their desire for personal recognition, (2) their focus on the faults of others, and (3) their preoccupation with externalities. The various traditions that now make up Matthew 23 and parallels bring out each of these sins: hypocrites (1) love to be seen publicly as possessing positions of prestige (Mark 12:37-40), (2) find minor faults in the lives of others but neglect their own obvious weaknesses (Luke 6:42//Matt. 7:4-5), and (3) become entangled with externalities and neglect their own hearts — like cups that are outwardly spotless but inwardly filthy (Matt. 23:25-26// Luke 11:39-41) and like tombs that have been whitewashed (Matt. 23:27-28//Luke 11:44). They become so preoccupied with "micro-ethics," such as tithing small quantities of herbs, that they forget "macroethics" — things like justice, mercy, and faithfulness (Matt. 23:23-24//Luke 11:42). For Jesus, the law of Moses, the statement of God's will for the nation, is thereby distorted and turned into an impossible burden.[31]

Jesus' accusing contemporary Jewish leaders of hypocrisy (and he no doubt leveled this criticism especially at certain branches of the Pharisees) may well have been inspired by their influence and their leading of other Israelites astray (cf. Matt. 23:13, 15). Whatever the reason, Jesus found hypocrisy to be a fundamental misperception of what God wanted for the Israelite who desired God's kingdom for Israel. The hypocrites saw the external world as the real battlefield, while Jesus saw the heart as a battlefield between self and God. His followers, however, were to bring their inner self into line with their external behavior so that dignity and personal integrity could rule their lives. Their obedience to laws, their acts of mercy, and their whole life before others were to be a sincere reflection of a heart transformed from the inside out. They were to embody what Jeremiah anticipated: the law written on the heart of God's restored people.

31. See Caird, *New Testament Theology,* 393.

Self-love

The concept of self-love, which is implicitly taught at Mark 12:31 and explicitly at Matt. 7:12, has almost no other parallel ideas or expressions in the teachings of Jesus and might best be seen as a practical expedient. Grounded in the reality of how humans operate and how they can be motivated, Jesus urged his disciples to love others in a way consistent with how they loved themselves. On the other hand, Mark 8:35 ("save their life," "lose their life") and the command to do to others what one wants done to oneself (cf. Matt. 7:12//Luke 6:31) may well have emerged from a more central concern about the self as a ground for moral exhortation. Jesus evidently anchored loving actions for others in an observation about the reality of human conduct: all people take care of themselves. Jesus used his awareness of the natural human proclivity toward self-care as a basis for exhorting people to love others. His teaching on love of self represents an uncommon insight into the realities of human motives in ethical matters, as well as a positive affirmation of the self created by God and therefore responsible to him.[32]

Relation to Others

When we speak of "the other" in discussing the ethic of Jesus, we must bear in mind the various "others" with whom the followers of Jesus had a relationship: other disciples, the wider movement around Jesus, fellow Jews who did not follow Jesus, Rome, and the wider world. It also needs to be kept in mind that "the other" includes various institutions as well: family, marriage, government, temple, and the like. To provide a full sketch of what Jesus said about each of these others and the institutions they represented would require a lengthy book in itself.[33] Our

32. It ought to be noted, however, that Mark 12:31 also affirms the Torah when it speaks of loving the neighbor *as oneself,* a notion that is found in Aristotelian ethics (*Nic. Eth.* 9.4) and in some sense in the later rabbis (*m. Abot* 1:14). See Moffatt, *Love,* 97-100.

33. See R. A. Horsley, *Jesus and the Spiral of Violence: Popular Jewish Resistance in Roman Palestine* (San Francisco: Harper & Row, 1987) and J. D. Crossan, *The Historical Jesus: The Life of a Mediterranean Jewish Peasant* (San Francisco: HarperSanFrancisco, 1991).

purpose here can best be served by focusing on four central themes: love, forgiveness, mercy, and peacemaking.

Love

Jesus' teaching about love centered on the relation to God and the relation to others.[34] It is this second relation that needs to be examined here. Just as love is the fundamental requirement for faithful Israelites (and therefore for the followers of Jesus) in their relation to God, so it is in their relation to other Israelites and other followers of Jesus:

> One of the scribes came near and heard them disputing with one another, and seeing that he answered them well, he asked him, "Which commandment is the first of all?" Jesus answered, "The first is, 'Hear, O Israel: the Lord our God, the Lord is one; you shall love the Lord your God with all your heart, and with all your soul, and with all your mind, and with all your strength.' The second is this, 'You shall love your neighbor as yourself.' There is no other commandment greater than these." (Mark 12:28-31 pars.)

Jesus here affirms Lev. 19:18, a principle of love for the neighbor (the fellow Israelite) that animates several ethical injunctions in Levitical law: respect for parents (19:3); provision for the poor (19:9-10; cf. 19:34); prohibitions against stealing, cheating, and lying (19:11); prohibitions against various sorts of fraud (19:13); behavior toward the physically challenged (19:14); justice for the powerless (19:15); prohibitions against slandering (19:16); and prohibitions against hate and vengeance (19:17-18). In this appropriation of a Levitical tradition, Jesus affirmed love as the governing ethic for his followers. For him, love meant treating others with respect, dignity, integrity, mercy, and justice.

A second aspect of love of others evolved out of what Jesus said about loving God: as God's love for Israelites generates their love for God, so the love of others is an imitation of God's love for them.[35] We

---

34. See Moffatt, *Love*, 97-130; Jeremias, *Proclamation of Jesus*, 211-14; Schottroff, *Essays*.

35. On imitation of God, cf. Schnackenburg, *Die sittliche Botschaft*, 1.85-86; Vermes, *Religion*, 200-206; see also S. Schechter, *Aspects of Rabbinic Theology* (reprint, Woodstock, Vt.: Jewish Lights Publishing, 1993) 199-218.

find this principle in Jesus' command to love one's enemies (Luke 6:27//Matt. 5:44), the logically extreme implication of God's love for unworthy Israelites and pagans:[36]

> "But I say to you that listen, Love your enemies, do good to those who hate you. . . ."

Jesus' call for love of the enemy was not an innovation in Israelite-Jewish tradition (cf., e.g., Exod. 23:4-5; 1 Sam. 24:1-15; 2 Kings 6:1-23; Prov. 25:21-22), even if his teaching struck at the very root of current understandings of Israel's identity. The scriptures of Israel stand behind his exhortation. The argument is simple, but persuasive, for the Israelite: if God showers his goodness and providential care upon all, regardless of their social, ethnic, or religious status, then surely those who have experienced God's love will do the same (cf. the larger tradition at Luke 6:27-28, 32-33//Matt. 5:43-47; see also Luke 23:34).[37] God's love dictates the Israelite's love, and his love is directed toward a nation that has been anything but wholeheartedly and consistently faithful to him.[38]

But who exactly did Jesus have in mind when he spoke of the "enemy"? Though interpreters in the past inclined toward romanticizing the referent of this term in Jesus' teaching, making him an advocate of universal philanthropy, contemporary scholars tend to identify the "enemy" with Rome, or perhaps with the Jewish authorities that were in league with Rome and who opposed the ministry of Jesus.[39] The heritage of Jesus favors an interpretation that particularizes the term "enemy" so that it refers to a specific socio-political entity rather than to some generic personal adversary. Among the more recent historic ene-

---

36. Jesus counters the idea of "hating your enemy" in Matt. 5:43. See A. E. Harvey, *Strenuous Commands: The Ethic of Jesus* (Philadelphia: Trinity Press International, 1990) 97.

37. J. Becker, *Jesus von Nazaret* (New York: de Gruyter, 1996) 312-19, is surely justified here in seeing a theology of creation shaping the ethic of Jesus.

38. Again, however, the ground of loving others is not altruistic, the supposed goodness of the action, or even the needs of others, but God. See Bornkamm, *Jesus*, 114; M. Borg, *Conflict, Holiness and Politics in the Teachings of Jesus* (SBEC 5; New York: Edwin Mellen, 1984) 125; Morris, *Covenants of Love*, 150; E. Lohse, *Theological Ethics of the New Testament* (trans. M. E. Boring; Minneapolis: Fortress, 1991) 56.

39. See L. Schottroff, "Non-Violence and the Love of Enemies," in Schottroff, et al., eds., *Essays*, 9-15; Horsley, *Jesus and the Spiral of Violence*, 255-73.

mies of Israel were the Babylonians, the Samaritans, the Greeks, the Ptolemies, and the Seleucids. At the time of Jesus, Rome was identified as the enemy (cf. Luke 1:71, 74; 19:43). In the words of Marcus Borg, Jesus' call to "love your enemies" would have meant "'Love the Romans — do not join the resistance movement'"; it would have been a call "to eschew acts of terrorism and revenge."[40] Jesus did not reduce love for the enemy to a gentle disposition; he expected it to be expressed in concrete actions for the benefit of the Romans. When he called on his followers to "do good to those who hate you, bless those who curse you, pray for those who abuse you" (Luke 6:27-28), he was calling them to move actively toward their enemies and to perform acts of mercy for the benefit of those same enemies. This kind of love needs to be distinguished from toleration. Toleration denies the value of others by avoiding their place in community; love, by contrast, includes, understands, and acts for the benefit of the other. These actions are concrete and, at times, aggressive. This is how God relates to the Romans; if God acts that way, so should those who are included in the new vision for Israel.[41]

Although Jesus' call to love one's enemies was not radically innovative, there is solid evidence to suggest that this kind of love was an about-face for many in Israel (cf. Luke 9:52-56; 10:30-36; John 4:9). It became a mark of social identity among his followers as it stood in contrast to the behavior of other groups (cf. John 13:34-35).[42]

Jesus also called upon his followers to love their neighbor.[43] The story of the Good Samaritan illustrates what Jesus meant by "neighbor":

> But wanting to justify himself, he asked Jesus, "And who is my neighbor?" Jesus replied, "A man was going down from Jerusalem to Jericho, and fell into the hands of robbers, who stripped him, beat him, and went away, leaving him half dead. Now by chance a priest was going down that road; and when he saw him, he passed by on the

40. Borg, *Politics,* 130. See also Bonhoeffer, *Cost,* 162-63.
41. On how this worked in the earliest churches, see J. Piper, *'Love Your Enemies': Jesus' Love Command in the Synoptic Gospels and in the Early Christian Paraenesis* (SNTSMS 38; Cambridge: Cambridge University Press, 1979) 4-65.
42. See Schottroff, "Non-Violence," 15-28, esp. 24-25.
43. See Moffatt, *Love,* 103-4, 120-23.

other side. So likewise a Levite, when he came to the place and saw him, passed by on the other side. But a Samaritan while traveling came near him; and when he saw him, he was moved with pity. He went to him and bandaged his wounds, having poured oil and wine on them. Then he put him on his own animal, brought him to an inn, and took care of him. The next day he took out two denarii, gave them to the innkeeper, and said, 'Take care of him; and when I come back, I will repay you whatever more you spend.' Which of these three, do you think, was a neighbor to the man who fell into the hands of the robbers?" He said, "The one who showed him mercy." Jesus said to him, "Go and do likewise." (Luke 10:29-37)

Jesus evidently thought that everyone whom his followers encountered was to be seen as a neighbor. But Jesus' response is more than a quantitative numbering. It is not just that the man who asked Jesus the question restricted the numbering to his fellow Israelites, whereas Jesus included everyone (Israel plus others). Rather, Jesus placed the whole issue on another footing: the neighbor cannot be defined or quantified; one can either be a neighbor or choose not to be a neighbor. In other words, it is not the *encountered* that concerned Jesus but the *person who encounters.* Jesus turned the question to a deeper issue: not "Who am I to love?" but "What kind of person am I?" In Jesus' reforming vision for Israel, it is no longer a question of "Who is my neighbor?" but "To whom can I be neighborly?"[44]

A particular manifestation of this theme in Jesus' own life goes beyond the Samaritan to the kinds of people who accompanied Jesus. This applies especially to Jesus' attitude toward women, in which he evidently pushed against Jewish custom.[45] Jesus' love of neighbor manifested itself in treating women in a neighborly manner, in treating them as one might treat oneself, in treating them as God treats them. He included women in his company, enlisting them in his ranks and

---

44. Bornkamm, *Jesus,* 113.

45. See B. Witherington, *Women in the Ministry of Jesus: A Study of Jesus' Attitudes to Women and Their Roles as Reflected in His Earthly Life* (SNTSMS 51; Cambridge: Cambridge University Press, 1984); see also T. Ilan, *Jewish Women in Greco-Roman Palestine* (Peabody, Mass.: Hendrickson, 1996); D. M. Scholer, "Women," *DJG,* 880-87; J. Schaberg, "A Feminist Experience of Historical-Jesus Scholarship," in W. E. Arnal and M. Desjardins, eds., *Whose Historical Jesus?* (SCJ 7; Waterloo, Ont.: Wilfrid Laurier University Press, 1997) 146-60.

spending time with them in a manner that probably rankled custom. The Jewish context is well known,[46] though scholars have too often exaggerated the ugliness of Jewish treatment of women in order to cast Jesus' practice in a more favorable light. The reality of Jewish practice was probably far more humane than some of the ancient texts assert. Jesus himself was not so bold as to include women in the apostolic band, even though on other occasions he was not afraid to counter his culture. Yet he consistently treated women kindly and accorded them equal status with men as they found in him the solution to Israel's problems.

Jesus' discussions of religious matters with the woman at the well (John 4:7-26) and with Mary and Martha (Luke 10:38-42) epitomize his teaching on love of neighbor as an imitation of God, even if the historicity of these traditions is doubted. Women accompanied Jesus and supported him (Luke 8:1-3), and he healed them (Matt. 8:14-15; Mark 5:21-43; Luke 13:11-17). Although most scholars regard the passage as an addition to the text of the Fourth Gospel, the story of the woman caught in adultery but then forgiven by Jesus in John 7:53–8:11 crystallizes the kind of thing Jesus did and is consistent with his association with prostitutes (Matt. 21:28-32). Jesus' position on divorce shows mercy toward women (cf. Mark 10:1-12; Matt. 5:31-32). His treatment of women, though not explicitly prescribed for his followers, is a natural effect of what he thought about God, about the advent of the kingdom, and about the new community he was establishing for Israel.

To return to our original point, Jesus taught that his followers were to live a life that imitates God, who is merciful and loving toward all. If love of others is an imitation of God, it follows that loving others is in a similar sense *imitation of Jesus,* since he is the messenger of God to the Israel being formed around him. There is an undeniable element of serving others in Jesus' perception of what love is. Jesus loved by serving others in doing good things for them. When the Evangelists, in all strands and forms of the Gospel tradition, describe Jesus as one who was "filled with compassion," they are saying that he performed loving deeds of service on behalf of his fellow Israelites.

Consistent with this picture of compassion in performance is a Markan passage that connects Jesus' mission with service:

46. See Witherington, *Women,* 1-10.

James and John, the sons of Zebedee, came forward to him and said to him, "Teacher, we want you to do for us whatever we ask of you." And he said to them, "What is it you want me to do for you?" And they said to him, "Grant us to sit, one at your right hand and one at your left, in your glory." But Jesus said to them, "You do not know what you are asking. Are you able to drink the cup that I drink, or be baptized with the baptism that I am baptized with?" They replied, "We are able." Then Jesus said to them, "The cup that I drink you will drink; and with the baptism with which I am baptized, you will be baptized; but to sit at my right hand or at my left is not mine to grant, but it is for those for whom it has been prepared." When the ten heard this, they began to be angry with James and John. So Jesus called them and said to them, "You know that among the Gentiles those whom they recognize as their rulers lord it over them, and their great ones are tyrants over them. But it is not so among you; but whoever wishes to become great among you must be your servant, and whoever wishes to be first among you must be slave of all. For the Son of Man came not to be served but to serve, and to give his life a ransom for many." (Mark 10:35-45 pars.)

Regardless of one's assessment of the historical reliability of the Johannine tradition, the coherence of the Johannine message of Jesus' loving service toward others and their need to follow him in the same loving service with traditions found in the Synoptics only serves to demonstrate that, no matter how much editorial work the Gospel of John has undergone, that work was done on a tradition that goes right back to the bedrock tradition of Jesus' own practice of serving others (cf., e.g., John 13:1-15, 34; 15:13).[47]

This service is not some romantic ideal but a principle embodied in concrete actions. We find Jesus praying for others, showing kindness to others, healing others, helping the hurting, and caring for those who have been imprisoned (Matt. 5:43-47 par.; 25:31-46; Luke 10:30-37; John 13:12-17). Love for Jesus amounted not only to imitating God but also to following his own example in relating to others. His disciples are to follow him in his loving mission by following the Golden Rule:

47. See Moffatt, *Love*, 281-308.

"Do to others as you would have them do to you." (Luke 6:31//Matt. 7:12)[48]

It is well known that Hillel made a similar point, though in negative form: "What is hateful to you, do not do to your fellow" (*b. Šabbat* 31a). But it is also found in a slightly different form in the apocryphal book of Tobit 4:15: "And what you hate, do not do to anyone."[49] This Golden Rule of Jesus, though now in a more positive shape, represents the actualization of love in a concrete principle. What we said about love for God not being expressed solely through loving others now needs its own reversal: neither is love for God possible without loving others. And love of others is not some feigned act of love for God. Rather, in the humdrum tedium of real life, a follower of Jesus is to act lovingly by treating others as persons and doing good for them in concrete actions determined by the person, the relation, and the moment.[50]

Forgiveness

Recent scholarship has shown the tight connection between forgiveness and the end of the exile: when God acts at the end of history to restore the fortunes of Israel, he will do so by forgiving Israel's sins, healing her iniquities, and removing her transgressions against the covenant (cf. Lam. 4:22; Jer. 31:31-34; 33:4-11; Ezek. 36:24-26, 33; 37:21-23; Isa. 40:1-2; 43:25–44:3; Dan. 9:16-19).[51] This aspect of forgiveness runs directly against centuries of Christian interpretation, which has viewed forgiveness in strictly individualistic terms. Increasingly, though, scholars have begun to locate the primary significance of eschatological forgiveness in God's removal of the barriers that prevent divine blessing from restoring the land and reclaiming the people of Is-

---

48. Matthew's version has evidently been edited both to fit the context of Matt. 5:17–7:12 and to express the theology Matthew sees in the logion ("for this is the law and the prophets").

49. On the context, see Vermes, *Religion*, 38-41.

50. See Moffatt, *Love*, 107, 109; E. Schweizer, *Jesus* (trans. D. E. Green; London: SCM, 1971) 34-39.

51. J. Jeremias, *Prayers of Jesus* (trans. J. Bowden, C. Burchard, and J. Reumann; London: SCM, 1967) 102-3; Wright, *Jesus and the Victory of God*, 268-74, from whom these references are taken.

rael.[52] And Jesus offered just this forgiveness — not so much a private religious experience of God's grace as a national offer of revival and reform that follows on the heels of his announcement of the kingdom. Forgiveness and love are, then, the two primary eschatological blessings that Jesus offered to Israel (Matt. 13:16-17//Luke 10:23-24).

A discussion of the eschatological nature of forgiveness raises the issue of the year of jubilee. Leviticus 25 stipulates that every fifty years Israelites are to be released from debts and parcels of land are to return to the original owners, on the principle of divine ownership: "the land is mine; with me you are but aliens and tenants" (Lev. 25:23). In the unfolding history of Israel, the year of jubilee was connected with both the return from exile and forgiveness (cf. Isaiah 42; 58; 61). Jesus' inaugural sermon in Galilee as recorded in Luke 4:16-30 may well entail an evocation of the jubilee theme.[53] And the use of "debts" (rather than "sins") in Matt. 6:12, which is surely the earliest form of the Lord's Prayer, suggests that economic liberation was one goal of Jesus' mission.[54] At the very least, it is safe to say that Jesus expected his followers to live by the principles of the jubilee.[55]

Even if Jesus did not reflect often on the interrelation of love and forgiveness, we can be confident that forgiveness of others figured prominently in his ethical teachings.[56] There is one tradition, found only in Luke, that does connect the two themes: the story of Jesus forgiving the sinful woman who bathes his feet with her tears and ointment (Luke 7:36-50):

> "Therefore, I tell you, her sins, which were many, have been forgiven; hence she has shown great love. But the one to whom little is forgiven, loves little." Then he said to her, "Your sins are forgiven." But those who were at the table with him began to say among themselves,

---

52. See Wright, *Jesus and the Victory of God*, 271.

53. See esp. R. B. Sloan, *The Favorable Year of the Lord: A Study in Jubilary Theology in the Gospel of Luke* (Austin: Schola Press, 1977); idem, "Jubilee," *DJG*, 396-97; S. H. Ringe, *Jesus, Liberation, and the Biblical Jubilee* (OBT; Philadelphia: Fortress, 1985); J. H. Yoder, *The Politics of Jesus: Behold the Man! Our Victorious Lamb* (2d ed.; Grand Rapids: Eerdmans, 1994) 60-75.

54. See Horsley, *Jesus and the Spiral of Violence*, 246-55.

55. So Wright, *Jesus and the Victory of God*, 295; cf. Wiebe, *Messianic Ethics*, 128-29.

56. See Moffatt, *Love*, 103-10.

"Who is this who even forgives sins?" And he said to the woman, "Your faith has saved you; go in peace." (Luke 7:47-50)

The historicity of this tradition has been intensely debated.[57] The tradition as we now have it has been shaped by the tradition about the anointing at Bethany (Mark 14:3-9 pars.) and influenced by early Christian debates over forgiveness, grace, and love. But it does reflect an incident in Jesus' ministry.

Jesus also taught that his followers must forgive others.[58] The theme is found in several independent strands of the Gospel tradition, including the following:

> "And forgive us our sins [debts], for we ourselves forgive everyone indebted to us." (Luke 11:4//Matt. 6:12)

> "Whenever you stand praying, forgive, if you have anything against anyone; so that your Father in heaven may also forgive you your trespasses." (Mark 11:25//Matt. 6:14-15)[59]

Forgiveness here, as we can tell from a later tradition in Matt. 18:15-20, pertains to personal offenses that are pardoned by the wronged person in the interests of a reconciled community. It would be accurate to see in these acts of forgiveness an intentional dispensing of eschatological pardon as a way of ending exile and restoring the blessings to Israel — even if debts in an economic sense may also be in view. Those who follow Jesus are to extend God's forgiveness to others, and to do so beyond measure even to enemies (cf. Matt. 5:38-42//Luke 6:29-30; Matt. 5:43-47//Luke 6:27-28, 32-33).

Finally, we find the extreme claim of Jesus that those who do not forgive will ultimately not be forgiven by God. In other words, there is both reciprocity and responsibility when one has been forgiven. By virtue of its extreme nature, this teaching deserves to be considered as lying at the very root of the Jesus tradition. The critical idea is found in two logia:

---

57. See Fitzmyer, *Luke*, 1.684-88.

58. Jeremias, *Prayers of Jesus*, 102-4.

59. Cf. also the independent (perhaps redactional) tradition at Matt. 5:23-24 and the early Christian formulation at Matt. 18:15-20.

"Whenever you stand praying, forgive, if you have anything against anyone; so that your Father in heaven may also forgive you your trespasses." (Mark 11:25//Matt. 6:14-15)

"So my heavenly Father will also do to every one of you, if you do not forgive your brother or sister from your heart." (Matt. 18:35)

The latter tradition, which comes at the end of the parable of the unforgiving servant (Matt. 18:21-35), could be a redactional application within the developing tradition; if so, however, it is an application of an authentic logion found now at Mark 11:25, which itself is implied in the Lord's Prayer (Matt. 6:12//Luke 11:4). Christian theology has long struggled with the implication of this teaching, since God's forgiveness of persons appears contingent upon humans forgiving humans, even though Jewish tradition has its share of the dialectic of God and human forgiveness.[60] This instinct within Christian theology is undoubtedly sound, but the sentiment is also thoroughly Jewish: what Matt. 18:35 asserts, namely, that the followers of Jesus must be willing to forgive from the heart, surely clarifies what is left somewhat more ambiguous in Mark 11:25//Matt. 6:14-15. Jewish theology does not teach that forgiveness is earned by forgiving others. On the other hand, Christian theology has too frequently dismissed the integral relation that comes to the surface in these logia of Jesus.[61] The one who is unwilling to forgive others has not sensed what God has done in acting at the end of history to redeem Israel.[62]

Mercy

Treating others mercifully is a manifestation of love for others, since mercy is defined as loving compassion that acts for a person to alleviate

60. See Sirach 28:2-5; *T. Zebulun* 5:3; 8:1-2; *T. Joseph* 18:2; *m. Yoma* 8:9; *t. Baba Qamma* 9:29; *b. Šabbat* 151b; *b. Megilla* 28a.
61. See D. A. Hagner, *Matthew 1–13* (WBC 33; Waco, Tex.: Word, 1993) 152; Jeremias, *Prayers of Jesus,* 103; Piper, 'Love of Enemies,' 83-85.
62. See also C. F. D. Moule, "'. . . As We Forgive . . .': A Note on the Distinction between Deserts and Capacity in the Understanding of Forgiveness," in E. Bammel, C. K. Barrett, and W. D. Davies, eds., *Donum Gentilicium: New Testament Studies in Honour of David Daube* (Oxford: Clarendon, 1978) 68-77, esp. 71-72.

a need. Jesus both practiced acts of mercy and called upon those who subscribed to his vision for Israel to practice deeds of mercy. This is seen in Gospel texts describing the concrete deeds that Jesus envisioned for the kingdom and in actual statements about mercy. In recent scholarship, "mercy" has become an important category for understanding the mission of Jesus. According to one scholar, Jesus offered a "politics of mercy" in contrast to the reigning "politics of holiness."[63] Although "mercy" need not be pitted against "holiness," the former nevertheless remains an important element in Jesus' vision for a restored Israel. Jesus' balancing of God's holiness and love reveals an unusual capacity to sustain both the quest for holiness and the quest for mercy within the scope of his grand vision for the nation.

Jesus treated needy Israelites with mercy. This is reflected in his utter disregard for "status" in Jewish society and culture as he healed those on the margins of that society (e.g., Mark 1:40-45 pars.; Matt. 8:5-13//Luke 7:1-10; Mark 1:32-34 pars.; 2:1-12 pars.; 2:13-17 pars.; 5:1-20 pars.; 5:21-43 pars.; Matt. 9:27-34), his decision to place human need above the sacred custom of the Sabbath (Mark 2:23-28 pars.), and his advocacy of the poor (Luke 6:20//Matt. 5:3; Luke 7:22//Matt. 11:5; Mark 10:21 pars.; Luke 14:13, 21; 19:8). Surely the parables of Luke 15, however much they have been incorporated into the theology of Luke, witness to the concern Jesus had for those in need ("the lost").[64]

It follows that Jesus both expected and taught his disciples to be merciful toward others. The fifth beatitude ("Blessed are the merciful, for they will receive mercy," Matt. 5:7), though found only in Matthew, reflects the same logic as that found in the matter of forgiveness and for that reason alone is firmly anchored to the historical Jesus. As with forgiveness, mercy is shown by God to those who are merciful to others.[65] An original Q tradition, now seen in Luke 6:36,[66] commands the followers of Jesus to be merciful and grounds the command in the very nature of God (he, too, is merciful). Not only are both of these themes anchored in Judaism (on God as merciful, cf. Exod. 34:6; Deut. 4:31; 10:18-19; Joel 2:13; Jonah 4:2), they both express themes coherent with what we have seen elsewhere about Jesus.

63. See esp. Borg, *Politics*, 123-43; idem, *Jesus*, 86-93, 129-42.
64. Matthew's use of the parable of the lost sheep at 18:10-14 has Jesus' ministry of mercy in view but is directed at contemporary wayward Christians.
65. See the similar connection at *1 Clement* 13:1-2 and Polycarp, *Philippians* 2:3.
66. Matthew edits this to "perfect" at 5:48 (cf. 19:21).

Peace

A final theme in Jesus ethical teaching about relating to others is peace-making, an important motif in his overall vision for Israel as it awaited the imminent coming of God.[67] One of the political options in the Palestinian Judaism of Jesus' day was a revolutionary movement often called the Zealots, though many debate the precise date for the origin of this movement.[68] Jesus practiced his ministry in a day when armed revolution against foreign occupying powers in the name of God and Israel was on the horizon. Many of the leading figures in the various revolutionary movements of his day drew their inspiration from national heroes like the Maccabees.[69] It is wrong to narrow these revolutionary movements to the group Josephus describes as the Zealots, which had its defining origin in A.D. 66-67. Whatever the origin of the Zealots, Jesus faced the choice of using or denouncing violence to usher in the kingdom of God. The earliest traditions about Jesus bear univocal witness to a figure who opposed the use of violence to restore Israel.[70]

Scholars are fond of seeing the Greek understanding of political peace in a negative sense (the absence of war) and of seeing in the Jewish perspective a condition of wholeness and health, especially national blessing and physical well-being (cf. Gen. 26:29; 42:27; Judg.

67. On "peace," see esp. Schnackenburg, *Die sittliche Botschaft*, 1.125-35; Borg, *Conflict, Holiness, and Politics*, 73-143, 163-99.

68. The classic study is M. Hengel, *The Zealots: Investigations into the Jewish Freedom Movement in the Period from Herod I until 70 A.D.* (trans. D. Smith; Edinburgh: T & T Clark, 1988). See also E. Schürer, *The History of the Jewish People in the Age of Jesus Christ* (3 vols.; rev. G. Vermes, et al.; Edinburgh: T & T Clark, 1973-87) 2.598-606; W. J. Heard, "Revolutionary Movements," *DJG*, 688-98; Horsley, *Jesus and the Spiral of Violence*; R. A. Horsley and J. S. Hanson, *Bandits, Prophets, and Messiahs: Popular Movements in the Time of Jesus* (Minneapolis: Winston, 1985); M. Goodman, *The Ruling Class of Judaea: The Origins of the Jewish Revolt against Rome, A.D. 66-70* (Cambridge: Cambridge University Press, 1987).

69. See Wright, *Jesus and the Victory of God*, 170-81.

70. Two books that see Jesus in Zealot categories are S. G. F. Brandon, *Jesus and the Zealots: A Study in the Political Factor in Primitive Christianity* (Manchester: Manchester University Press, 1967) and G. W. Buchanan, *Jesus: The King and His Kingdom* (Macon, Ga.: Mercer University Press, 1984). This perception of Jesus was dealt a fatal blow in E. Bammel and C. F. D. Moule, eds., *Jesus and the Politics of His Day* (Cambridge: Cambridge University Press, 1984). However, to exonerate Jesus of the Zealot charge does not eliminate "politics" from Jesus' vision for Israel.

19:20; 1 Chron. 12:16-18; Ps. 4:8; 73:3 [where the Hebrew *šālôm* probably means "prosperity" or "blessing"]; Isa. 48:17-19; 57:19; Hag. 2:9; Sir. 1:18).[71] In Israelite tradition, the classic expression of peace comes in the priestly benediction of Numbers 6, ". . . the LORD lift up his countenance upon you, and give you peace" (Num. 6:26). Israel is blessed, is given peace, when it lives according to the covenant YHWH has with it. "Peace" served as a focal term for Israel's standing before God as a nation. Individualism plays little role here. When the Hebrew prophets looked forward to the final days of restoration, when God would reclaim Israel and walk tenderly with her, when God's people would live according to the covenant, when Israel would be delivered from oppressive governments and exile, when Jerusalem would be the talk of the world, they looked forward to the day when peace would reign in Israel (Isa. 9:5-6; 11:6-9; 29:17-24; 54:10; 60:17; 61:1-4; 62; Ezek. 34:25; Micah 5:4; Zech. 8:16; 9:10; cf. 1QS 2:4; 4:7; 1QH 4:32; 11:9). The vision of Isaiah 60 crystallizes this longing:

> I will appoint Peace as your overseer
>   and Righteousness as your taskmaster.
> Violence shall no more be heard in your land,
>   devastation or destruction within your borders;
> you shall call your walls Salvation,
>   and your gates Praise. (Isa. 60:17-18)

The images here of God's final act of delivering Israel are the basis upon which Jesus constructed his vision for Israel. Jesus shared Isaiah's vision, or rather appropriated Isaiah's vision and made it his own. And if the coming deliverer, a messianic figure to be sure, is the Prince of Peace (Isa. 9:6; cf. Ezek. 34:25; Micah 5:4; Zech. 9:10), then surely Jesus, if he saw himself inaugurating those days, must have been concerned with the peace of Israel (Luke 1:79; 2:14, 29; cf. Gen. 46:30).

If Jesus looked for Israel's eschatological day of salvation and saw the restoration of Israel being realized in his mission, then it is highly likely that he used the term "peace" to describe one goal of his national

---

71. See C. Spicq, "Peace," *TLNT,* 1.424-38; W. Klassen, "'A Child of Peace' (Luke 10.6) in First-Century Context," *NTS* 27 (1981) 488-506.

mission.[72] The traditions do not disappoint on this score. The seventh beatitude, which neither betrays any early Christian vocabulary nor highlights a significant theme in the Gospel of Matthew, perhaps originally belonged to the Q traditions:[73]

> "Blessed are the peacemakers, for they will be called children of God." (Matt. 5:9)

In the teaching of Jesus, peacemaking meant ending broken relationships and social tensions (Matt. 5:23-24), but it also entailed repudiating violence as a means of securing deliverance from Rome (cf. Luke 9:51-56; 22:38; Matt. 13:24-30).

When Jesus sent out the Twelve, he instructed them:

> "Whatever house you enter, first say, 'Peace to this house!' And if anyone is there who shares in peace, your peace will rest on that person; but if not, it will return to you." (Luke 10:5-6//Matt. 10:10-13)

It is possible that only the typical Jewish greeting is meant here by "peace" (cf., e.g., Luke 7:50; Mark 5:34 par.), but it is far more likely that the offer of eschatological peace is to be construed in the sense of release from captivity to Rome, the end of exile, and the salvation of Israel. The one "who shares in peace" (literally, "is a son of peace") is the one who sees in the disciples' mission of offering peace the final deliverance of Israel through Jesus.

As Jesus approached Jerusalem, "the whole multitude of the disciples" greeted him with the words:

---

72. The force of the logion in Matt. 10:34//Luke 12:51 ("Do not think that I have come to bring peace on the earth; I have not come to bring peace, but a sword") is rhetorical and should not be taken as a denial that Jesus' mission involved peacemaking. Jesus knew that his mission would create division and strife within the nation, but he forged ahead with that mission at the call of God. His steady determination and bitter disappointment led to this hyperbolic statement, as did a desire to let his followers in on what loomed in the future. See, e.g., R. A. Horsley, *Jesus and the Spiral of Violence*, 156-66.

73. See W. D. Davies and D. C. Allison, Jr., *A Critical and Exegetical Commentary on the Gospel According to St. Matthew* (3 vols.; Edinburgh: T & T Clark, 1988-97) 1.457-58 (though the authors do not anchor this beatitude in the life of Jesus).

"Blessed is the king
   who comes in the name of the Lord!
Peace in heaven,
   and glory in the highest heaven!" (Luke 19:38)

There are good grounds for attributing these words to the pilgrims when Jesus entered Jerusalem. The acclamation expresses their view of Jesus as the realization of their dreams for their nation, not for their individual redemption. As they saw it, God was about to arrive and to set Israel free. This is confirmed by what comes next in the Lukan narrative (19:41-44):

> As he came near and saw the city, he wept over it, saying, "If you, even you, had only recognized on this day the things that make for peace! But now they are hidden from your eyes. Indeed, the days will come upon you, when your enemies will set up ramparts around you and surround you, and hem you in on every side. They will crush you to the ground, you and your children within you, and they will not leave within you one stone upon another; because you did not recognize the time of your visitation from God."

This tradition, found only in Luke, coheres with the whole picture of Jesus' mission that we have sketched thus far. Jesus' vision for Israel built on the foundation of what the prophets of Israel and Judah had said about their nation when it was faced with capture and exile. On his entry into Jerusalem, Jesus issued his last and fatal call to the nation to turn from unfaithfulness, from foreign alliances as a means to strength, and from disregard of God's messengers. If Israel would only see Jesus for who he is, for what he is offering, for what he has for her in his vision from God, she would "recognize on this day the things that make for peace!" (19:42). And this peace is to be understood in precisely the same terms as those in which the Hebrew prophets understood it: the end of exile and the restoration of the nation.

Jesus envisioned a restored Israel — a nation at peace with God, with other nations, and with itself. Peace for Jesus was not a warm feeling in the individual heart but a state of affairs for the entire nation, for the remnant who saw in him the end-time savior. Peacemaking for him was a process of establishing this state of affairs without the use of violence. Those who followed him would be reconciled to other Israelites as peacemakers and would offer to other Israelites an opportunity to participate in this restoration process.

Reward for Obedience

Before drawing this chapter to a close, we must ask what place reward had in the teaching of Jesus.[74] What did Jesus think awaited those who accepted his call to discipleship after counting the costs and who then carried through to live according to the ethic of the kingdom in relation to God, self, and others? What did he think they would gain? "Heaven" is not the right answer, since Jesus spoke so seldom about it. The Christian vision, derived from Old Testament metaphors, of a heaven beyond, of quiet pastures and gurgling streams, of formerly ferocious beasts transformed into household pets, or of luxurious dwellings with all the amenities — on none of this did Jesus focus. For him, the future reward for conversion to his vision for Israel would be the grand and glorious revitalization of Zion, the flocking of Gentiles to Jerusalem to acknowledge Israel's God, the defeat of Israel's national enemies, the total restoration of Jewish society, and the complete moral transformation of the people of Israel, so that every Israelite would do the will of God from the inside out.

Although Christians today may be uncomfortable with the notion of reward,[75] Jesus nevertheless spoke of it. To begin with, he promised *present* rewards for those who accepted his vision for Israel and followed him in obedience and love. Two can be mentioned here: physical provisions and community relations. When Jesus taught his fol-

---

74. See A. N. Wilder, *Eschatology and Ethics*, 86-115; G. Bornkamm, "Der Lohngedanke im Neuen Testament," in his *Studien zum Neuen Testament* (Munich: Kaiser, 1985) 72-95; Schnackenburg, *Die sittliche Botschaft*, 1.76-88; E. P. Sanders, *Paul and Palestinian Judaism: A Comparison of Patterns of Religion* (Philadelphia: Fortress, 1977) 107-25; G. F. Moore, *Judaism in the First Centuries of the Christian Era: The Age of the Tannaim* (2 vols.; New York: Schocken, 1971) 2.89-111; Becker, *Jesus von Nazaret*, 297-305; Jeremias, *Proclamation of Jesus*, 214-18.

75. See Schrage, *Ethics*, 27, who traces Protestant discomfort with reward to the influence of idealist ethics (doing good is its own reward) and the doctrine of merit through good works. See also Wilder, *Eschatology and Ethics*, 89, who seems to regard Jesus' teaching on reward as an accommodation to Jewish modes of discourse.

lowers to pray for daily bread (Luke 11:4//Matt. 6:11), he certainly expected them to get what they prayed for. After all, he taught his disciples that God knew what they needed before they even asked (Matt. 6:8; Luke 12:30//Matt. 6:32). According to a tradition from Q, the disciples are to seek the kingdom and let God take care of their everyday needs (Luke 12:22-31//Matt. 6:25-34). Though Jesus warned would-be followers of the precariousness of his own existence (Luke 9:57-58//Matt. 8:19-20), he also promised that they would find adequate provisions for their mission (cf. Mark 6:7-13 pars.; Luke 10:1-16 pars.). These sayings, found in various forms and traditions, suggest that Jesus regarded God's provision for his followers as a tangible reward for obedience.

Accompanying this provision was an alternative community for those who forfeited their own families when they followed Jesus:

> Peter began to say to him, "Look, we have left everything and followed you." Jesus said, "Truly I tell you, there is no one who has left house or brothers or sisters or mother or father or children or fields, for my sake and for the sake of the good news, who will not receive a hundredfold now in this age — houses, brothers and sisters, mothers and children, and fields with persecutions — and in the age to come eternal life." (Mark 10:28-30)

> Then his mother and his brothers came; and standing outside, they sent to him and called him. A crowd was sitting around him; and they said to him, "Your mother and your brothers and sisters are outside, asking for you." And he replied, "Who are my mother and my brothers?" And looking at those who sat around him, he said, "Here are my mother and my brothers! Whoever does the will of God is my brother and sister and mother." (Mark 3:31-35)

Jesus' mission for Israel intentionally formed a new community for those who believed that John and Jesus had been called by God to announce to Israel the dawn of salvation and the threat of judgment. Many have called this community an eschatological remnant; whatever one calls it (and "church" would not be wholly inappropriate), Jesus regarded this community as a present reward for obedience to compensate those who had left their current social location by abandoning their family, their community status, and their economic security. Jesus also promised his followers a *future* reward. The predominant image he used for the final reward that God would give his people was that of eternal table fellowship with God:

> "I tell you, many will come from east and west and will eat with Abraham and Isaac and Jacob in the kingdom of heaven." (Matt. 8:1 // Luke 13:28)

> "Truly I tell you, I will never again drink of the fruit of the vine until that day when I drink it new in the kingdom of God." (Mark 14:25// Matt 26:29)

As we have seen, table fellowship was a central feature of Jesus' ministry. He promised those who sat with him in the evenings in various homes throughout the land that their current eating was but a foretaste of the future meal of God.

In short, Jesus promised his followers that their reward for following him would be participation in the kingdom of God. Those who showed acts of mercy to others would get to enjoy the kingdom prepared for them (Matt. 25:31-46); those who were poor would inherit the kingdom (Luke 6:20//Matt. 5:3); those who did the will of God, as Jesus taught it, would enter the kingdom (Matt. 7:21); those who were humble, like children, would enter the kingdom (Mark 10:15 pars.); and those who turned away from the idolatry of possessions would enter the kingdom (Mark 10:23 pars.).

What then do we make of Jesus' teaching on rewards? To begin with, we must accept it as both very Jewish and very typical of him. It will not do to dismiss his teaching of this subject as an accommodation to Judaism by someone who actually knew better but had to have a way of communicating with his fellow Jews.[76] We must also recognize that Jesus believed in a correspondence between one's life — what one does and what one is in relation to his announcement to Israel — and one's eternal standing before God. Furthermore, Jesus taught that, though there is a correspondence between one's life and one's eternal standing in the kingdom, that eternal standing is a gracious gift of God that far exceeds what one "deserves." This conviction comes through in the notoriously difficult parable of the workers in the vineyard (Matt. 20:1-

---

76. As does, e.g., Jeremias, *Proclamation of Jesus,* 216.

16), where the final payment for some far outweighs what they have done (cf. also Mark 10:29-30; Matt. 25:21; Luke 6:38). It also comes to expression in the recommended quip of the servant who says, after performing the assigned task, "We are worthless slaves; we have done only what we ought to have done!" (Luke 17:10).

Finally, it needs to be observed that what Jesus taught about reward is intimately tied to the gift of God; God is the one who has revealed his word to Israel in the last days, who has sent Jesus to announce the end of exile and the reversal of Israel's fortunes, and who acts in mercy and power to save and heal. This kingdom context shapes the whole discussion, and it is the reward of the kingdom that ultimately drives the entire ethic of Jesus.

Conclusion

When placed in context, the ethic of Jesus is far more specific than is often noted. Jesus' call to follow him, to convert to him, and to follow his ethical directives is inextricably bound up with his teaching about God and the kingdom. It is wrong to force Jesus into the mold of a professional philosopher or a modern pastor; the most important model for understanding him is that of *a messianic prophet.* Jesus' prophetic vision and call were shaped by his understanding of God. As God is holy, so Jesus calls his followers to live in line with God's very nature: they are to persevere in wholehearted commitment to him, to abide by the covenant that is now being restored, to follow the teachings of Jesus in a new obedience to the Torah, and to live in light of a coming judgment. Though Jesus rarely spelled out the theological foundation of his ethics, we can be sure that his perception of God determined his perception of right living before God. As God is loving, so his followers are to enjoy that love by trusting in God and loving him; out of that relation to God they are also to live in love and service toward others by performing deeds of mercy, forgiving one another, and seeking the peace of Israel.

In Jesus' teaching, God's holiness and love are to shape the individual Israelite's understanding of the self: God's holiness drives the Israelite to see his or her need and unworthiness before God, and God's love inspires hope in the heart of the Israelite so that trust of and love for God are awakened as the primary ways of relating to God.

Jesus' teaching centered on the nation of Israel — for the end of her exile and for her restoration. He saw himself as the last of God's messengers to the nation, a charismatically endowed prophet who knew that Israel was facing its last opportunity to be reconciled to her Creator God. And so he stepped forward out of the movement of John the Baptist and called Israel to repent, to turn from the current condition and back to faithfulness to the Torah as God had given Jesus to understand it.

Some responded; most did not. In light of that division, Jesus promised hope for those who embraced his vision and threatened a horrible judgment for those who refused to accept his offer. His vision of the impending judgment recapitulated what the prophets of old had seen before him: war, destruction, captivity, and exile. His hope reactualized the hope of the prophets as well: deliverance, peace, righteousness, an obedient community, and most especially the kingdom as God wanted it to be. The judgment did come in many of the ways that he had anticipated; Josephus lived to tell his readers about it in *The Jewish War*. The hope came about as well, but over the course of the next four decades it took on a life of its own. And it is that very hope that sustains the vision of countless Christians who live under Jesus' lordship in the prayer, "May your kingdom come!"

Bibliography

Agrell, Goran. *Work, Toil and Sustenance: An Examination of the View of Work in the New Testament.* Translated by Stephen Westerholm. Lund: Håkan Ohlsson, 1976.

Allison, Dale C., Jr. *The End of the Ages Has Come: An Early Interpretation of the Passion and Resurrection of Jesus.* Philadelphia: Fortress, 1985.

———. "Jesus and the Covenant: A Response to E. P. Sanders." *JSNT* 29 (1987) 57-78.

———. *The Jesus Tradition in Q.* Harrisburg, Penn.: Trinity Press International, 1997.

Applebaum, S. "Economic Life in Palestine." In *The Jewish People in the First Century: Historical Geography, Political History, Social, Cultural, and Religious Life and Institutions,* edited by S. Safrai and M. Stern, et al., 631-700. CRINT 1.2. Philadelphia: Fortress, 1974-.

Arnal, William E. and Michel Desjardins, eds. *Whose Historical Jesus?* SCJ 7. Waterloo, Ont.: Wilfrid Laurier University Press, 1997.

Bailey, Kenneth E. *Poet and Peasant: A Literary-Cultural Approach to the Parables in Luke.* Grand Rapids: Eerdmans, 1976.

Bammel, Ernst and C. F. D. Moule, eds. *Jesus and the Politics of His Day.* Cambridge: Cambridge University Press, 1984.

Banks, Robert. *Jesus and the Law in the Synoptic Tradition.* SNTSMS 28. Cambridge: Cambridge University Press, 1975.

Barbour, R. S. "Uncomfortable Words. 8: Status and Titles." *ExpTim* 82 (1970-71) 137-42.

Barnett, Paul W. "The Jewish Sign Prophets — A.D. 40-70 — Their Intentions and Origins." *NTS* 27 (1981) 679-97.

Barr, James. "Abba Isn't Daddy." *JTS* 39 (1988) 28-47.

Barton, Stephen C. *Discipleship and Family Ties in Mark and Matthew.* SNTSMS 80. Cambridge: Cambridge University Press, 1994.

Bauckham, Richard. "The Sonship of the Historical Jesus in Christology." *SJT* 31 (1978) 245-60.

Beasley-Murray, G. R. *Jesus and the Kingdom of God*. Grand Rapids: Eerdmans, 1986.

———. *Jesus and the Last Days: The Interpretation of the Olivet Discourse*. Peabody, Mass.: Hendrickson, 1993.

———. *John*. WBC 36. Waco, Tex.: Word, 1987.

Becker, Jürgen. *Jesus von Nazaret*. New York: de Gruyter, 1996.

Berkey, R. F. "ΕΓΓΙΖΕΙΝ, ΦΘΑΝΕΙΝ and Realized Eschatology." *JBL* 82 (1963) 177-87.

Berkhof, Louis. *Systematic Theology*. 4th ed. Grand Rapids: Eerdmans, 1941.

Bernstein, Alan E. *The Formation of Hell: Death and Retribution in the Ancient and Early Christian Worlds*. Ithaca, N.Y.: Cornell University Press, 1993.

Blidstein, G. *Honor Thy Father and Mother: Filial Responsibility in Jewish Law and Ethics*. New York: Ktav, 1975.

Bloomquist, L. G. "The Rhetoric of the Historical Jesus." In *Whose Historical Jesus?* edited by William E. Arnal and Michel Desjardins, 98-117. SCJ 7. Waterloo, Ont.: Wilfrid Laurier University Press, 1997.

Bock, Darrell L. "The Son of Man Seated at God's Right Hand and the Debate over Jesus' Blasphemy." In *Jesus of Nazareth: Lord and Christ: Essays on the Historical Jesus and New Testament Christology*, edited by Joel B. Green and Max Turner, 181-91. Grand Rapids: Eerdmans, 1994.

Bonhoeffer, Dietrich. *The Cost of Discipleship*. Rev. ed. Translated by Reginald H. Fuller and Irmgard Booth. New York: Macmillan, 1963.

———. *Nachfolge*. DBW 4. Edited by M. Kuske and I. Tödt. Munich: Kaiser, 1989.

Borg, Marcus. *Conflict, Holiness and Politics in the Teachings of Jesus*. SBEC 5. New York: Edwin Mellen, 1984.

———. *Jesus: A New Vision: Spirit, Culture, and the Life of Discipleship*. San Francisco: Harper & Row, 1988.

Bornkamm, Günther. *Jesus von Nazaret*. 12th ed. Stuttgart: Kohlhammer, 1980.

———. *Jesus of Nazareth*. Translated by Irene and Fraser McLuskey with James M. Robinson. New York: Harper, 1960.

———. "Der Lohngedanke im Neuen Testament." In *Studien zum Neuen Testament*, 72-95. Munich: Kaiser, 1985.

Brandon, S. G. F. *Jesus and the Zealots: A Study in the Political Factor in Primitive Christianity*. Manchester: Manchester University Press, 1967.

Briggs, C. A. *The Ethical Teaching of Jesus*. New York: Charles Scribner's Sons, 1904.

Brooks, Roger. *The Spirit of the Ten Commandments: Shattering the Myth of Rabbinic Legalism*. San Francisco: Harper & Row, 1990.

Brown, Michael L. *Israel's Divine Healer*. SOTBT. Grand Rapids: Zondervan, 1995.

Brown, Raymond E. *The Death of the Messiah: From Gethsemane to the Grave*. 2 vols. ABRL. New York: Doubleday, 1994.

———. *The Semitic Background of the Term "Mystery" in the New Testament*. FBBS. Philadelphia: Fortress, 1968.

———, et al. *Mary in the New Testament*. Philadelphia: Fortress, 1978.

Buchanan, George W. *Jesus: The King and His Kingdom*. Macon, Ga.: Mercer University Press, 1984.

Bultmann, Rudolf. *The History of the Synoptic Tradition.* Rev. ed. Translated by John Marsh. New York: Harper & Row, 1963.

————. *Jesus and the Word.* Translated by Louise P. Smith and Erminie H. Lantero. New York: Charles Scribner's Sons, 1958.

————. *Theology of the New Testament.* 2 vols. Translated by K. Grobel. New York: Charles Scribner's Sons, 1951-55.

Caird, G. B. *Jesus and the Jewish Nation.* Ethel M. Wood Lecture. London: Athlone, 1965.

————. *The Language and Imagery of the Bible.* Philadelphia: Westminster, 1980; reprint, Grand Rapids: Eerdmans, 1997.

————. *Saint Luke.* WPC. Philadelphia: Westminster, 1977.

————. *New Testament Theology.* Completed and edited by L. D. Hurst. Oxford: Clarendon, 1994.

Campbell, J. Y. "The Kingdom of God Has Come." *ExpTim* 48 (1936-37) 91-94.

Camponovo, Odo. *Königtum, Königsherrschaft und Reich Gottes in den frühjudischen Schriften.* OBO 58. Göttingen: Vandenhoeck & Ruprecht, 1984.

Charlesworth, James H. "A Caveat on Textual Transmission and the Meaning of *Abba:* A Study of the Lord's Prayer." In *The Lord's Prayer and Other Prayer Texts from the Greco-Roman Era,* edited by James H. Charlesworth, Mark Harding, and Mark Kiley, 1-14. Valley Forge, Penn.: Trinity Press International, 1994.

Chilton, Bruce D. *A Galilean Rabbi and His Bible.* GNS 8. Wilmington, Del.: Glazier, 1984.

————. *God in Strength: Jesus' Announcement of the Kingdom.* SNTSU B:1. Freistadt: Plöchl, 1979.

————. "Jesus within Judaism." In *Judaism in Late Antiquity. II: Historical Syntheses,* edited by Jacob Neusner, 262-84. HO 17. Leiden: Brill, 1994.

————. "Jesus and the Repentance of E. P. Sanders." *TynBul* 39 (1988) 1-18.

————, ed. *The Kingdom of God.* IRT 5. Philadelphia: Fortress, 1984.

————. *Pure Kingdom: Jesus' Vision of God.* Grand Rapids: Eerdmans, 1996.

————. "The Purity of the Kingdom as Conveyed in Jesus' Meals." *SBLASP* (1992) 473-88.

————. *The Temple of Jesus: His Sacrificial Program within a Cultural History of Sacrifice.* University Park, Penn.: Pennsylvania State University Press, 1992.

————, and Craig A. Evans. "Jesus and Israel's Scriptures." In *Studying the Historical Jesus: Evaluations of the State of Current Research,* 281-335. Leiden: Brill, 1994.

Conzelmann, Hans. *Jesus.* Translated by J. R. Lord. Introduction by John Reumann. Philadelphia: Fortress, 1973.

Cothenet, Edouard, et al. *Imitating Christ.* RES 5. St. Meinrad, Ind.: Abbey, 1974.

Crossan, John Dominic. *The Historical Jesus: The Life of a Mediterranean Jewish Peasant.* San Francisco: HarperSanFrancisco, 1991.

Cullmann, Oscar. *Christ and Time: The Primitive Christian Conception of Time and History.* Rev. ed. Translated by Floyd V. Filson. Philadelphia: Westminster, 1964.

D'Angelo, Mary Rose. "*Abba* and 'Father': Imperial Theology and the Jesus Traditions." *JBL* 111 (1992) 611-630.

Dalman, Gustaf. *Jesus-Jeshua: Studies in the Gospels.* Translated by Paul P. Levertoff. New York: Macmillan, 1929.

————. *The Words of Jesus Considered in the Light of Post-Biblical Jewish Writings and the Aramaic Language.* Translated by D. M. Kay. Edinburgh: T & T Clark, 1902.

Davies, W. D. *The Gospel and the Land: Early Christianity and Jewish Territorial Doctrine.* Berkeley: University of California Press, 1974.

———— and Dale C. Allison, Jr. *A Critical and Exegetical Commentary on the Gospel According to St. Matthew.* 3 vols. Edinburgh: T & T Clark, 1988-97.

Deissmann, Adolf. *The Religion of Jesus and the Faith of Paul.* Translated by William E. Wilson. London: Hodder and Stoughton, 1923.

Dillistone, Frederick W. *C. H. Dodd: Interpreter of the New Testament.* Grand Rapids: Eerdmans, 1977.

Dobschütz, Ernst von. *The Eschatology of the Gospels.* London: Hodder and Stoughton, 1910.

Dodd, C. H. *The Founder of Christianity.* New York: Macmillan, 1970.

————. *The Parables of the Kingdom.* London: Nisbet, 1936.

Donaldson, Terence L. *Paul and the Gentiles: Remapping the Apostle's Convictional World.* Minneapolis: Fortress, 1997.

Douglas, Mary. "Deciphering a Meal." *Daedelus* 101 (1972) 61-81.

Downing, Francis G. *Jesus and the Threat of Freedom.* London: SCM, 1987.

Dunn, James D. G. *Christology in the Making: A New Testament Inquiry into the Origins of the Doctrine of the Incarnation.* 2d ed. London: SCM, 1989; Grand Rapids: Eerdmans, 1996.

————. *Jesus' Call to Discipleship.* Cambridge: Cambridge University Press, 1992.

————. *Jesus and the Spirit: A Study of the Religious and Charismatic Experience of Jesus and the First Christians as Reflected in the New Testament.* Philadelphia: Westminster, 1975. Reprint, Grand Rapids: Eerdmans, 1997.

————. "Jesus, Table-Fellowship, and Qumran." In *Jesus and the Dead Sea Scrolls,* edited by James H. Charlesworth, 254-72. New York: Doubleday, 1992.

————. "Matthew 12:28/Luke 11:20 — A Word of Jesus?" In *Eschatology and the New Testament: Essays in Honor of George Raymond Beasley-Murray,* edited by W. Hulitt Gloer, 29-49. Peabody, Mass.: Hendrickson, 1988.

————. "Messianic Ideas and Their Influence on the Jesus of History." In *The Messiah: Developments in Earliest Christianity,* edited by James H. Charlesworth, 365-81. PSJCO. Minneapolis: Fortress, 1992.

————. *The Partings of the Ways between Christianity and Judaism and Their Significance for the Character of Christianity.* Philadelphia: Trinity Press International, 1991.

————. "Pharisees, Sinners, and Jesus." In *The Social World of Formative Christianity and Judaism: Essays in Tribute to Howard Clark Kee,* edited by Jacob Neusner et al., 264-89. Philadelphia: Fortress, 1988.

————. *The Theology of Paul the Apostle.* Grand Rapids: Eerdmans, 1997.

Ellis, E. Earle. *The Old Testament in Early Christianity: Canon and Interpretation in the Light of Modern Research.* Grand Rapids: Baker, 1992.

Elmore, W. E. "Linguistic Approaches to the Kingdom: Amos Wilder and Norman Perrin." In *The Kingdom of God in 20th-Century Interpretation,* edited by Wendell Willis, 53-65. Peabody, Mass.: Hendrickson, 1987.

Estep, William R. *The Anabaptist Story: An Introduction to Sixteenth-Century Anabaptism.* 3d ed. Grand Rapids: Eerdmans, 1996.

Evans, Craig A. "Jesus' Action in the Temple: Cleansing or Portent of Destruction?" *CBQ* 51 (1989) 237-70.

———. *Jesus and His Contemporaries: Comparative Studies.* AGJU 25. Leiden: Brill, 1995.

Fitzmyer, Joseph. "Abba and Jesus' Relation to God." In *À cause de L'Évangile: Etudes sur les Synoptiques et les Actes offertes au P. Jacques Dupont,* edited by F. Refoulé, 16-38. LD 123. Paris: Cerf, 1985.

———. *The Gospel according to Luke.* AB 28-28A. 2 vols. Garden City, N.Y.: Doubleday, 1981-85.

Flusser, David. "Jesus, His Ancestry, and the Commandment of Love." In *Jesus' Jewishness: Exploring the Place of Jesus within Early Judaism,* edited by James H. Charlesworth, 153-76. New York: Crossroad, 1991.

Forkman, Goran. *The Limits of the Religious Community: Expulsion from the Religious Community within the Qumran Sect, within Rabbinic Judaism, and within Primitive Christianity.* Lund: Gleerup, 1972.

France, R. T. "Development in New Testament Christology." In *Crisis in Christology: Essays in Quest of Resolution,* edited by William R. Farmer, 63-82. Livonia, Mich.: Dove, 1995.

———. *The Gospel according to Matthew.* TNTC. Grand Rapids: Eerdmans, 1985.

———. *Jesus and the Old Testament: His Application of Old Testament Passages to Himself and His Mission.* London: Tyndale, 1971.

Freyne, Sean. "Galilean Questions to Crossan's Mediterranean Jesus." In *Whose Historical Jesus?* edited by William E. Arnal and Michel Desjardins, 63-91. SCJ 7. Waterloo, Ont.: Wilfrid Laurier University Press, 1997.

———. *Galilee from Alexander the Great to Hadrian: A Study of Second Temple Judaism.* Wilmington, Del.: Glazier, 1980.

———. *Galilee, Jesus, and the Gospels: Literary Approaches and Historical Investigations.* Philadelphia: Fortress, 1988.

Fuller, Reginald H. "The Double Commandment of Love: A Test Case for the Criteria of Authenticity." In *Essays on the Love Commandment,* edited by Luise Schottroff, et al., 41-56. Translated by Reginald H. and Ilse Fuller. Philadelphia: Fortress, 1978.

———. *The Mission and Achievement of Jesus: An Examination of the Presuppositions of New Testament Theology.* SBT 12. London: SCM, 1954.

Garland, David E. *The Intention of Matthew 23.* NovTSup 52. Leiden: Brill, 1979.

Geffré, C. "'Father' as the Proper Name of God." In *God as Father?* edited by Johannes-Baptist Metz and Edward Schillebeeckx, 43-50. New York: Seabury, 1981.

Gerhardsson, Birger. *Memory and Manuscript: Oral Tradition and Written Transmission in Rabbinic Judaism and Early Christianity.* ASNU 22. Lund: Gleerup, 1961. Reprint, Grand Rapids: Eerdmans, 1998.

Glasson, T. F. "Schweitzer's Influence — Blessing or Bane?" *JTS* 28 (1977) 289-302.

Gnilka, Joachim. *Jesus von Nazaret: Botschaft und Geschichte.* Rev. ed. Freiburg: Herder, 1993.

Goodman, Martin. *The Ruling Class of Judaea: The Origins of the Jewish Revolt against Rome, A.D. 66-70.* Cambridge: Cambridge University Press, 1987.

Goppelt, Leonhard. *Theology of the New Testament.* 2 vols. Translated by John E. Alsup. Edited by Jürgen Roloff. Grand Rapids: Eerdmans, 1981-82.

Gräßer, Erich. "Zum Verständnis der Gottesherrschaft." *ZNW* 65 (1974) 3-26.

Gray, Rebecca. *Prophetic Figures in Late Second Temple Jewish Palestine: The Evidence from Josephus.* New York: Oxford University Press, 1993.

Guelich, Robert A. *The Sermon on the Mount: A Foundation for Understanding.* Waco, Tex.: Word, 1982.

Gundry, Robert H. *Mark: A Commentary on His Apology for the Cross.* Grand Rapids: Eerdmans, 1993.

Hagner, Donald A. *Matthew 1–13.* WBC 33A. Dallas: Word Books, 1993.

———. *Matthew 14-28.* WBC 33B. Dallas: Word Books, 1995.

Hamerton-Kelly, R. G. "God the Father in the Bible and in the Experience of Jesus: The State of the Question." In *God as Father?* edited by Johannes-Baptist Metz and Edward Schillebeeckx, 95-102. New York: Seabury, 1981.

———. *God the Father: Theology and Patriarchy in the Teaching of Jesus.* Philadelphia: Fortress, 1974.

Harnack, Adolf. *What Is Christianity?* Translated by Thomas B. Saunders. New York: Harper, 1957.

Harvey, A. E. *Jesus and the Constraints of History.* Philadelphia: Westminster, 1982.

———. *Strenuous Commands: The Ethic of Jesus.* Philadelphia: Trinity Press International, 1990.

Hawthorne, Gerald F. *The Power and the Presence: The Significance of the Holy Spirit in the Life and Ministry of Jesus.* Dallas: Word, 1991.

Hays, Richard B. *The Moral Vision of the New Testament: Community, Cross, New Creation: A Contemporary Introduction to New Testament Ethics.* San Francisco: HarperSan Francisco, 1996.

Hengel, Martin. *The Atonement: The Origins of the Doctrine in the New Testament.* Translated by John Bowden. Philadelphia: Fortress, 1981.

———. *The Charismatic Leader and His Followers.* Translated by James Greig. SNTW. Edinburgh: T & T Clark, 1981.

———. *Crucifixion.* Translated by John Bowden. Philadelphia: Fortress, 1977.

———. "Mk 7,3 πυγμη: Die Geschichte einer exegetischen Aporie und der Versuch ihrer Lösung." *ZNW* 60 (1969) 182-98.

———. *Property and Riches in the Early Church: Aspects of a Social History of Early Christianity.* Translated by John Bowden. Philadelphia: Fortress, 1974.

———. *The Zealots: Investigations into the Jewish Freedom Movement in the Period from Herod I until 70 A.D.* Translated by D. Smith. Edinburgh: T & T Clark, 1988.

Hiers, Richard H. *Jesus and Ethics: Four Interpretations.* Philadelphia: Westminster, 1968.

Holman, C. L. *Till Jesus Comes: Origins of Christian Apocalyptic Expectation*. Peabody, Mass.: Hendrickson, 1996.

Hooker, Morna D. *The Signs of a Prophet: The Prophetic Actions of Jesus*. Harrisburg, PA: Trinity Press International, 1997.

Horsley, Richard A. *Galilee: History, Politics, People*. Valley Forge, Penn.: Trinity Press International, 1995.

———. *Jesus and the Spiral of Violence: Popular Jewish Resistance in Roman Palestine*. San Francisco: Harper & Row, 1987.

———, and John S. Hanson. *Bandits, Prophets, and Messiahs: Popular Movements in the Time of Jesus*. Minneapolis: Winston, 1985.

Ilan, Tal. *Jewish Women in Greco-Roman Palestine*. Peabody, Mass.: Hendrickson, 1996.

Jeremias, Joachim. *The Eucharistic Words of Jesus*. Philadelphia: Fortress, 1964.

———. *Jerusalem in the Time of Jesus: An Investigation into Economic and Social Conditions during the New Testament Period*. Philadelphia: Fortress, 1969.

———. *New Testament Theology: The Proclamation of Jesus*. Translated by John Bowden. New York: Charles Scribner's Sons, 1971.

———. *The Parables of Jesus*. 2d ed. New York: Charles Scribner's, 1972.

———. *Prayers of Jesus*. London: SCM, 1967.

———. *The Sermon on the Mount*. Translated by Norman Perrin. FBBS 2. Philadelphia: Fortress, 1963.

Jonge, Marinus de. *Jesus, The Servant-Messiah*. New Haven: Yale University Press, 1991.

Kingsbury, Jack Dean. "The Verb AKOLOUTHEIN ("To Follow") as an Index of Matthew's View of His Community." *JBL* 97 (1978) 56-73.

Klassen, W. "'A Child of Peace' (Luke 10.6) in First-Century Context." *NTS* 27 (1981) 488-506.

Klausner, Joseph H. *Jesus of Nazareth: His Life, Times, and Teaching*. Translated by Herbert Danby. New York: Macmillan, 1926.

Kloppenborg, John S. *The Formation of Q: Trajectories in Ancient Wisdom Collections*. SAC. Philadelphia: Fortress, 1987.

———. *Q Parallels: Synopsis, Critical Notes, and Concordance*. Foundation and Facets Reference Series. Sonoma, Calif.: Polebridge, 1988.

Kümmel, Werner G. *Promise and Fulfillment: The Eschatological Message of Jesus*. Translated by Dorothea M. Barton. London: SCM, 1957.

———. *The Theology of the New Testament According to Its Major Witnesses: Jesus — Paul — John*. Translated by John E. Steely. Nashville: Abingdon, 1973.

Künzi, Martin. *Das Naherwartungslogion Markus 9,1 par: Geschichte seiner Auslegung, mit einem Nachwort zur Auslegungsgeschichte von Markus 13,30*. BGBE 21. Tübingen: Mohr Siebeck, 1977.

———. *Das Naherwartungslogion Matthäus 10,23: Geschichte seiner Auslegung*. BGBE 9. Tübingen: Mohr Siebeck, 1970.

Lachs, Samuel T. *A Rabbinic Commentary on the New Testament: The Gospels of Matthew, Mark, and Luke*. Hoboken, N.J.: Ktav, 1987.

Ladd, George E. *A Theology of the New Testament*. Rev. ed. Edited by Donald A. Hagner. Grand Rapids: Eerdmans, 1993.

———. *The Presence of the Future: The Eschatology of Biblical Realism*. Grand Rapids: Eerdmans, 1974.

Lane, William L. *The Gospel according to Mark*. NICNT. Grand Rapids: Eerdmans, 1974.

Lang, Bernhard. "The Roots of the Eucharist in Jesus' Praxis." *SBLASP* (1992) 467-72.

Lattke, M. "Zur jüdischen Vorgeschichte des synoptischen Begriffs der 'Königsherrschaft Gottes.'" In *Gegenwart und kommender Reich*, edited by P. Fiedler and D. Zeller, 9-25. Stuttgart: Katholisches Bibelwerk, 1975.

Liefeld, Walter L. "The Wandering Preacher as a Social Figure in the Roman Empire." Ph.D. diss., Columbia University, 1967.

Lissarrague, Francois. *The Aesthetics of the Greek Banquet: Images of Wine and Ritual (Un Flot d'Images)*. Translated by A. Szegedy-Maszak. Princeton: Princeton University Press, 1990.

Lohse, Eduard. *Theological Ethics of the New Testament*. Translated by M. Eugene Boring. Minneapolis: Fortress, 1991.

Longenecker, Richard N., ed. *Patterns of Discipleship in the New Testament*. MNTS. Grand Rapids: Eerdmans, 1996.

Lövestam, Evald. *Jesus and 'This Generation.'* CBNT 25. Stockholm: Almqvist & Wiksell, 1995.

MacLaurin, E. C. B. "The Semitic Background of the Use of 'EN SPLANCHNOIS.'" *PEQ* 103 (1971) 42-45.

Malina, Bruce J. *The New Testament World: Insights from Cultural Anthropology*. Rev. ed. Louisville, Ky.: Westminster John Knox, 1993.

——— and Richard L. Rohrbaugh. *Social-Science Commentary on the Synoptic Gospels*. Minneapolis: Fortress, 1992.

Mánek, J. "Fishers of Men." *NovT* 2 (1958) 138-41.

Manson, T. W. *Ethics and the Gospel*. London: SCM, 1960.

———. *Only to the House of Israel? Jesus and the Non-Jews*. FBBS 9. Philadelphia: Fortress, 1955.

———. *The Sayings of Jesus*. London: SCM, 1949.

———. *The Teaching of Jesus: Studies of Its Form and Content*. Cambridge: Cambridge University Press, 1939.

Marxsen, Willi. *New Testament Foundations for Christian Ethics*. Translated by O. C. Dean, Jr. Minneapolis: Fortress, 1993.

Matera, Frank J. *New Testament Ethics: The Legacies of Jesus and Paul*. Louisville: Westminster John Knox, 1996.

Mathews, Shailer. *Jesus on Social Institutions*. Edited by K. Cauthen. Philadelphia: Fortress, 1971.

McKnight, Scot. "Eternal Consequences or Eternal Consciousness?" In *Through No Fault of Their Own? The Fate of Those Who Have Never Heard*, edited by William V. Crockett and James G. Sigountos, 147-57. Grand Rapids: Baker, 1991.

———. "Jesus and the End-Time: Matthew 10:23." *SBLASP* (1986) 501-20.

———. *A Light among the Gentiles: Jewish Missionary Activity in the Second Temple Period.* Minneapolis: Fortress, 1991.

———. "Public Declaration or Final Judgment? Matthew 10:26//Luke 12:2-3 as a Case of Creative Redaction." In *Authenticating the Words of Jesus,* edited by Craig A. Evans and Bruce D. Chilton. NTTS. Leiden: Brill, forthcoming.

———. "Who is Jesus?" In *Jesus under Fire,* edited by Michael J. Wilkins and J. P. Moreland, 51-72. Grand Rapids: Zondervan, 1995.

Meadors, Edward P. *Jesus the Messianic Herald of Salvation.* Peabody, Mass.: Hendrickson, 1997.

Meeks, Wayne A. *The Origins of Christian Morality: The First Two Centuries.* New Haven: Yale University Press, 1993.

Meier, John P. *A Marginal Jew: Rethinking the Historical Jesus.* ABRL. 3 vols. New York: Doubleday, 1991-.

Mendels, Doron. *The Rise and Fall of Jewish Nationalism.* ABRL. New York: Doubleday, 1992. Reprint, Grand Rapids: Eerdmans, 1997.

Merklein, Helmut. *Jesu Botschaft von der Gottesherrshaft.* SBS 111. Stuttgart: KBW, 1983.

Meyer, Ben F. *The Aims of Jesus.* London: SCM, 1979.

———. *Christus Faber: The Master-Builder and the House of God.* Allison Park, Penn.: Pickwick, 1992.

Miller, John W. *Jesus at Thirty.* Minneapolis: Fortress, 1997.

Moffatt, James. *Love in the New Testament.* New York: Smith, 1930.

Montefiore, Hugh. "God as Father in the Synoptic Gospels." *NTS* 3 (1956-57) 31-46.

Moore, George F. *Judaism in the First Centuries of the Christian Era: The Age of the Tannaim.* 2 vols. New York: Schocken, 1971.

Morris, Leon L. *Testaments of Love: A Study of Love in the Bible.* Grand Rapids: Eerdmans, 1981.

Moule, C. F. D. "'. . . As we forgive . . .': A Note on the Distinction between Deserts and Capacity in the Understanding of Forgiveness." In *Donum Gentilicium: New Testament Studies in Honour of David Daube,* edited by E. Bammel, C. K. Barrett, W. D. Davies, 68-77. Oxford: Clarendon, 1978.

———. "The Manhood of Jesus in the New Testament." In *Christ, Faith and History: Cambridge Studies in Christology,* edited by S. W. Sykes and J. P. Clayton, 95-110. Cambridge: Cambridge University Press, 1972. Reprinted in *Crisis in Christology: Essays in Quest of Resolution,* edited by W. R. Farmer, 47-62. Livonia, Mich.: Dove Booksellers, 1995.

Neusner, Jacob. *From Politics to Piety: The Emergence of Pharisaic Judaism.* Englewood Cliffs, N.J.: Prentice-Hall, 1973.

Neyrey, Jerome H. "Loss of Wealth, Loss of Family, and Loss of Honour." In *Modelling Early Christianity: Social-scientific Studies in the New Testament in Its Context,* edited by Philip F. Esler, 139-58. London: Routledge, 1995.

Otto, Rudolf. *The Kingdom of God and the Son of Man.* London: Lutterworth, 1938.

Parrott, R. "Entering the Door: Matt 7:13-14//Luke 13:22-24." *Forum* 5 (1989) 111-20.

Pax, E. "Beobachtungen zum biblischen Sprachtabu." *SBFLA* 12 (1961-62) 66-112.

Perrin, Norman. *Jesus and the Language of the Kingdom: Symbol and Metaphor in New Testament Interpretation.* Philadelphia: Fortress, 1976.

————. *The Kingdom of God in the Teaching of Jesus.* London: SCM, 1963.

————. *Rediscovering the Teaching of Jesus.* New York: Harper & Row, 1967.

Phillips, Paul T. *A Kingdom on Earth: Anglo-American Social Christianity, 1880-1940.* University Park, Penn.: Pennsylvania State University Press, 1996.

Pilch, John J. and Bruce J. Malina, eds. *Biblical Social Values and Their Meaning: A Handbook.* Peabody, Mass.: Hendrickson, 1993.

Piper, John. *'Love Your Enemies': Jesus' Love Command in the Synoptic Gospels and in the Early Christian Paraenesis.* SNTSMS 38. Cambridge: Cambridge University Press, 1979.

Priest, J. "A Note on the Messianic Banquet." In *The Messiah: Developments in Earliest Christianity,* edited by James H. Charlesworth, 222-38. PSJCO. Minneapolis: Fortress, 1992.

Przybylski, Benno. *Righteousness in Matthew and His World of Thought.* SNTSMS 41. Cambridge: Cambridge University Press, 1980.

Rambo, Lewis R. *Understanding Religious Conversion.* New Haven: Yale University Press, 1993.

Reimarus, Hermann Samuel. *Concerning the Intention of Jesus and His Teaching.* Translated by R. S. Fraser. Edited by Charles H. Talbert. Lives of Jesus Series. Philadelphia: Fortress, 1970.

Reiser, Marius. *Jesus and Judgment: The Eschatological Proclamation in Its Jewish Context.* Translated by L. M. Maloney. Minneapolis: Fortress, 1997.

Reynolds, S. M. "A Note on Dr. Hengel's Interpretation of Πυγμῇ in Mark 7,3." *ZNW* 62 (1971) 295-96.

————. "Πυγμῇ (Mark 7,3) as 'Cupped Hand.'" *JBL* 85 (1966) 87-88.

Ridderbos, Herman. *The Coming of the Kingdom.* Translated by H. de Jongste. Edited by Raymond O. Zorn. St. Catharines, Ont.: Paideia, 1962.

Ringe, Sharon H. *Jesus, Liberation, and the Biblical Jubilee: Images for Ethics and Christology.* OBT. Philadelphia: Fortress, 1985.

Safrai, S. "Home and Family." In *The Jewish People in the First Century: Historical Geography, Political History, Social, Cultural, and Religious Life and Institutions,* edited by S. Safrai and M. Stern, 728-92. CRINT 1.2. Assen: Van Gorcum; Philadelphia: Fortress, 1976.

Safrai, Z. *The Economy of Roman Palestine.* New York: Routledge, 1994.

Sanday, William. "Jesus Christ." In *A Dictionary of the Bible,* edited by James Hastings, 2.603-53. New York: Charles Scribner's Sons, 1902.

————. *Outlines of the Life of Christ.* 2d ed. Edinburgh: T & T Clark, 1906.

Sanders, E. P. *Jesus and Judaism.* Philadelphia: Fortress, 1985.

————. *Jewish Law from Jesus to the Mishnah: Five Studies.* Philadelphia: Trinity Press International, 1990.

————. *Judaism: Practice and Belief 63 BCE–66 CE.* Philadelphia: Trinity Press International, 1992.

———. *Paul and Palestinian Judaism: A Comparison of Patterns of Religions.* Philadelphia: Fortress, 1977.

Sanders, Jack T. *Ethics in the New Testament: Change and Development.* Rev. ed. London: SCM, 1986.

Schaberg, Jane. "A Feminist Experience of Historical-Jesus Scholarship." In *Whose Historical Jesus?* edited by William E. Arnal, Michel Desjardins, 146-60. SCJ 7. Waterloo, Ont.: Wilfrid Laurier University Press, 1997.

Schechter, Solomon. *Aspects of Rabbinic Theology.* Introduction by N. Gilman. Reprint. Woodstock, Vt.: Jewish Lights Publishing, 1993.

Schlatter, Adolf. *The History of the Christ: The Foundation for New Testament Theology.* Translated by A. J. Köstenberger. Grand Rapids: Baker, 1997.

Schlosser, Jacques. *Le Régne de Dieu dans les dits de Jésus.* Paris: Gabalda, 1988.

Schnackenburg, Rudolf. *The Moral Teaching of the New Testament.* New York: Seabury, 1965.

———. *Die sittliche Botschaft des Neuen Testaments.* 2 vols. HTKNTS 1-2. Freiburg: Herder, 1986-88.

Schottroff, Luise. "Non-Violence and the Love of Enemies." In *Essays on the Love Commandment,* edited by Luise Schottroff et al., 9-15. Translated by Reginald H. and Ilse Fuller. Philadelphia: Fortress, 1978.

Schrage, Wolfgang. *The Ethics of the New Testament.* Translated by David E. Green. Philadelphia: Fortress, 1988.

Schuller, Eileen M. *Post-Exilic Prophets.* Wilmington, Del.: Glazier, 1988.

———. "The Psalm of 4Q372 1 within the Context of Second Temple Prayer." *CBQ* 54 (1992) 67-79.

Schürer, Emil. *The History of the Jewish People in the Age of Jesus Christ (175 B.C.–A.D. 135).* 3 vols. Revised and edited by Geza Vermes, Fergus Millar, Matthew Black, et al. Edinburgh: T & T Clark, 1973-87.

Schürmann, Heinz. *Gottes Reich — Jesu Geschick: Jesu ureigener Tod im Licht seiner Basileia-Verkündigung.* Freiburg: Herder, 1983.

Schweitzer, Albert. *The Kingdom of God and Primitive Christianity.* New York: Seabury, 1968.

———. *The Mystery of the Kingdom of God: The Secret of Jesus' Messiahship and Passion.* Translated by Walter Lowrie. New York: Schocken, 1964.

———. *The Quest for the Historical Jesus: A Critical Study of Its Progress from Reimarus to Wrede.* Translated by W. Montgomery. Introduction by James M. Robinson. New York: Macmillan, 1968.

Schweizer, Eduard. *Jesus.* Translated by David E. Green. London: SCM, 1971.

Scott, Bernard Brandon. *Jesus, Symbol-Maker for the Kingdom.* Philadelphia: Fortress, 1981.

Sloan, Robert B. *The Favorable Year of the Lord: A Study in Jubilary Theology in the Gospel of Luke.* Austin, Tex.: Schola Press, 1977.

Smith, C. W. F. "Fishers of Men: Footnotes on a Gospel Figure." *HTR* 52 (1959) 187-203.

Snaith, Norman H. *The Distinctive Ideas of the Old Testament.* New York: Schocken, 1964.

Snodgrass, Klyne. *The Parable of the Wicked Tenants: An Inquiry into Parable Interpreta-tion*. WUNT 27. Tübingen: Mohr Siebeck, 1983.

Sparks, H. F. D. "The Doctrine of the Divine Fatherhood in the Gospels." In *Studies in the Gospels: Essays in Memory of R. H. Lightfoot*, edited by D. E. Nineham, 241-62. Oxford: Basil Blackwell, 1955.

Spicq, Ceslas. *Theological Lexicon of the New Testament*. 3 vols. Translated by J. D. Er-nest. Peabody, Mass.: Hendrickson, 1994.

Stanton, Graham N. "Jesus of Nazareth: A Magician and a False Prophet Who Deceived God's People?" In *Jesus of Nazareth: Lord and Christ: Essays on the Historical Jesus and New Testament Christology*, edited by Joel B. Green and Max Turner, 164-80. Grand Rapids: Eerdmans, 1994.

Stein, Robert H. *The Method and Message of Jesus' Teachings*. Rev. ed. Louisville, Ky.: Westminster John Knox, 1994.

Strack, Hermann L., and Paul Billerbeck. *Kommentar zum Neuen Testament aus Talmud und Midrasch*. 5 vols. Munich: Beck, 1928.

Strobel, A. "Die Passa-Erwartung als urchristliches Problem in Lc 17.20f." *ZNW* 49 (1958) 157-96.

Tan, Kim Huat. *The Zion Traditions and the Aims of Jesus*. SNTSMS 91. Cambridge: Cambridge University Press, 1997.

Taylor, Joan E. *The Immerser: John the Baptist within Second Temple Judaism*. Grand Rapids: Eerdmans, 1997.

Theissen, Gerd. *Sociology of Early Palestinian Christianity*. Translated by John Bowden. Philadelphia: Fortress, 1978.

Tolstoy, Leo. *The Kingdom of God Is Within You: Chistianity Not as a Mystic Religion but as a New Theory of Life*. Translated by C. Garnett. Foreword by M. Green. Lin-coln, Nebr.: University of Nebraska Press, 1984.

Travis, Stephen H. *Christ and the Judgment of God: Divine Retribution in the New Testa-ment*. Basingstoke: Marshall Pickering, 1986.

Tuckett, Christopher M. *Q and the History of Early Christianity*. Peabody, Mass.: Hendrickson, 1996.

Twelftree, Graham H. *Jesus the Exorcist: A Contribution to the Study of the Historical Je-sus*. Peabody, Mass.: Hendrickson, 1993.

Urbach, Ephraim E. *The Sages: Their Concepts and Beliefs*. Translated by I. Abrahams. Jerusalem: Magnes, 1979.

Vermes, Geza. *Jesus the Jew: A Historian's Reading of the Gospels*. London: SCM, 1976.

————. *The Religion of Jesus the Jew*. Minneapolis: Fortress, 1993.

Ward, R. A. *Royal Theology: Our Lord's Teaching about God: Studies in the Divine Sever-ity and Kindness*. London: Marshall, Morgan & Scott, 1964.

Webb, Robert L. "John the Baptist and His Relationship to Jesus." In *Studying the His-torical Jesus: Evaluations of the State of Current Research*, edited by Bruce D. Chilton and Craig A. Evans, 179-229. NTTS 19. Leiden: Brill, 1994.

————. *John the Baptizer and Prophet: A Socio-Historical Study*. JSNTSup 62. Sheffield: JSOT Press, 1991.

Weiß, Johannes. *Die Idee des Reiches Gottes in der Theologie*. Giessen: Ricker, 1901.

————. *Die Predigt Jesu vom Reiche Gottes.* 3d ed. Edited by Ferdinand Hahn. Introduction by Rudolf Bultmann. Göttingen: Vandenhoeck & Ruprecht, 1964.

————. *Jesus' Proclamation of the Kingdom of God.* Translated and edited by Richard H. Hiers and D. L. Holland. Chico, Calif.: Scholars Press, 1985.

Weinfeld, M. *Social Justice in Ancient Israel and in the Ancient Near East.* Minneapolis: Fortress, 1995.

Wenham, David. *The Rediscovery of Jesus' Eschatological Discourse.* GP 4. Sheffield: JSOT Press, 1984.

Westerholm, Stephen. *Jesus and Scribal Authority.* CBNT 10. Lund: Gleerup, 1978.

Wheeler, Sondra E. *Wealth as Peril and Obligation: The New Testament on Possessions.* Grand Rapids: Eerdmans, 1994.

Wiebe, Ben. *Messianic Ethics: Jesus' Proclamation of the Kingdom of God and the Church's Response.* Scottdale, Penn.: Herald, 1992.

Wilder, Amos N. *Early Christian Rhetoric: The Language of the Gospel.* Cambridge, Mass.: Harvard University Press, 1971.

————. *Eschatology and Ethics in the Teaching of Jesus.* Rev. ed. New York: Harper and Bros., 1950.

Wilken, Robert L. *The Land Called Holy: Palestine in Christian History and Thought.* New Haven: Yale University Press, 1992.

Wilkins, M. J. *Following the Master: Discipleship in the Steps of Jesus.* Grand Rapids: Zondervan, 1992.

Williams, George H. and Angel M. Mergal. *Spiritual and Anabaptist Writers: Documents Illustrative of the Radical Reformation.* LCC. Philadelphia: Westminster, 1967.

Willis, Wendell, ed. *The Kingdom of God in 20th-Century Interpretation.* Peabody, Mass.: Hendrickson, 1987.

Windisch, Hans. *The Meaning of the Sermon on the Mount.* Translated by S. M. Gilmour. Philadelphia: Westminster, 1961.

————. "Die Sprüche vom Eingehen in das Reich Gottes." *ZNW* 27 (1928) 163-92.

Witherington, Ben. *The Christology of Jesus.* Minneapolis: Fortress, 1990.

————. *Jesus, Paul, and the End of the World: A Comparative Study in New Testament Eschatology.* Downers Grove, Ill.: InterVarsity, 1992.

————. *Jesus the Sage: The Pilgrimage of Wisdom.* Minneapolis: Fortress, 1994.

————. *Women in the Ministry of Jesus: A Study of Jesus' Attitudes to Women and their Roles as Reflected in His Earthly Life.* SNTSMS 51. Cambridge: Cambridge University Press, 1984.

Wright, N. T. *Jesus and the Victory of God.* Christian Origins and the Question of God, vol. 2. Minneapolis: Fortress, 1996.

————. *The New Testament and the People of God.* Christian Origins and the Question of God, vol. 1. Minneapolis: Fortress, 1992.

Wuellner, Wilhelm H. *The Meaning of "Fishers of Men."* Philadelphia: Westminster, 1967.

Yoder, John Howard. *The Politics of Jesus: Behold the Man! Our Victorious Lamb.* 2d ed. Grand Rapids: Eerdmans, 1994.

Young, Brad H. *Jesus the Jewish Theologian.* Peabody, Mass.: Hendrickson, 1995.

Index of Names and Subjects

ble fellowship of, 41-49; and the
unlikely, 98-100; and women, 221-
22. *See also* ethics; God; John the
Baptist; kingdom; Rome
Johanan b. Zakkai, 54
John the Apostle, 179
John the Baptist, 3-6, 29, 39, 46, 62,
81, 89, 91, 94, 96, 106, 112, 115,
116, 122-23, 149, 174, 179, 184,
202-3, 212
Joseph (father of Jesus), 1-2, 208
Joseph of Arimathea, 124
jubilee, 225
Judah b. Tema, 59
Judaism, 2-3, 24, 25, 33-34, 41, 49,
52, 55, 56, 78, 100-101, 105-6, 149,
157, 160-61, 201, 228; God in, 50-
54; and Jesus, 20
Judea, 189
judgment: agents of, 145-47; final
consequences of, 147-48; and the
nations, 148-49

kingdom, 70-155; and *'abbā'*, 154;
and death of Jesus, 115-18; and
ethics, 110-15, 132-33; as fellowship with the Father, 149-54; future
dimensions of, 120-55; as imminent, 122-25, 128-39; inauspicious
nature of, 95-103; and Jesus, 78-79,
89-95; nature of, 77-78, 149; and
politics, 82-84, 85-89, 96-97, 100-
102, 104, 106-7, 110, 116-18, 126-
28, 139-49; present dimensions of,
84-119; and Protestant liberalism,
74; scholarship on, 71-84, 120-21;
strength of, 103-10; as symbol, 79-
80; and time, 80-81
Klausner, Joseph, 161
Kümmel, Werner Georg, 75-77

Ladd, George E., 17, 41, 102
love: of enemy, 218-20; and forgiveness, 225-26; of God, 206-10; as

imitation, 222-24; and Leviticus,
218; of neighbor, 220-22; of others,
218-24; of self, 217; and toleration,
220
Luther, Martin, 24

Maccabees, 101, 184, 191, 229
Malina, Bruce J., 183
Manson, T. W., 15, 18, 50, 55, 75n.20,
81, 87
marriage, 180, 184, 186-87, 200
Mary, 1-2, 187, 208
Meier, John P., 6, 26, 120, 125
mercy, 227-28
Meyer, Ben F., 79, 83, 121, 128n.19,
138
Moore, George F., 50
Moses, 4, 10, 19, 23, 24, 31, 32, 84,
198, 209

Naaman, 93
Nazareth, 2

Otto, Rudolf, 79, 89

Paul, 159, 168, 197, 201-2, 205-6, 215
peace, 229-33; nature of, 230, 232-33
Perrin, Norman, 48-49
Peter, 19, 89, 92, 127, 135, 177, 193
Pharisees, 3, 24, 42, 45, 47, 48, 92,
114, 200, 205, 216
poor, 211
possessions, 187-94
prophecy, 12-13, 130-33, 137-39

Rabbi, 2
Rambo, Lewis R., 183
repentance, 172-76; external and internal, 173-74
reward, 33-35, 233-36
righteousness, 200-206
Ritschl, Albrecht, 71
Rohrbaugh, R. L., 183

Index of Scripture
and Other Ancient Writings